Contents

Foreword

American as well as British students will find much that is interesting and illuminating in this British view of the Reagan presidency. David Mervin writes as an experienced American politics specialist whose study includes first-hand observation in the United States. Putting aside policy substance and concentrating on effectiveness in using the political process, Mervin portrays Reagan's presidential record more favorably than may be common in the British community. Indeed, Mervin explicitly addresses an expected anti-Reagan readership among the British students for whom the book is primarily intended. I doubt whether an American political scientist writing about the Thatcher prime ministership would similarly have to ask American students to overcome an anti-Thatcher bias. Understanding how Ronald Reagan could have reached the presidency may have been hard for Britons or any other people whose leaders customarily reach the top after long careers in national government. Mervin, however, appreciates that Reagan provides only one example of the capacity of the American nomination and election processes to put outsiders in the White House.

Where Mervin's view is British, and advantageously so, is in its concentration on the limitations of presidential leadership in comparison with executive leadership in Britian. An American president certainly has some powers that a British prime minister lacks, in relation to the cabinet, but, as Mervin makes clear, a president suffers distinctive policy-making constraints. These include general anti-government traditions, frequently hostile partisan majorities in Congress, and relatively weak parties as means for exerting leadership even among a president's own partisan members of Congress. In describing each constraint, Mervin gives special attention to congressional and party developments that have imposed new obstacles to executive leadership during the last few decades. For Mervin, these features of the American political culture are not defects to be remedied by the substitution of British parliamentary institutions for the separation of powers. Refreshingly, he suggests reasons why the established arrangements, no matter how frustrating for chief executives, nevertheless suit American circumstances.

It is very much in the context of constraints on presidential power that Mervin evaluates Reagan's record as a strategist. That record began, Mervin reminds us, when presidential authority was at a low ebb. At the end of the 1970s, there was doubt that a presidential authority was at a low ebb. At the end of the 1970s, there was doubt that a president could accomplish anything requiring major congressional action. Given such low expectations, Mervin sees Reagan as effective in securing much of what he sought in tax and appropriation legislation in 1981, and in the Tax Reform Act of 1986. He argues convincingly that it was politically unrealistic for David Stockman to expect a great deal more budget-cutting than Reagan secured in the early 1980s. But he does not say that Stockman was wrong on policy grounds to worry about the budget deficits that resulted from Reagan's dealing with Congress. Nor does Mervin show Reagan as regularly successful in achieving his policy goals, meritorious or not.

Whether another president can be even as effective as Mervin regards Reagan is now an open question. Constraints were slightly relaxed for Reagan because his first election appeared linked to a new partisan majority in the Senate and a *de facto* coalitional majority in the House. Such linkage, suggesting a policy mandate, may now be highly exceptional. Electing a president of one party and a Congress with clear majorities for the other party looks like the usual order of things. In that case, party responsibility, long the favored means for achieving at least temporarily coherent policy-making, would not be clearly relevant.

Leon D. Epstein
University of Wisconsin-Madison

Acknowledgements

My interest in the politics of the United States now extends back over nearly three decades. It is my hope that this book will, in part, be seen to reflect my admiration for a beautiful and fascinating country and its people.

It was my good fortune as an undergraduate to be taught by a gifted and dedicated teacher, Professor Lucian Marquis. He inspired my early study of American politics and encouraged me to pursue it further. Subsequently, as a graduate student at Cornell University, I completed a PhD under the guidance of an eminent presidential scholar, the late Professor Clinton Rossiter. Some years later I received an American Council of Learned Societies fellowship enabling me to spend a year at the University of Wisconsin-Madison. At Madison my understanding of American politics was much enhanced by my conversations with Professor Leon Epstein. I am most grateful to Professor Epstein not only for his generosity in contributing a foreword to this book, but also for his reading of the manuscript which has saved me from a number of errors of fact and interpretation. Any that remain are, of course, my responsibility alone.

I would like to acknowledge also the stimulation and help in developing my ideas provided by many generations of students who have taken my courses in American politics at the University of Warwick. I am also grateful to staff at Longman for their help and guidance with this project. I owe an especial debt of gratitude to Mrs Gill Lamb, formerly Secretary of the University of Warwick Summer School. Without her assistance I could not have met my responsibilities as Director of the School while also writing this book.

My thanks are also due to Alice Mervin and John Mervin both of whom have given me more help and inspiration than they realise. My greatest debt of all is to Dr Kathleen McConnell Mervin. Her professional skill eliminated some of the worst imperfections of my English, but although important, that was only a small part of her overall contribution. Without her constant support and encouragement this book could not possibly have been written.

David Mervin
University of Warwick

Abbreviations

ACLU	American Civil Liberties Union
AMA	American Medical Association
CIA	Central Intelligence Agency
CBS	Columbia Broadcasting System
CBO	Congressional Budget Office
EPA	Environmental Protection Agency
FBI	Federal Bureau of Investigation
GE	General Electric
GOP	Grand Old Party (the Republican Party)
GNP	Gross National Product
INF	Intermediate-Range Nuclear Forces
LSG	Legislative Strategy Group
NAACP	National Association for the Advancement of Colored People
NLRB	National Labor Relations Board
NOW	National Organization for Women
NSC	National Security Council
OMB	Office of Management and Budget
SAG	Screen Actors Guild
SALT II	Strategic Arms Limitation Treaty
START	Strategic Arms Reductions Talks
SDI	Strategic Defense Initiative (Star Wars)
WIN	Whip Inflation Now

To Kathleen

CHAPTER ONE
Introduction

Most books published by academics, textbooks apart, seem to be written for other academics; this is a book primarily for students. Naturally, I hope that my interpretation of Reagan's presidency in the later chapters will prove of interest to my professional colleagues, but, in preparing this study, I have tried to keep in mind the needs of students and those who come to the subject matter with no more than an elementary understanding of American politics. It is also my hope that the book will serve, in a limited sense, as an introduction to the politics of the United States even though much of the ground that would be dealt with in a conventional textbook is not covered here.

The introductory nature of this book will be especially apparent in Chapters Two and Three where I attempt to place the presidency of the 1980s in its systemic and historical context. It is impossible to understand the office of president in isolation; some comprehension of the nature of the political system and some sense of historical perspective are essential. It should also be immediately apparent that this book is, in no sense, a conventional biography; it is rather a study of the presidency with particular reference to Ronald Reagan. He provides the focus of the work rather than the subject of it.

While the book is written by a British university teacher of American politics mainly for a non-American audience, it should also afford a perspective useful to American readers. A comparative viewpoint can advance native understanding and the detachment of a foreign observer can be a useful aid to analysis.

On the other hand, those who are looking at a political system from the outside need to be aware of some major hazards. There is, for instance, the danger that their analyses will be distorted by alien predispositions and preferences. Even those polities with which we feel we have much in common are likely to be profoundly different in many respects – for example, differences of geography and historical experience as well as quite different constitutional arrangements and political institutions. Oliver Wright, a former British ambassador in Washington, has commented on the differences between the United Kingdom and the United States

> What we must understand is that the United States is a foreign country, with a history and traditions and a culture and a way of doing things which are different from our own (neither better nor worse, but different). . . . It is natural to view the other country as a mirror image, to suppose that because both Britain and America are democracies, we organize our political affairs in much the same way. Nothing could be further from the truth.[1]

Anyone remotely interested in politics will be aware that the British and American political systems differ in a number of respects. It will have come to their attention that parties are far less meaningful in the one than in the other; they will know that in the United States the legislature is not the captive of the executive in the way that is the case in the United Kingdom. What will be less apparent, however, are differences of political culture.

There are many definitions of political culture, some of which are very broad in their scope, but the term will be used quite narrowly here. Simply stated, political culture is concerned with how people think and react in the political context. In reference to the United States, William Mitchell suggests that political culture is about, 'the ways in which the American people view politics and its place in their lives . . . how they see politics both in terms of what *is* and what *ought* to be . . . (it also includes) what the typical American views as his own proper role in the politics of the nation.'[2] The norms, values, emotions and beliefs that comprise the political culture of a society can be found in 'the explicit statements of leaders of the nation, newspaper commentary, the Constitution, the texts of political science and civics, the art of the nation and of course the everyday expressions of the mass of the citizenry.'[3]

Political culture, it should be emphasized, is not concerned with differences of political affiliation or policy preferences, but with the consensual framework within which the political activity of a nation takes place. By definition political culture is very elusive and there are many hazards involved in trying to make use of the concept; nevertheless, it is of particular value in comparative politics. Those of us who view the United States from the outside are obliged to recognize that in that country there exists a pattern of political values, norms, attitudes, emotions and beliefs that, taken together, comprise a political culture significantly different from that found elsewhere. It does make sense to speak of an 'American creed' or an 'American ethos,' a political culture that can be distinguished from that that exists in Britain.[4]

This can be briefly illustrated: a suspicion of governmental authority in all its forms and a marked antipathy towards the concentration of political power is widespread in the United States to a degree not found in the United Kingdom.[5] Cultural attitudes and norms require American national legislators to be deferential to their constituents in a manner that would not be acceptable in Britain. Secrecy in government is tolerated in the British context to an extent that would be wholly unacceptable on the other side of the Atlantic – a political culture difference to which Edward Shils drew attention: 'The United States has been committed to the principle of publicity since its origin. . . . Repugnance for governmental secretiveness was the offspring of the distrust of aristocracy. [Whereas] the acceptance of hierarchy in British society permits the government to retain its secrets, with little challenge or resentment.'[6]

In approaching the study of the American presidency and the career of a particular incumbent, therefore, it is essential to bear in mind not only institutional differences, but also those of political culture. Neither the institution nor the individual should be measured against values, standards and assumptions appropriate to another polity. As Harold Laski, a distinguished British student of American politics of an earlier era, remarked:

> How careful one must be in seeking to estimate, especially as an Englishman, an institution so intricate and psychologically unfamiliar as the American Presidency . . . the essence of [this office] is the fact that it is an American institution, that it functions in an American environment, that it must be judged by American criteria of its response to American needs.[7]

Laski argues that the role of the chief executive of the United States is radically different from that of a prime minister. A president must contend with a fundamentally different constitutional framework and is the focus of a different set of popular expectations. Ronald Reagan's performance in office, therefore, cannot reasonably be assessed using criteria applicable to Mrs Thatcher. Those of us who observe American politics from outside must, for analytical purposes, endeavour to set aside the values, norms, attitudes, emotions and beliefs of our native political culture and constantly bear in mind the peculiar 'Americanness' of the political system in that country.

Partly because so many observers tend to view Ronald Reagan through British spectacles, he has been held in particularly low esteem in this country in contrast to his extraordinary popularity at home. A few months prior to his landslide re-election victory in 1984, Gallup found that only 32 per cent of Britons answered in the affirmative when asked, 'Do you think Mr Reagan is or is not proving a good president of the United States.'[8] In much the same vein, Simon Hoggart, writing in a serious, influential newspaper, *The Observer*, reflected supposedly informed British public opinion when he said in the wake of the Iran–Contra revelations, 'The Reagan administration is in an appalling and conceivably terminal crisis. The main reason is that the President's aides are incompetent and arrogant. He himself is incompetent and lazy. All this has been true for six years. But in the past calamitous November the American people have been forced to recognize and come to terms with the fact.'[9] There was indeed a sharp drop in Reagan's approval ratings at home following the crisis in question, yet subsequently he recovered and retained his position as one of the most consistently popular presidents.

The extraordinarily low view of Reagan that persists in Britain even amongst the so-called 'thinking classes' can be attributed in part to the highly popular, satirical television programme, *Spitting Image*. Ronald Reagan and Margaret Thatcher have been principal targets of this clever programme, but in the case of the prime minister the work of the satirists may have backfired. By portraying her as a loud-mouthed woman, wearing a man's suit and tyrannizing over pusillanimous cabinet colleagues, the satirists, by their own admission, may have done their victim a favour.[10] The impression created is that of an unpleasant, dictatorial, but intelligent and able woman – one who has a very clear idea of where she wants to go and is fully in command. The image of a strong, dynamic leader evokes favourable responses among many British voters. They may not like her, but she commands their respect.

The same satirists were devastatingly successful in undermining popular perceptions of Ronald Reagan in Britain. Not only *Spitting Image*, but also a small army of TV impressionists, conveyed an image of a president in an advanced stage of senile dementia, a vacuous, grinning idiot incapable of coherent thought and completely in the grip of image-makers and manipulators. The television satirists' image of Reagan was reinforced by constant press references to his former status as a Grade B film actor and derogatory comments about his alleged laziness and inattention to detail. Such unremittingly hostile interpretations distort understanding while pandering and adding strength to the virulent currents of anti Americanism that are never far from the surface in Britain.

British and American perceptions of Ronald Reagan as president have also been influenced by ideological considerations. He was flayed because he was a conservative and had been responsible for pursuing foreign and domestic policies which his critics happened to deplore. Needless to say, this is an entirely legitimate position; however, such reactions need to be set on one side by those who aspire to objectivity in their analysis. This touches on some important questions about the role of the student of politics and what it is that he or she is concerned with by comparison with partisans and political journalists. Academic analysts are obliged to suppress their personal preferences; complete objectivity is an unattainable ideal, yet it must be approached as far as it is in our power to do so. Unless, that is, it is assumed that there is no important distinction between the work of political activists and journalists on the one side and academic students of politics on the other. Our approval or disapproval of the American political system, whether or not we like Reagan personally or agree or disagree with his policies, are all matters irrelevant to our purposes.

The distinct possibility of personal preferences obscuring the assessments of professional students of politics was raised by a poll among members of the American Political Science Association. This revealed, first of all, that the overwhelming proportion of political scientists in the US were Democrats; no less than 76 per cent of American politics specialists. Of even greater interest were those figures that showed that, in assessing Reagan's 'overall performance in office', 71 per cent of respondents who identified as Republicans rated him as 'excellent' or 'good' while 29 per cent found him to be 'fair' or 'poor'. Of the Democratic identifiers, meanwhile, 96 per cent found him to be 'fair' or 'poor', whereas only 4 per cent rated him as 'excellent' or 'good'.[11] How are we to account for these sharply contrasting evaluations amongst political 'scientists', men and women trained in political analysis, with some special claim, it might be thought, to be taken seriously in such matters? It seems reasonable to assume that most of those who responded to this poll assessed Reagan primarily in respect of the content of his policies. Their evaluations, in other words, were likely to have turned in large part on whether they approved or disapproved of Reaganomics or of the direction of the president's foreign or defence policies. By and large, these experts seem to have responded as any man or woman in the street would do – as Democrats or Republicans rather than as objective analysts.

The problem of bias in the study of politics surfaces at all levels, from the most distinguished professor to the novice student, but it can be minimized by restricting the scope of what is to dealt with under the heading of politics. The ideal of objective analysis can be brought closer if the policy process becomes the main focus of attention and the partisan minefield of policy substance is avoided. This leads us into more general questions about the nature and scope of what is usually grandly referred to as 'political science'. This is a contentious subject area. All would agree that it is not possible to deal with everything that touches on politics and the scope of enquiry must therefore be limited. There is, however, little agreement about where to draw the line. The position adopted here is close to that of Frederick Watkins who, some years ago, made what he saw as an important distinction between

> the *process* of decision-making and the *content* of the decisions made. If economics were the science of wealth production, all knowledge would be its proper concern. If political science were the science of determining public policies, it would need to be at least as comprehensive. But political science, like economics, has a less ambitious purpose. It is concerned not with the potentially infinite content of all public decisions, but with the process by which those decisions are reached.[12]

In studying American politics, I am concerned with process rather than policy substance; my role, as I see it, is that of an observer of the national, political decision-making machinery in Washington, trying to comprehend, amongst other things, the context within which that machinery operates, the relationships between its component parts, and the reasons why it occasionally produces policy outcomes, but more frequently does not. The nature of those outcomes, their consequences and the merits of possible alternatives are for me, if not for others, matters of secondary concern.

In looking at the presidency, my interest is in trying to understand what the man in the White House must do to get a notoriously, cumbersome, inefficient, irrational and difficult piece of machinery to work. The successful president is the one who overcomes these difficulties and masters the policy process sufficiently to bring about significant public policy change. We are impressed that he has moved the country in new directions at all, irrespective of our own views as to the desirability of those directions.

Not all political scientists see their role in these terms. Some argue that the distinction between policy process and the substance of policy is meaningless. Others contend that to focus on process alone is to narrow excessively the area of study. Some even go so far as to claim that the political scientist has prescriptive responsibilities: 'If political science concerns itself with politics and governments, it is not simply concerned with how governments operate. It should make every effort to deal also with what governments ought to do.'[13]

While these objections are not without merit, there are two very good reasons for limiting the inquiry to matters of process. First, it minimizes, although certainly does not eliminate, the problem of bias. Second, by declining to delve into the substance of policy the danger of being drawn into areas where we have little or no expertise is avoided. I am not qualified to pass judgement on the merits of alternative economic policies and my opinions on military strategy are no better informed than those of other laymen. There are plenty of experts in these fields and evaluations of particular policies are best left to them . Whatever expertise I have to contribute lies in the realm of policy process. Each of us, it might be said, should keep to his own last.

My interest in the presidency as an institution, and in Ronald Reagan's incumbency, has everything to do with process and very little to do with the substance of policy. In considering the career of any president the interesting questions for me are: How effective was he as chief executive? How far was he able to master the decision-making process? How successful was he in moving the country in new directions, irrespective of whether that movement was desirable? My approach is similar to that of Barbara Kellerman who, in an outstanding book *The Political Presidency*, writes

> When I speak of an effective presidency, or effective presidential leadership, I am speaking here in terms of functional criteria only. I am not asking if the leadership was, for example, courageous, wise or moral, or if it led the country down the proper path. I am asking only if it was effective in the sense that the president was able to accomplish what he wanted to accomplish.[14]

Similarly Aaron Wildavsky, in an essay, 'President Reagan as Political Strategist' says,

> When I speak of politicians as strategists, I mean that they have a vision, a broad sense of direction toward which they wish the nation to move, and that they use effective and creative (nonobvious) means in pursuing these ends. *Nothing is implied about the desirability of the directions chosen, for then the politicians could be strategists only by being in accord with the preferences of the analyst.*[15] (*My italics*)

He goes on to characterize Reagan as a 'superb political strategist', a sentiment with which I broadly agree. In my experience, however, British undergraduates miss the point when prevailed upon to read Wildavsky's piece. They are likely to be irritated by what they see as pro-Reagan proclivities. To perceive Reagan as an exceptional political strategist or as a notably effective president says nothing about his economic policy or the activities of his administration in Central America. Such considerations are irrelevant for the purposes of this discussion and must be treated as such if we wish to be taken seriously as political analysts.

To summarize, those seeking to understand the American political system must be alert to a number of dangers. They should be aware that the United States has a political culture quite different from that of other countries. Politicians are the subject of different expectations and operate according to different norms of behaviour. The institutional mechanisms are quite unlike those in the United Kingdom and the functions of political leaders are, accordingly, profoundly different.

In evaluating Ronald Reagan's presidency we must forget our own policy preferences, direct our attention to considerations of effectiveness and not allow ourselves to be seduced by the charms of often amusing, but nevertheless grotesque, caricatures that have been so fashionable in the media outside the United States in the 1980s. Particularly in the later chapters of this book, I shall endeavour to show that, contrary to such perceptions Reagan has to be taken very seriously as President of the United States. He had many shortcomings and his incumbency was not without scandals, crises and disasters, but he cannot be written off as an ill-qualified and incompetent chief executive who, by some fluke, fell into the White House. There was much more to him than that.

No doubt some readers will find my treatment of Ronald Reagan unduly charitable. They will be troubled by my lack of attention to what they perceive as the adverse consequences of his policies, but that, I must emphasize, is to miss the point of this book. I have my own doubts about the content and the effects of Reagan's policies. I deplore, as much as anyone, such developments during his tenure as the widening of the gap between rich and poor, the increase in homelessness, the worsening of the plight of many black people, the evidence of corruption in high places and the bullying of Nicaragua. However, my interest as a student of politics is not whether Reagan was right or wrong in what he did, but whether he was effective in turning his policy intentions into governmental action. His policies may be considered morally wrong, or wrong in the sense that they will not achieve the objectives sought. His administration's economic policy, for instance, may prove disastrous for the American economy in the long run, but speculation of this sort and judgements of this nature are outside the scope of this study.

The next two chapters of this book contain introductory material designed to provide new students of American politics with some essential background. It is not possible to comprehend any presidency without first acquiring some understanding of the parameters within which every incumbent must work. In Chapter Two, therefore, the myth of the all-powerful president is confronted and the limits of presidential power are examined, and we also consider what chief executives must do if they are to be effective leaders.

To come to grips with the presidency in the 1980s it is necessary to understand the political upheavals of the previous decade and these will be the subject of Chapter Three. The 1970s were marked by two of the great traumas of American history – Vietnam and Watergate – these had consequences of the greatest importance for the presidency. Partly in reaction to these events congress strove vigorously in the 1970s to reclaim power lost to the executive branch. It embarked on a feverish bout of congressional reform – again with major consequences for the presidency. It is necessary to understand these matters and the three failed presidencies of Nixon, Ford and Carter as a preliminary to a study of Reagan.

In Chapter Four Reagan's background, experience and qualifications are considered to show that, contrary to the assumptions of many commentators in Europe, Reagan was, in many respects, rather well qualified for the special needs of the presidency in the 1980s. This chapter also charts Reagan's quest for the Republican nomination and explores the circumstances of his landslide election victory in 1980.

In considering Reagan's record in the White House, I have made no attempt to survey eight years of activity. I have been heavily selective, directing my attention to issues of especial significance. Thus, Chapter Five deals almost exclusively with 1981. In that first year even Reagan's sternest critics in the United States were stunned by his apparent mastery of congress, his success in bringing the bureaucracy under control and his spectacular reversal of long-standing policy directions. The central question addressed here is: Why was Reagan initially so effective in the White House? The following two chapters provide an instructive contrast with what has gone before: if Reagan enjoyed some great triumphs in his first term, his second term brought him to the edge of catastrophe. In Chapter Six two major, second-term, domestic policy issues – tax reform and the Bork nomination – are examined. Chapter Seven focuses on failure and achievement in foreign policy – the Iran–Contra affair and the INF Treaty.

Ronald Reagan's style of leadership is considered in Chapter Eight. The starting point for this discussion is the overwhelmingly predominant Roosevelt model of presidential power. After a brief look at the Eisenhower example, the chapter considers Reagan's personality, his management style and his strategy of leadership. In the concluding chapter there is an overall assessment of the Reagan legacy, one that takes account of the limits on presidential power discussed in earlier chapters, considers his strengths as well as his weaknesses and evaluates him against yardsticks that make possible comparisons between one president and another.

No doubt all authors believe that their subject is of special significance, but there are good reasons for concluding that the Reagan presidency was one of the more important of the twentieth century. It was important first of all in terms of institutional history. When Reagan entered the White House the American political system in general, and its central guiding institution, the presidency, in particular, were in bad repair. Public confidence in presidential leadership was at a perilously low ebb and the presidency itself had come to be widely regarded as an inadequate institution. Reagan, however, revitalized the office and did much to restore confidence in the political system at large. In addition, Reagan's contribution to the development of the presidency is not to be underestimated. Since World War II, the Franklin Roosevelt model of the presidency had reigned supreme, but, in the 1980s, new research on Eisenhower in conjunction with Reagan's example in office led to a recognition that other models were possible. Reagan, furthermore, added new dimensions to the presidency by his command of television and other skills as a communicator.

The Reagan presidency is also important because, more than most, it made a difference. By that I mean that under Reagan's stewardship the United States moved in new directions in both domestic and foreign policy. How far this can be attributed to the president himself, to his staff, to shifts in American public opinion or to changes in the world outside are all questions open to debate, but the fact that real movement occurred when Reagan was at the helm is indisputable. And this, it should be emphasized, is most unusual; almost all presidents fail to accomplish any significant public policy change.

NOTES AND REFERENCES

1. '"Understanding America": Impressions of a Departing Ambassador', *Government and Opposition*, **22**, No. 2, (Spring 1987), pp. 163–74.
2. *The American Polity*. Free Press, Glencoe 1962, p. 105.
3. Ibid. p. 106.
4. Samuel Huntington, *American Politics: The Promise of Disharmony*. Harvard University Press, Cambridge, Mass. 1981; Herbert McCloskey and John Zaller, *The American Ethos*. Harvard University Press, Cambridge, Mass. 1984.
5. For the 'anti governmental cast of American society' see H.G. Nicholas, *The Nature of American Politics*, Oxford University Press, Oxford 1986, p. 10.
6. Quoted in Huntington, op. cit., p. 48.
7. *The American Presidency*, George Allen and Unwin, London 1940, p. 19.
8. Ivor Crewe, 'Britain Evaluates Ronald Reagan', *Public Opinion*, **7**, No.5 (Oct./Nov. 1984), pp. 46–49.
9. *Observer* (30 Nov. 1986), p. 13.
10. Alan Rusbridger, 'Funny Peculiar', *The Guardian* (23 July 1988).
11. Walter B. Roettger and Hugh Winebrenner, 'Politics and Political Scientists', *Public Opinion* (Sept./Oct. 1986), pp. 41–44.
12. 'Comments on Professor Van Dyke's Paper', Monograph 6, American Academy of Political and Social Science, Philadelphia 1966, pp. 28–33.
13. David Spitz, ibid., p. 39.
14. Oxford University Press, Oxford 1984, p. x.
15. *Society* (May/June 1987), pp. 56–62.

CHAPTER TWO

The Limits on Presidential Power

The President of the United States is, at first sight, an extraordinarily powerful figure. He is the principal leader of one of the largest, wealthiest and mightiest nations on earth. In theory, he commands a formidable array of armed forces and in his hands lie the means for destroying the human race. Yet for all that he is a political leader of remarkably limited powers. Within his own country, he is not so much a Leviathan as a Gulliver figure hemmed in and tied down by a complex network of restraints that must be thrown off if he is to be more than a helpless giant in the White House. The principal purpose of this book is to examine Ronald Reagan's efforts to deal with these problems; to examine the techniques he and his staff used as they sought to break free from the ties that bound them; and to assess how successful Reagan was in mastering the system of government and in achieving his policy objectives.

This chapter is the first of two devoted to providing background essential to an informed assessment of the Reagan presidency. I shall first review some of the main impediments to the exercise of power that confront all modern presidents and then consider what can be done to overcome these difficulties. This will encompass American political culture; the role and structure of the legislative branch; the place of political parties, problems of bureaucratic control; and the nature of presidential power. Before turning to these matters, however, I shall use as my starting point the rather more advantageous conditions for executive leadership that exist in the United Kingdom.

EXECUTIVE HEGEMONY IN THE UNITED KINGDOM

The distribution of political power in the UK is broadly centrepetal. The national entities of England, Scotland, Northern Ireland and Wales are organized in a unitary rather than a federal structure and parliamentary government in practice provides for the supremacy of the executive branch. In the 1980s, the tendency for political power to be concentrated at the centre has been carried a stage further by a prime minister sufficiently determined and resourceful to achieve a high level of dominance over her cabinet colleagues. However, Mrs Thatcher is by no means a typical prime minister; her approach to the job has been quite unlike that of most of her modern predecessors who, with one or two exceptions, have adopted a less ambitious, more pragmatic consensual style.[1] Nevertheless, if British governments usually provide leadership that is more authentically collective than at present, the possibility of executive branch hegemony is always there. Assuming that the government of the day has a comfortable majority in the House of Commons, executive dominance over the legislature and control over the processes of decision making becomes possible.

The case should not, of course, be overstated. Nowhere does the exercise of political power come about easily. All British governments, however large their majority, must have an eye to the next election and an effective opposition will take maximum advantage of that fact. In recent years, moreover, the incidence of backbench revolts among government supporters has increased and the House of Lords has more than once demonstrated an inclination to go its own way. For all that, executive branch dominance continues to be one of the striking characteristics of the British political system.

That dominance thrives on the enthusiasm for positive and effective goverment that is embedded in our political culture. Public opinion polls reveal a powerful popular distaste for divided political parties and an aversion to coalitions, both of which are assumed to detract from effective government.[2] Executive hegemony is also facilitated by institutional arrangements that combine, rather than separate, the legislative and executive branches . More than a hundred members of the legislature are simultaneously part of the executive and they provide a large phalanx of obedient support for cabinet initiatives. The almost automatic acceptance of those same initiatives by the legislature as a whole is assured by the formidable mechanisms of party. Executive branch 'henchmen' in the whips' office armed with inducements and sanctions can, in almost all cases, ensure that rank and file members of the legislature will follow the injunctions of the party leadership.

As a consequence, the executive branch in the United Kingdom, provided it is fortified by a working majority in the legislature, has a comparatively awesome command of the political process. For all sorts of reasons it may fail to fulfil its potential. It may be divided within itself; it may lose bye-elections, or it may lack resolution or competence. But, providing it survives these and other perils, it will be possible for the executive to bring about significant public policy change. No such guarantees are available in the United States where the political culture is fundamentally different, the separation of powers principle is alive and well and political parties are notoriously weak and undisciplined.

THE CONSTRAINED PRESIDENT

Presidents, no less than prime ministers, normally enter office bent on making things happen. They are typically determined to bring about change, to introduce reforms and to reverse what they see as the mistakes of the past. Reasonably enough, newly elected or re-elected presidents interpret their success at the polls as a mandate to move the country in new directions. Richard Nixon, for example, after his re-election in 1972, said at his Inauguration[3],

> When a new administration comes in, it comes in with new ideas, new people, new programs . . . we feel that we have a mandate, a mandate not simply for approval of what we have done in the past, but a mandate to continue to provide change that will work in our foreign policy and in our domestic policy, change that will build a better life, that will mean progess at home toward our great goals here, just as we have been making progress in the field of international affairs.

Nixon's ambitions were to crash on the rock of Watergate, but even without that disaster it is most unlikely that he would have come even close to fulfilling his mandate, In that, he would not, by any means, have been alone. Indeed very few presidents in the last half century have accomplished much in the way of substantial policy change. Fred Greenstein argues that 'the impact of modern presidents on public policy need not be apocalyptic to be important' and no doubt this is true.[4] However, a distinction surely has to be made between those presidents who alter the terms of the debate and change the course of history and those who achieve no more than marginal change. Franklin Roosevelt could be said to fall into the former category, but it should not be forgotten that he took office at a moment of great crisis in American history and was aided by unusually large majorities in both houses of the legislature. Roosevelt, furthermore, was almost certainly the most gifted man to sit in the White House in the twentieth century. Lyndon Johnson initiated a considerable amount of legislation and several other modern presidents could claim some limited success in the realm of foreign policy. However, of Truman, Eisenhower, Kennedy, Nixon, Ford and Carter, none could be said to have had a decisive impact on the direction of domestic policy. How do we explain all these paltry records? Why is it that presidents come and go and yet accomplish so relatively little?

The procedures whereby political decisions are made in the United States surely have much to answer for. These are so ponderous and unwieldy and so vulnerable to obstruction that it seems remarkable that major decisions are ever made outside of crisis situations. The decision making process can be likened to one of those great lumbering steam locomotives seen in Western films. The president is ostensibly the driver of this large complex machine, but at the beginning of each new administration the question is: Will the man temporarily in charge of this unwieldy, temperamental vehicle be able to master its tricky controls and get it to move at all? The odds are that the engine of public policy change will, in fact, make few significant journeys and will spend most of the time hissing and panting in a siding.

The truth is that it is monumentally difficult to galvanize the American political system into action. The president, in the modern age, is the key political actor and the public constantly looks to him for initiatives, services and solutions. In other words, they demand that he give a lead; meanwhile, however, countless obstacles are placed in his path to prevent him from actually exercising leadership. If he is to meet his responsibilities, the chief executive must impose his will, his preferences, his policy choices on that 'maze of personalities and institutions called the government of the United States'.[5] In order to understand what a president has to do to master that maze we must first briefly consider some relevant features of the American political culture.

POLITICAL CULTURE

The people of the United States tend to be instinctively wary and suspicious of government in all its forms. These attitudes arise from the American historical experience. Many of those who founded the country had fled to the New World to escape the oppressiveness of traditional societies marked by hierarchy, inequality and the absence of freedom. The architects of the Constitution were accordingly intent upon constructing political mechanisms that would allow for the essential minimum level of government without encroaching on their hard-won liberties. There was to be no all-powerful central state apparatus, and political leaders were to be given no blank cheques; on the contrary, they were to be hedged in by a complex, decentralized and fragmented system designed to prevent any one leader or group of leaders from becoming excessively powerful.

The Constitution has undergone much development in the last two centuries, but the concerns and fears that motivated the Founding Fathers have not lost their relevance. Americans continue to be sceptical about the virtues of government and are almost paranoid in their attitudes towards political leaders. Presidents are obliged to tread carefully; as we noted, they are expected to lead, but they must do so without stirring up age-old resentments and suspicions.

Given this ambivalence towards political authority, there is little scope in the United States for heroic leadership. Strong leaders are sometimes the subject of admiration, but typically they are long dead, like Washington, Lincoln or Roosevelt, or they can be safely admired from a distance, like Margaret Thatcher or Mikhail Gorbachev; Winston Churchill has the advantage of falling into both categories. It is also the case that the American people have occasionally, in crisis situations, been prepared to shelve their traditional fears and to tolerate strong leadership from the White House. Thus, Lincoln during the Civil War, Wilson during World War I and Franklin Roosevelt in an era of domestic and international crisis were all temporarily accorded a leeway that non-crisis presidents have not enjoyed. It is worthy of note, however, that these presidents were all followed by periods of anti-executive backlash. Witness the attempt to use the impeachment process against Lincoln's successor, Andrew Johnson; the defeat of Wilson over the Treaty of Versailles and the routing of his party in the 1920 election. Finally, and perhaps most significant of all, there is the passage of the 22nd Amendment to the Constitution prohibiting third terms and clearly designed to guard against the possibility of another Franklin Roosevelt emerging.

In normal circumstances the American political culture is a restraint on leaders in general and on chief executives in particular. The latter must be careful to avoid giving an impression of revelling in the trappings of power, and they must beware of appearing to threaten the prerogatives of other political actors such as the Supreme Court or the Congress. Strident, overbearing leadership is inadvisable in this political culture. Those who seek to lead must act with subtlety and caution or they will meet with strong negative reactions.

CONGRESSIONAL POWERS

In institutional terms, the major potential obstacle to presidential leadership is normally the United States Congress. In most Western democracies in the twentieth century, legislatures have lost a great deal of ground to executive branches. This has occurred in America too, but to nowhere near the same extent as elsewhere. Congress has not become a parliamentary poodle or a mere captive of the executive branch; it remains an imposing and fractious body, fully capable of defending its position and thwarting presidential ambitions.

The exceptional importance of the legislature in the American system is provided for by a constitution that makes Congress the 'first' branch of government; endows it with the legislative power; gives it control over the purse strings; allows it a considerable role in the making of foreign policy; and makes senior executive appointments subject to its approval. To be sure, the president is usually the dominant partner in the legislative process; most major legislative initiatives come from him and little legislation of real consequence is likely to pass without his support. Nevertheless, if congress has largely surrendered the positive power to initiate legislation to the executive, it remains a formidable negative force. Any bill proposed must navigate a complex network of committees and sub-committees that offer innumerable opportunities for delaying, diluting or defeating legislation. Even a president whose party controls both the House and the Senate is obliged to approach the legislature more or less cap in hand as he seeks approval for his programme.

Similarly, the legislature's 'power of the purse' is not to be underestimated. Important policy changes will invariably carry revenue and expenditure implications and Congress jealously guards its constitutional rights in such matters. The Budget committees, the Senate Finance Committee, the House Ways and Means Committee, the Appropriations committees in both houses and their sub-committees are all major power centres well capable of inflicting severe damage on the executive branch.

In the domestic policy arena, there can be no doubt that the legislature remains an institution of great consequence; however, in the overlapping realms of foreign and defence policy, the pendulum of power has swung rather more sharply in the direction of the president. From the beginning, the president's constitutional position in these areas has been strong.[6] He is designated Commander-in-Chief, making him responsible for the safety of US troops abroad and for dealing with any threat to the nation's security at home. In addition, the president is constitutionally responsible for the making of treaties and the appointment of ambassadors and is effectively put in charge of foreign policy. In the modern age, furthermore, the role of congress has been undermined by the special needs of this policy arena. Congress, so it is argued, lacks the information resources of the executive and is neither capable of keeping secrets nor of providing the sort of instant response to crises that modern technology and weaponry demands. It is also claimed that the irrational and inefficient procedures of pluralistic decision making are inappropriate in foreign and defence policy, where considered rational responses in the national interest are required.

The weight of these and other arguments has, without question, sharply shifted the balance in favour of the president in this century. In crisis situations, the initiative inevitably rests with the executive – it is the president who authorizes immediate military responses and in so doing he may not be as carefully respectful of the Constitution as some purists would like. Nevertheless, there is much more to foreign and defence policy than crisis response, and in these circumstances Congress can play a more meaningful role. Executive officials can be hauled before Congressional committees and asked to justify their conduct of policy. New weapons programmes cannot proceed without Congressional authorization. Military adventures abroad that extend for any length of time depend on the legislature being willing to provide the necessary funding and the Senate's approval of treaties can, by no means be taken for granted. In short, despite some loss of power congress remains an institution of genuine weight unlike the situation in Britain where

> The Prime Minister appoints people to office without worrying about parliamentary confirmation, concludes treaties without worrying about parliamentary ratification, declares war without obtaining parliamentary assent, is safe from parliamentary investigation and in many respects has inherited the authority that once belonged to absolute monarchs.
> Congress, pusillanimous as it often is, is far more independent of the head of government, far more open to a diversity of ideas, far more capable of affecting executive policies, far better staffed and paid and far more disposed to check, balance, challenge and investigate the executive branch than Parliament.[7]

THE STRUCTURE OF CONGRESS

The president's difficulties in dealing with the legislature are compounded by the structure of the institution. Power is intensely fragmented and dispersed rather than being centred in a small group of party leaders as in a parliamentary system. Thus, in the UK power is concentrated in the cabinet, a situation made possible by a weak legislature and strong political parties . No such luxuries are available to presidents who confront a legislative branch of imposing strength that has chronically weak political parties and a near chaotic distribution of power.

In trying to meet his responsibility to govern, a president must deal not with a select group of leaders but with a multiplicity of party and committee leaders. His starting point will be the congressional leaders of his own party, but their cooperation alone will not get him very far. The influence of such leaders on their followers is limited and they may be quite helpless in the face of recalcitrant committee and sub-committee chairmen. In specific policy areas, moreover, these committee leaders are likely to be the more important political actors, fully capable of destroying a president's legislative proposals.

In parliamentary systems with strong parties, party leaders can control committees by ensuring that only good party loyalists are appointed as chairmen, but this is not possible in the US. For many years all major committee chairmen acquired their posts solely from their seniority, and even now this is true of almost all chairmen. That is to say, chairmen are invariably the most senior member of the majority party on that committee. It should be noted that these arrangements have important consequences for the distribution of power in congress. Seniority provides committee chairmen with an independent power base and helps to insulate them from control by party leaders and presidents.[8]

Even if a president and his staff are successful in obtaining the cooperation of party and committee leaders, there are no guarantees that they will be able to deliver the votes of rank-and-file members. This has become especially the case in the 'new' congress of the 1980s, where congressmen and senators have become even more individualistic and less amenable to control than before. Since the 1950s and 1960s there has been a weakening of the norms of 'good' congressional behaviour which, by obliging most members to conform, had in the past helped to bring some order into the legislature. In addition, procedural reforms in the 1970s transformed the relationship between chairmen and their committee colleagues. Rank-and-file members now participate far more fully in committee proceedings and are no longer subordinate to chairmen to the degree that they were in the past.[9] These changes have made congress more democratic, but they have also added immeasurably to the difficulties that presidents face in trying to obtain congressional cooperation.

Individualism among today's members of congress has also been heightened by electoral considerations. At the present time, success at the polls turns primarily on effective personnel rather than party organization and on the establishment of a good personal relationship between legislators and their constituents. Particularly in the House of Representatives, constituency service is regarded as the key to re-election and arguably, as a consequence of their single-minded pursuit of this strategy, almost all incumbents seeking re-election to the House are successful.[10] The relentlessly parochial orientations of congressmen and senators inevitably give them perspectives on issues at variance with presidents responding to a national electorate.

Another potentially troublesome difference in perspective between presidents and members of the legislature arises from the separation of powers. In the American system there is no career link between the executive and legislative branches. Legislators will not normally have had prior experience of governing, nor do they provide a government-in-waiting, as in the United Kingdom. In the latter, 'in criticism, proposal and debate, the leading members of the opposition are . . . guided by their own previous experience in the various ministries and their expectation that one day they themselves may have to administer the policies now under debate.'[11] Members of congress, by contrast, enjoy great power without responsibility; it is possible for them to wallow in carping criticism and to engage in other negative tactics free from the anxiety of ever having to shoulder the responsibility for government – a burden that the president cannot escape.

The intense diffusion of power that characterizes the American national legislature is one of the principal difficulties facing every president. In other systems, parties facilitate the work of executive branches by concentrating power at the centre. Party leaders, moreover, are provided with an array of rewards and sanctions that can be used to bring rank-and-file members into line. US parties are, by comparison, broken-backed organizations incapable of fulfilling the functions performed by parties elsewhere and providing relatively little assistance to a president trying to bring about public policy change.

BUREAUCRATIC CONTROL

Presidents and their staff must come to terms with a powerful, but formless and undisciplined, legislative branch; however, this will not, by itself, be sufficient. Persuading legislators is essential to the policy-making process but, in addition, non-elected officials holding pivotal positions in the bureaucracy must also be convinced of the justification of the president's proposals.

Leaving aside those bodies that, for the purposes of this discussion will be treated as presidential staff agencies – the White House Office, the Office of Management and Budget and the National Security Council and other agencies within the Executive Office of the President – there are approximately three million civilian and two million military personnel in the employ of the federal government. Annual editions of the *Government Organization Manual* provide neat schematic diagrams of the federal administration with the president at the top, above thirteen executive departments and innumerable independent agencies. Taken at their face value, such diagrams convey the impression that the president is the chief administrator of the federal government with all its employees directly answerable and accountable to him; the reality, however, is very different. Constitutionally the president is, without doubt, the chief executive, but what is seriously in question is his freedom to direct and control those who work in 'his' administration. That vast organization is as amorphous and as difficult to impose discipline on as the legislature; from the most senior to some quite junior levels, there are many opportunities for bureaucrats to undermine and defeat a president's purposes.

A president cannot even be sure of the loyalty of cabinet members to his programme. He appoints them to run departments and expects them to use their positions to aid the fulfilment of his purposes, but cabinet secretaries and departments are not answerable only to the White House. Members of the cabinet are nominated by the president, but their appointments have to be confirmed by the Senate. Departments are established in the first place by Act of Congress and they remain subject to Congressional oversight. Their budgets are closely controlled by Congress and any departmental legislative proposals will have to run the gauntlet of Congressional scrutiny.

Departments, moreover, are not easily moved in new directions by the outsiders that presidents set over them. Indeed, there is an ever-present danger of those outsiders – cabinet and sub-cabinet appointees – 'going native' and accepting departmental rather than presidential priorities.[12] Within departments, career bureaucrats exercise great influence and these men and women may well not share the partisan or policy preferences of their supposed political masters. Furthermore they will inevitably develop close relationships with important members of relevant congressional committees and with the leaders of constituent groups served by the department. This will lead to the formation of issue networks or sub-governments – essentially triangular groupings of élites embracing bureaucrats, congressmen and pressure group leaders who share a common interest and are in a position to distort the policy making process to their collective advantage. The most notorious of these powerful informal alliances is the military industrial complex, but this is only one of many such groupings that a president must accommodate as he seeks to bring about policy change. [13]

It is with good reason that presidents constantly complain of the large problems they face in trying to get the bureaucracy to do what they want it to do. Even the outstanding president of the twentieth century, Franklin Roosevelt, armed with a massive popular mandate and large majorities in both houses of the legislature, had grave difficulties in moving bureaucrats in the directions he, rather than they, wanted to go:

> The Treasury is so large and far-flung and ingrained in its practices that I find it almost impossible to get the action and results I want – even with Henry [Morgenthau] there. But the Treasury is not to be compared with the State Department. You should go through the experience of trying to get any changes in the thinking, policy,and action of the career diplomats and then you'd know what a real problem was. But the Treasury and the State Department put together are nothing compared with the Na-a-vy. The admirals are really something to cope with – and I should know. To change anything in the Na-a-vy is like punching a feather bed. You punch it with your right and you punch it with you left until you are finally exhausted, and then you find the damn bed just as it was before you started punching. [14]

Roosevelt, however, was president in a relatively uncomplicated era and since his time government has become vastly more complex and expansive with the problems of bureaucratic control increasing by quantum leaps.[15] In recent decades, moreover, the difficulties in these matters have been especially acute for Republican presidents for the simple reason that few senior civil servants are Republicans. According to one study, published in 1971, only 5 per cent of career foreign service officers in the State Department regarded themselves as Republicans. Another source established that no more than 17 per cent of senior career administrators in a range of departments and agencies dealing with domestic affairs, were Republicans.[16] Richard Nixon repeatedly expressed his exasperation at having to work with an unresponsive bureaucracy. On one occasion, for instance, with typical pungency he commented to John Ehrlichman; 'We have no discipline in this bureaucracy! We never fire anybody. We never reprimand anybody. We always promote the sons-of-bitches that kick us in the ass!'[17] Since Watergate, Nixon has been a discredited figure and some of his attempts to bring order to the fragmented system of government stepped beyond the bounds of legality. Nevertheless, his conviction that the federal bureaucracy was packed with administrators holding policy views antithetical to his own was founded in fact and was an experience common to Republican presidents.

Ensuring that non-elected officals conform to the wishes of their elected superiors presents difficulties in all democratic systems of government. The *Yes Minister* television series obviously deals in caricature, yet it has been said by insiders to be alarmingly close to the realities of the British political system. In comic and overdrawn form, this programme presents many instances where civil servants manipulate government ministers and play an improper part in determining policy outcomes. At a more serious level, Richard Crossman and others have shown that, in the right circumstances, civil servants in the UK may have an undesirably large role in policy-making.[18]

On the other hand, the civil service in Britain is much more centralized and hierarchical in its structure and, consequently, is more easily subject to control by elected officials. This is made possible by different cultural attitudes, secrecy in government and the sinews of party. Senior administrators are not above attempting to influence the shape of policy, but once the policy has been made they accept that it is their responsibility to bring about its implementation. There is little incentive in the British context for disaffected administrators to try to achieve their ends by making informal alliances with members of the legislature. Budgetary and legislative control lies with a cabinet backed by the formidable mechanisms of party, and few parliamentary committees have real teeth. Even those committees so bold as to demand to see papers and witnesses are unlikely to receive the cooperation they require. The opportunities for bureaucrats in the UK to subvert or negate the wishes of elected officials are far fewer and more limited in scope than is the case in the diffused, more open and non-hierarchical structures of the federal administration in the United States.

PRESIDENTIAL POWER

The American presidency, despite appearances, is a much constrained and limited office. Onerous responsibilities are heaped upon the man in the White House, but many obstacles are placed in his way as he attempts to meet those responsibilities. According to Godfrey Hodgson: 'Never has so powerful a leader been so impotent to do what he wants to do, what he is pledged to do, what he is expected to do, and what he knows he must do'. [19] Presidents must operate in a political culture that is riddled with anti-governmental attitudes and is hostile to political leadership. It is imperative that they establish a good working relationship with a legislative branch that has real teeth and is characterized by a deeply fragmented structure of power. A chief executive must also subdue an enormous and amorphous federal administration packed with individuals who, if not restrained, may thwart a president's plans. And this is not the end of the story. We have concentrated here on the formal institutions of government and the political culture context, but there are other constraints on presidential power. There are pressure groups (which were alluded to under bureaucratic control, but not discussed in any detail), the media, international organizations and the governments of other nations. No wonder Lyndon Johnson remarked in exasperation, 'The only power I've got is nuclear and I can't use that.'[20]

Some presidents, however, do come to terms with the multiplicity of constraints that confront them and manage to compile reasonable records of achievement. How is this to be explained? What are the secrets of presidential power? The first thing to be said is that the 'circumstantial variables' of a president's incumbency may give him important advantages. The tenor of the times may be favourable to presidential action. He may take office during a period of crisis when the American people are willing to suspend their paranoia about leadership. In such a situation members of congress may also be prepared to forego their usual concern with constitutional niceties in the interest of allowing the president to cope with an international or domestic crisis. A president may also benefit from movements in the cycles of American history, by taking office at a moment advantageous to his policy preferences. Some presidents are favoured with sweeping personal victories at the polls and that success may be flanked by considerable success for their party in congressional elections. By no means will the latter guarantee the president success in his constant struggles with the legislature, but it will provide him with an invaluable starting point.[21] His chances of accomplishing policy change will also be enhanced if he maintains high levels of support in public opinion polls.

Armed with some or, very rarely, all of the above resources, presidents may achieve some degree of mastery over the American political system. Such mastery, however, will normally be brief; it is unlikely to outlast the passing of crisis and/or movement in the cycles of history; it will not survive substantial loss of congressional or popular support and it will be relentlessly eroded by the passage of time. And if only fleeting mastery is possible for exceptionally advantaged presidents, what of the generality, of those who possess few resources?

All presidents must move carefully and skilfully if they are to be effective leaders. Even those with many advantages will have precious few opportunities for issuing commands with the expectation that they will actually be executed. Harry Truman summed up the central dilemma of presidential power when, in reference to his successor, he said, 'He'll sit here, and he'll say, "Do this! Do that!" *And nothing will happen.* Poor Ike, it won't be a bit like the Army. He'll find it very frustrating.'[22] It was, of course, absolutely correct to assert that the government of the United States bore little resemblance to the army. Military organizations possess hierarchical structures; senior officers at the apex of a pyramid issue commands which are relayed down to those who are obliged to carry them out. Even in military organizations subordinates are not above evading or diluting orders from on high, but given the extent of relatively rigid discipline the scope for such activity will be very restricted.

Presidents, on the other hand, can rarely issue plausible, self-executing commands; for the most part they must persuade rather than order other political actors to do what they want them to do. To implement his programme, a president must gain the cooperation or acquiesence of other members of the political élite, but such people are unlikely to be responsive to presidential directives for the relationship between them and the president is not one of simple dependency. Members of congress, senior bureaucrats and other leaders share power with the president; they do not hold their jobs at his discretion and the fulfilment of their career objectives does not lie in his hands alone. As Richard Neustadt puts it, 'When one man shares authority with another, but does not gain or lose his job on the other's whim, his willingness to act upon the urging of the other turns on whether he conceives the action right for him.'[23] Legislators and civil servants in the US enjoy a degree of independence and freedom to go their own way that is unheard of in the UK.

Given the above circumstances it is hardly possible to dissent from Neustadt's assertion that 'presidential *power* is the power to persuade', what is more controversial, however, is his further statement, 'the power to persuade is the power to bargain.'[24] The notion of bargaining undoubtedly captures a great deal of what presidential power is all about, but it does not provide a complete explanation.

Bargaining occurs in all political systems, but nowhere is it more prevalent than in the United States – 'The necessity for constant bargaining is . . . built into the very structure of American government.'[25] Bargaining is synonomous with trading or dealing and may be briefly defined as participation in mutually beneficial transactions. *A* seeks the cooperation of *B*, but lacks the means to impose his will. *B* may be willing to cooperate in return for an inducement offered by *A*. Political life in America sometimes seems only to be about bargaining in one form or another:

> The politician is, above all, the man whose career depends upon successful negotiation of bargains. To win office he must negotiate electoral alliances. To satisfy his electoral alliance he must negotiate alliances with other legislators and administrators, for his control depends on negotiation. Most of his time is consumed with bargaining. That is the skill he cultivates; it is the skill that distinguishes the master politician from the political failure.[26]

Bargaining skill is indispensable in a chief executive obliged to operate in a pluralist system of decison-making where power is diffused and decentralized, and where there is a multiplicity of significant power holders rather than just a few. The president is the chief bargainer in the American political system. Without bargaining skills, a president will be a nonentity in the White House, unable to control other political leaders and incapable of meeting his responsibilities as the principal public policy-maker.

Suppose, for the purposes of illustration, that a president and his advisers are convinced of the essential need for a new weapons system. At some stage this will require the passage of authorizing legislation and a key figure in the legislative process in this case will be the chairman of the House Armed Services Committee; without his or her agreement the president's bill will not pass. This major congressional leader may not be a member of the president's party, but, even if he is, his cooperation cannot be guaranteed. Whether this chairman goes along with the president or not may turn on many factors, but bargaining is very likely to play a part.

What this hypothetical committee chairman has to offer a president is self-evident, but what favours can the latter trade in return for the chairman's support? Some of the benefits used by chief executives for negotiating purposes may be quite trivial, although of great importance to the recipient. Congressmen value invitations to White House functions and enjoy receiving presidential pens at bill-signing ceremonies. Similarly, a photograph of the congressman with the president at his side may be invaluable for electoral purposes.

> A president can bestow on a member of Congress many other personal amenities, including a walk around the White House grounds (with a picture for the hometown newspaper), hints from White House sources of the value of the person's advice, designation as the sponsor of important legislation, appointment to a special presidential delegation or commission, a ride on Air Force One, baseball tickets in the presidential box seats, and recognition in speeches. President Kennedy sent congratulatory birthday notes to members of Congress, as did Johnson.[27]

At a more substantial level, a president might agree to appear in the constituency of a key congressman at election time to provide him with highly visible and, possibly, crucial support. Patronage in the form of federal jobs for the friends and followers of members of congress is useful for bargaining purposes. The president can use his influence to channel campaign contributions in the direction of favoured legislators; by working through party leaders, he may help a congressman to achieve a desirable committee post. A president's support for a legislator's pet bill may be vital to its passage. Similarly, success in obtaining appropriations for projects in a member's constituency may depend on signals from the White House

The president has at his disposal an array of bargaining counters that he must ceaselessly and skilfully deploy in countless negotiating situations. Often, of course, bargains are implicit rather than explicit. A congressman's support for the president on a particular issue may not represent a straightforward *quid pro quo*; it could well be a mark of his gratitude for favours bestowed upon him in the past.

Bargaining might be said to help fill the vacuum that in other systems is occupied by disciplined political parties. To put it another way, bargaining provides the cement essential if the American polity is to be anything more than a conglomeration of unintegrated fragments. Only by constant bargaining can a president hope to bring order to the inherent chaos of the US political system and thereby give it direction and purpose. On the other hand, there are disadvantages in a decision making system that depends so much on bargaining. Such arrangements are not conducive to rational problem-solving; solutions turn not on principle and reasoned argument, but on compromises, accommodation and, on occasion, rather sordid 'wheeling and dealing'.[28] The rooting out of inefficiency and waste in government becomes extremely difficult, because a reforming president, will soon be in trouble if he is insensitive to the needs of congressmen demanding patronage and other benefits for their constituents.

Another difficulty that arises in a system where public policy emerges primarily out of a clash of partial interests, crudely resolved by bargaining, is that the national interest is likely to be neglected. Furthermore, those with the most resources, the most bargaining counters, will be at an advantage; the organized, the wealthy and the privileged are likely to gain while the problems of the unorganized, the poor and the underprivileged may be given insufficient attention.[29] In political systems heavily dependent on trading and dealing, matters of principle get short shrift, long-standing problems are not faced and there is little scope for more than modest incremental change.

Bargaining is an unavoidable necessity in American politics and negotiating skill is a central component of presidential power. It would be a mistake, however, to assume that the latter is about nothing else. To assume that everything turns on the exchanging of benefits is to cast an unwarranted slur on many honourable, and sometimes courageous, public officials. By no means are all such men and women impervious to the claims of rational problem-solving and the demands of the national interest – the politics of principle also has its place.

We must also remember that human motivation is a very complex matter and monist explanations are rarely adequate. There are many reasons, apart from the trading of favours, for a legislator or bureaucrat going along with the wishes of the man in the White House. They may be responsive to his charm, his charisma, his intellectual quality or his symbolic position as Chief of State. Members of the political élite may give a president their support out of friendship or because they find him to be a likeable person. They may be moved by a sense of party loyalty. They may be intimidated by the president's apparent command over public opinion – a position he may seek to reinforce by using television, radio and public speaking in general.

Members of congress are, in any event, likely to be in awe of the president; a direct telephone call from him will carry special weight as Tip O'Neill reports: 'The men and women in Congress love nothing better than to hear from the head guy. So they can go back to their districts and say, "I was talking to the president the other day." '[30]

When congressmen visit the president in the White House, surrounded by the trappings of his great office, they are hardly likely to perceive him as just another bargainer. For his part the president, as he tries to get the cooperation he needs, will not restrict himself to offering inducements. He will use the arts of cajolery and flattery, possibly deferring to the experience and expertise of congressmen and pandering to their keen sense of constitutional importance.

To summarize, presidents do not depend on the trading of favours alone. Members of Congress and senior administrators are moved by considerations other than the carrots and sticks available to a chief executive. The latter and his staff will use an amalgam of strategems and techniques, many of which do not fall within a satisfactory definition of bargaining. Nevertheless, a willingness and an ability to bargain are essential in a president who aspires, as they all must, to be 'on top in fact as well as name', and who hopes to bring about significant public policy change.

If we return to the point where this chapter began, it is surely evident that nothing approaching the executive hegemony found in the United Kingdom exists in the United States. In the former there is far greater scope for effective executive leadership, and public policy change can occur in an orderly, rational and efficient manner. By contrast, the decision making system in the United States can only be described as ramshackle; however, rationality and efficiency are not necessarily the first priorities of a democratic political system, especially one as vast and heterogeneous as the United States. In such a country consensus does not come about easily and in many policy areas may be impossible. From this side of the Atlantic we may raise our eyebrows at the opportunities for obstruction and procrastination and the constant search for the lowest common denominator, but arguably these are part of the price of freedom and democracy in the American context.

NOTES AND REFERENCES

1. Anthony King, 'Mrs Thatcher as a Political Leader' in Robert Skidelsky (ed), *Thatcherism*. Chatto and Windus, London 1988, pp. 51–64.
2. Gallup.
3. Richard Nathan, *The Administrative Presidency*. Macmillan, New York 1986, p. 141.
4. *Leadership*.
5. Richard Neustadt, 'Preface to the Original Edition' in *Presidential Power*. John Wiley and Son, New York 1976 (edition).

6. See, for example, David Mervin, 'The President and Congress' in Malcolm Shaw (ed), *Roosevelt to Reagan: The Development of the Modern Presidency*. C. Hurst, London 1987, pp. 83–118.

7. Arthur Schlesinger, Jr, *The Imperial Presidency*. Popular Library, New York 1974, p. 463.

8. Barbara Hinckley, *The Seniority System in Congress*. Indiana University Press, Bloomington 1971, p. 3.

9. See, for example, David Mervin, 'Individualism and the New Congress' in Lynton Robins (ed), *The American Way*. Longman, London 1985, pp. 90–101.

10. In 1988, 402 of 409 House incumbents seeking re-election were returned. For the second successive election more than 98 per cent of incumbents were re-elected. Stuart Rothenberg, 'Election '88: the House and the Senate', *Public Opinion* **11**, No. 5 (Jan./Feb. 1989), pp. 8–11.

11. Robert Dahl, *Congress and Foreign Policy*. W.W. Norton, New York 1950, p. 136.

12. See William Safire, *Before the Fall*. Belmont Tower Books, New York 1975, p. 248.

13. Douglas Cater, *Power in Washington*. Random House, New York 1964.

14. Quoted in Neustadt, op. cit., p. 110.

15. See Robert Williams, 'The President and the Executive Branch' in Shaw, op. cit. Table 4.1, p. 120.

16. Joel Aberbach and Bert Rockman, 'Clashing Beliefs in the Executive Branch: The Nixon Administration Bureaucracy', *American Political Science Review* **LXX**, No. 2 (June 1976), pp. 456–68.

17. Richard Nathan, *The Plot that Failed; Nixon and the Administrative Presidency*. John Wiley and Son, New York 1975, p. 69.

18. Anthony Howard (ed), *The Crossman Diaries*. Hamish Hamilton and Johnathan Cape, London 1979, *passim*.

19. *All Things to all Men*. Weidenfield and Nicolson, London 1980, p. 13.

20. Ibid., p. 14.

21. Paul Light, *The President's Agenda*. The Johns Hopkins University Press, Baltimore 1982, p. 27.

22. Neustadt, op. cit. p. 77.

23. Ibid., p. 102.

24. Ibid., p. 104.

25. Robert Dahl and Charles Lindblom, *Politics Economics and Welfare*. Harper and Row, New York 1953, p. 336.

26. Ibid., p. 333.

27. George Edwards, *Presidential Influence in Congress*. W.H. Freeman, San Francisco 1980, p. 164.

28. Dahl and Lindblom, op. cit., p. 339.

29. Ibid., p. 340.

30. *Man of the House*. Random House, New York 1987, p. 342.

CHAPTER THREE

The Imperilling of the Presidency

Ronald Reagan's election to the White House occurred at a moment when the credibility of the American presidency was at a particularly low ebb. Of the previous four presidents one, Johnson, had been effectively driven from office by the failure of his Vietnam policy; one, Nixon, had resigned in disgrace and neither Ford nor Carter had been able to cope with the limits on presidential power. To place the Reagan presidency in context therefore, we need some understanding of the political history of the post-World War II period.

This chapter begins by considering the circumstances that brought about the so-called imperial presidency. This will lead into a discussion of the Nixon presidency including Watergate and the repercussions that followed, such as the widespread decline in public trust and a vigorous reassertion of congressional power. These and other factors – such as congressional reform, the increased importance of television in politics and the further weakening of political parties – combined to produce an environment in the middle and later 1970s even more hostile than usual to effective presidential leadership. Gerald Ford and Jimmy Carter were in office in conditions far removed from those that prevailed at the beginning of the decade. As Ford himself put it later the imperial presidency had been replaced by an, 'imperilled presidency'.[1]

THE IMPERIAL PRESIDENCY

In Chapter Two it was noted that although presidents face many difficulties in imposing their will on the American political system their chances of doing so are rather greater in foreign and defence policy than in domestic affairs. In the former areas the chief executive is sustained in his perennial struggle for mastery with congress by his claim to represent the nation as a whole and by the provisions of the Constitution that designate him as Commander in Chief and give him special responsibilites in international relations. In the early years of the republic these were factors of no great consequence, but they have assumed great importance since the movement of the United States on to the world stage in the twentieth century. Furthermore, for the past fifty years there has been a more or less perpetual state of international crisis, with America constantly involved as a leading player. Crisis situations invariably tend to tilt the balance of power in favour of the president at the expense of congress. As former Senator Fulbright remarked in 1966:

> In the past 25 years, American foreign policy has encountered a shattering series of crises and inevitably – or almost inevitably – the effort to cope with these has been executive effort, while the Congress, inspired by patriotism.importuned by Presidents and deterred by lack of information has tended to fall in line. The result has been an unhinging of traditional constitutional relationships.[2]

That unhinging extended back at least as far as the Japanese attack on the American fleet at Pearl Harbor in December 1941, a crisis which allowed Franklin Roosevelt finally to break free from the congressional restraints on executive action that had been operative in the inter war period. On this occasion congress exercised its constitutional right to declare war, but, in retrospect, this seems to have been no more than a case of going through the motions – the age of crisis was well underway and the constitutional balance of powers would never be the same again.

Just how far things had gone was demonstrated in 1950 when North Korea invaded South Korea. In a reaction with profound long-term implications President Truman promptly despatched American forces to support South Korea and, on the advice of Dean Acheson, his Secretary of State, deliberately chose not to seek congressional authorization for this act of war. Truman defended his response to the North Korean invasion as falling within his constitutional power as Commander in Chief and claimed the right to send US troops wherever in the world he thought necessary.[3]

What is remarkable is not so much Truman's sweeping claim, but the ease with which he gained support for his action in congress. Liberal senators – such as Wayne Morse of Oregon, Paul Douglas of

Illinois and J. William Fulbright of Arkansas – who were noted for their intellect and independence, all vigorously defended Truman against lonely critics like Robert Taft of Ohio. According to Douglas, 'With tanks, airplanes and the atom bomb, war can become instantaneous and disaster can occur while congress is assembling and debating.'[4] In emergency situations, it seemed, constitutional niceties had no place and the chief executive had to be allowed a free hand, an ominous precedent that was to be followed by a series of major military initiatives by presidents with little or no regard to the war power of congress.

Thus, in 1958 Eisenhower sent 14,000 troops into the Lebanon without congressional authority. The abortive attack on Cuba at the Bay of Pigs was set in train by the Eisenhower administration and implemented by Kennedy in 1961 without Congressional approval. Similarly, Congress played no role of consequence in the Cuban Missile crisis and Lyndon Johnson, by the end of his presidency, had more than half a million troops in Vietnam without Congress ever having declared war against the North Vietnamese. By the time Richard Nixon sent units of the US army into Cambodia in 1970 without the approval of the legislature the war power of congress appeared to be a dead letter and the age of the imperial presidency seemed to have arrived. That is to say, the position had been reached where, 'the constitutional balance between presidential power and presidential accountability [was] upset in favor of presidential power'.[5]

By no means had this state of affairs been brought about by presidents alone. Congress had willingly surrendered its prerogatives in the foreign policy field and both the media and the academic community had generally applauded the development. Historians and political scientists like Arthur Schlesinger and Clinton Rossiter repeatedly made the case for an all-powerful president well able to provide effective leadership not only in international affairs, but on the domestic front as well.[6]

In the wake of Watergate and other scandals, the pejorative connotations of the imperial presidency gained added weight, but the concept was always something of a cliché. The word 'imperial' summons up images of the president as an emperor, a supreme sovereign authority, a master of all he surveys. Roosevelt, at the beginning of the 1930s and at the height of World War II, may have briefly approached such a position of pre-eminence, but none of his successors has come even close to such a situation. In the 1950s and 1960s presidents were accorded, in American terms, great leeway in foreign policy, but even that came nowhere near the extraordinary freedom to manoeuvre enjoyed by British prime ministers in such matters. And in domestic affairs the power of the legislature continued to be formidable. 'Congress derided President Truman's domestic program, passed significant legislation over his veto and generally dismissed his hope of extending the Roosevelt New Deal into the Truman Fair Deal.'[7] Eisenhower, despite two terms, had little success in domestic policy; Kennedy was only briefly in office and even Lyndon Johnson's famed mastery of congress was very short-lived. Richard Nixon, meanwhile, was constantly driven into a fury by congressional and bureaucratic resistance to his domestic policy initiatives.

With some reason, former President Nixon has said, 'The "Imperial President" was a straw man created by defensive congressmen and by disillusioned liberals who in the days of FDR and John Kennedy had idolized the ideal of a strong presidency.'[8] This analysis could be said to be self-serving, yet it is not without justification; the president was never as powerful as the critics suggested. Nevertheless, the image of an out of control, imperial president became well established in the early 1970s and contributed much to the strong backlash against presidential power that bedevilled Ford and Carter.

THE NIXON PRESIDENCY

The name of Richard Nixon will forever be associated with the Watergate scandal. Nixon betrayed his trust in a number of ways and was justifiably forced to resign; however, the collapse of his presidency turned on relatively trivial matters. The burglary of the offices of the Democratic National Committee was a harebrained and quite unnecessary enterprise and the case against the president that eventually forced his resignation could never have been constructed without the re-installation of recording devices in the Oval Office.[9] The White House tapes provided dramatic evidence not only of a conspiracy to obstruct justice, but also of the existence of a seige mentality in the upper reaches of the executive branch. The president and his senior staff shared a fervent conviction that legislators, administrators and the national media were resolutely opposed to all that Richard Nixon stood for and were determined to prevent him from making a reality of his policy intentions.

The deep sense of frustration and resentment felt by leaders of the Nixon administration should not be dismissed as mere paranoia. In his memoirs the former president writes, 'At the beginning of my second term, Congress, the bureaucracy and the media were still working in concert to maintain the ideas and ideology of the traditional Eastern liberal establishment that had come down to 1973 through the New Deal, the New Frontier, and the Great Society.'[10] This is no more than a statement of fact; throughout the Nixon years the opposition party held large majorities in both Houses of Congress; the bureaucracy was thick with Democrats and the national media, at least, tended to be markedly hostile.

Notwithstanding these disadvantages, Nixon was determined to be an activist president. There was little he could do to combat the hostility of the media, but after the frustrations of his first term he decided to face up to the bureaucracy and the legislature. After his re-election in 1972 Nixon asked for the resignations of all non career employees in the executive branch and took steps to ensure that all those appointed or reappointed were loyal to him and his policies.

> No longer would the Cabinet be composed of men with national standing in their own right who were in a position to go their own way and were disposed by past experience to do so. Unprecedented changes were to be made in the designation (and removal) of appointed officials and in the assignment of their duties. The President's men – trusted lieutenants, tied closely to Richard Nixon and without national reputations of their own – were to be placed in direct charge of the major program bureaucracies.[11]

Nixon's strategy, in other words, was to *take over* the bureaucracy while, at the same time, he would *take on* the congress. Although he had been a member of both the US House of Representatives and the US Senate he had never been a true man of Congress. By the time he reached the White House, he shared fully the deep contempt for Congress that his hero Woodrow Wilson had repeatedly displayed. Like Wilson, Nixon believed that his national mandate gave him a legitimacy that the legislature lacked, a body that was, 'cumbersome, undisciplined, isolationist, fiscally irresponsible, overly vulnerable to pressures from organized minorities, and too dominated by the media'.[12]

John Ehrlichman, Assistant to the President for Domestic Affairs, has provided vivid testimony of the low esteem accorded the legislative branch in the Nixon White House. According to his view, congress was no more than a 'herd of mediocrities' where, 'members consume time in enormous quantities in their quaint Congressional processes. They recess; they junket; they arrive late and they leave early; they attend conferences out of town, fly off to give speeches, sip and chat and endlessly party. And only sometimes do they focus on legislation.' Gerald Ford, the leader of the Republicans in the House, 'might have become a pretty good Grand Rapids insurance agent; he played a good game of golf, but he wasn't excessively bright'. The Senate Republican leader, Hugh Scott, meanwhile, was 'a hack' and 'a rotund, owlish Pennsylvania machine politician'. Not surprisingly, meetings between Nixon and his staff and Republican Congressional leaders were not especially happy affairs. 'Our dynamic legislative leaders drank coffee and occasionally took notes, but they rarely were given a chance to say anything.'[13]

These remarks it should be noted were directed specifically at the Republican Congressional leadership by the man with the primary responsibility for persuading congress to accept the president's domestic programme. In their efforts to master Congress, presidents have normally given a high priority to working through their party's legislative leaders, but it is clear that an amicable and productive relationship with such leaders was not established during the Nixon years. It has been argued also that if the president and the Congress are to work well together, each branch must respect the other's legitimacy and competence; however, Nixon and his aides made no pretence of granting that much to the legislature.[14] Instead they set out to ride roughshod over the legislative branch, attempting to govern without congress rather than with it. Given these provocations, it is not surprising that Congress, when it got the chance, should strike back against the executive. Watergate was to provide just such an opportunity.

As that scandal unfolded during 1973 and 1974, foreign observers viewed the proceedings with some amazement. In the first place they were presented with a riveting demonstration of what a genuinely free press is capable of. Journalists such as Bob Woodward and Carl Bernstein of the *Washington Post* filed innumerable stories, often drawn from anonymous sources, and including less than completely substantiated allegations of criminal behaviour by public officials. Piece by piece, a picture emerged of wrong-doing in high places and eventually congress and law enforcement agencies were obliged to take action. Such stories would have never been published in the United Kingdom, for instance, where public officials can hide behind punitive laws of libel and press freedom is less assiduously protected. The Watergate hearings in Congress and the publication of the White House tapes also made possible an exposure of the inner workings of an administration to a degree inconceivable in Britain, where the shroud of secrecy that envelops matters of state is never lifted more than fractionally, even in moments of high crisis.

There was some tendency at the time to argue that the Watergate affair had revealed weaknesses in the American presidential system not found in parliamentary systems. A prime minister, so the argument went, who was the subject of such a massive loss of confidence among both the political élite and the public at large would swiftly have been removed from office. The boil of misgovernment would have been lanced very quickly and a long festering crisis of confidence in the integrity of the system would have been avoided. However, what such an analysis fails to take into account is that the evidence of wrong-doing that became so public in the United States would almost certainly have never surfaced in the United Kingdom, given the laws of libel and the willingness of the British people to tolerate secrecy in government.

European observers were also inclined to become impatient with the agonizingly slow pace at which congress appeared to move towards the impeachment of Richard Nixon. Television screens around the world seemed to show that the president and his associates were guilty as charged and there could be no doubt that public confidence in the Nixon administration had been shattered. Why, therefore, did congress not get on with the business of removing a patently guilty president? Impeaching a president, however, is not comparable to the removal of a prime minister. The latter is a mere politician, whereas the former is much more than that. He is also a symbolic figure who represents the unity of the nation and sits in the chair once occupied by folk heroes and demi gods such as Washington, Jefferson and Lincoln. To remove a president from office is comparable to removing a monarch, impeachment is closer to regicide than to the mere sacking of a prime minister.

Nixon's forced resignation, in other words, was a deeply traumatic episode in the history of the United States. It struck a devastating blow at the presidency as an institution and gave powerful new impetus to the collapse of trust in government that had begun some years previously. A famous study of comparative political culture, based on research in 1959 and 1960, revealed that, when Americans were asked what things they were most proud of in their country, 85 per cent had spontaneously mentioned governmental and political institutions. By comparison only 46 per cent of British respondents, 30 per cent of Mexicans, 7 per cent of Germans and 3 per cent of Italians expressed pride in their governmental and political institutions.[15] The 1960s and 1970s, however, saw, in the United States, a devastating erosion of public confidence in political institutions. Thus, in 1964 only 22 per cent of Americans held to the view that government could be trusted only, 'some of the time', whereas this had increased to 37 per cent by 1968, 45 per cent by 1972, 61 per cent by 1974 and 73 per cent by 1980. The collapse of trust in government that occurred in the 1970s cannot be attributed entirely to Watergate; the trend was established before 1973. Nevertheless, there was a particularly sharp increase in cynicism about political institutions in general between 1972 and 1974. During this same period there was also a precipitous fall from 76 per cent to 42 per cent in public confidence in the executive branch of the federal government.[16] It is clear that by the time Ronald Reagan entered office concerns generated by the spectre of the imperial presidency and intensified by the pattern of misgovernment symbolized by Watergate had had a seriously detrimental effect on public perceptions of the presidency.

CONGRESSIONAL REASSERTION

Congress has always posed major problems for the man in the White House. He must work in, 'a government of separated institutions *sharing* powers', and he will accomplish little without the cooperation of the legislative branch.[17] That cooperation, however, is not easily obtained; congress has become notably more difficult to master than before. In part, this may be attributed to Watergate and related scandals, but those events by no means provide a complete explanation. Many of the changes that helped to bring about in the 1970s a new, more fragmented and more intractable congress would have happened irrespective of the misdemeanours of the Nixon administration.

The invasion of Cambodia by US troops in 1970 can be seen as the high point in a twenty-year erosion of the legislature's role in the making of foreign and defence policy. However, as the United States began its ignominious withdrawal from South East Asia congress finally set about reclaiming the ground it had surrendered to the executive branch. During the 1970s there was to be a flood of legislation designed to limit the freedom of the president in these policy areas. The decade began with congress passing various bills that sought to cut off funding for the Vietnam War and in 1973 legislators moved on to pass the War Powers Act over President Nixon's veto.

The provisions of this act require a president to consult with congress about any commitment of American troops abroad and oblige him to withdraw those troops within 60 days (with the possibility of a 30-day extension) if a declaration of war is not forthcoming from Congress. When this act was debated, many doubted whether it would achieve its dual purpose of curbing presidents and giving teeth to the constitutional war power of Congress. With good reason some senators argued that the position of the president in these vital matters would be strengthened rather than weakened. He was effectively granted a blank cheque to conduct a war without Congressional authorization for up to 90 days. And, at the end of such a period, if American troops were still abroad it would be unthinkable for Congress to sabotage their position by denying the chief executive a declaration of war. In practice, moreover, presidents have shown the War Powers Act scant respect; nevertheless, in the context of 1973, it was a symbolically important reassertion of congressional prerogative.

Further evidence of a new mood in the legislature in this period can be seen in the steps taken to curtail the activities of the Central Intelligence Agency. High-powered investigations of intelligence agencies in the wake of Watergate had revealed much evidence of illicit and unconstitutional behaviour. With the Hughes–Ryan Act of 1974, Congress endeavoured to impose some discipline on the CIA by requiring the agency to obtain presidential approval before embarking on covert operations and obliging it to notify eight different Congressional committees either before, or soon after, such operations commenced. This was amended in 1980 – notice now only has to be given to the House and Senate Intelligence committees.

A determination to rein in the president also lay behind the Case Act that became law in 1972. Historically, the Senate's claim to a say in the making of foreign policy had depended on the provisions in the Constitution regarding treaty-making. Treaties with foreign powers were to be negotiated by the president, but were then subject to ratification by the Senate. In the twentieth century, however, presidents had increasingly made use of executive agreements as instruments of foreign policy. By definition, such agreements did not require approval by the legislature and 'In the year 1930 the United States made 25 treaties and only 9 executive agreements; in 1971, 214 executive agreements and only 17 treaties. The Nixon administration, up to May 1, 1972, had concluded 71 treaties and 608 executive agreements.'[18] It was argued in the Senate that presidents were using executive agreements not for minor matters, as originally intended, but as vehicles for entering into major foreign and defence policy commitments without reference to congress. The Case Act was devised to end such abuse; forthwith executive agreements, within 60 days of their negotiation, would have to be sent to the House and the Senate for approval.

By the War Powers Act, the Hughes–Ryan Act, the Case Act and a number of other bills in the 1970s, Congress made strenuous efforts to reclaim ground lost to the president in the realm of foreign policy. Similarly, the Congressional Budget and Impoundment Act of 1974 reflected the determination of the legislature to reassert its authority in domestic policy-making. Legislators had been deeply angered by Richard Nixon's assault on congress's most important and most treasured prerogative – the power of the purse. Bolstered by his landslide electoral victory in 1972, the President moved to take on the legislature. Central to his strategy was impoundment, a procedure whereby the chief executive chooses not to spend funds that have been appropriated by Congress. This was an entirely legitimate and historically well-founded practice, but Nixon carried it to extreme lengths, seeing it as a way both to cut back on federal expenditure and to impose his own order of spending priorities.

Impoundment may be justified when the administration of a programme reveals opportunities to save, or perhaps divert, funds without negating the policy intentions of the legislative branch. Impoundments that went beyond that and involved policy change had occurred in the past, but these were either justified under the Commander-in-Chief clause in the Constitution, or had been the subject of consultation with congressional leaders. President Nixon, however, used the weapon of impoundment without restraint, embarking 'on large scale impoundments in programs that he wanted to terminate or curtail. The impoundments – predominantly for policy purposes – totalled in excess of $18 billion, double the amount officially reported by the administration and far above the comparable action of any previous president.'[19] In response, Congress, in the 1974 Act, included provisions requiring the president to report impoundments to the legislature, making it possible for either the House or the Senate to compel the release of impounded funds, and obliging the executive to spend them in accordance with legislative intent. Once again Congress had struck back against an overweening executive branch.

The Budget and Impoundment Act also introduced major changes in congressional procedures for dealing with the president's budget. Reformers had long argued that the credibility of the legislature in the eyes of the public and its ability to compete with the executive were both weakened by a chaotic Congressional budgetary process. Budgets, on arrival from the White House, were dismantled and considered piecemeal with little attention to overall concerns about the state of economy, the need to balance expenditures against revenue or the national interest. The budget process in Congress, in other words, was deemed to be irrational, uncoordinated and inefficient. Under the new act these problems were to be addressed by setting up coordinating budget committees in the House and the Senate, drawing up a realistic timetable for dealing with the budget and establishing a Congressional Budget Office that would provide the staff and expertise necessary for dealing with the budget responsibly.

Like the War Powers Act, the budget reform act has not lived up to the expectations of those who crafted it. Nevertheless, the establishment of the CBO in particular had significant consequences for the balance of power between the legislature and the White House. Since the establishment of the modern presidency in the 1930s and the massive expansion of governmental activity, congress has always been at a disadvantage in its constant battles with the executive arising from the latter's superior access to information and expertise. This had been especially the case in budgetary matters and the foundation of the CBO went some way towards correcting the situation. In the words of Stuart Eizenstat, Jimmy Carter's domestic policy chief, 'One can trace from the time of the New Deal through the early and mid-parts of the Nixon administration, a clear, gradual, perceptible increase in presidential power relative to the legislative branch. The creation of the CBO began to redress the balance of power. It did that via one fundamental way – it ended the president's monopoly on information, on budget forecasts, on economic forecasts.'[20]

By the middle of the 1970s it was evident that a new mood was present in congress. Vietnam, Watergate and other horrors associated with the so-called imperial presidency had wrought severe damage on the standing of the executive branch. Those who, in the media and academe, had for years vaunted presidents amd expounded 'executive force' theories were now busily reconsidering their views. [21] In this new atmosphere the legislature displayed a determination to defend itself against executive encroachment, not seen for some years.

CONGRESSIONAL REFORM

The new posture was reflected in other steps that Congress took in an attempt to improve its procedures and which, ultimately, were to make life substantially more difficult for presidents. In the late 1960s the case for Congressional reform had gathered strength. The legislature was condemned as unrepresentative, as an institution dominated by a minority of rural and small town based conservatives, usually from the South, out of touch with the needs of the majority, located largely outside the South and living mainly in urban areas.[22]

The structure of the 'old' Congress was found badly wanting. In both houses, the reformers claimed, committee chairmen exercised disproportionate power. Secure in their seniority, these Congressional 'barons' determined when and if committee meetings were held; controlled the appearance of witnesses; decided the speaking opportunities of their colleagues on the committee; hired and fired committee staff; decreed whether or not their would be sub-committees; appointed sub-committee chairmen; reported the deliberations of the committee to the full House and appointed committee representatives to conference committees. By no means were all chairmen tyrants, but the opportunities were there and had made possible the emergence of uncontrollable 'powerhouse' figures such as Judge Howard Smith of Virginia, the chairman of the House Rules Committee, and Wilbur Mills of Arkansas, the chairman of the Ways and Means Committee.

The undue power of committee chairmen in relation to their colleagues was more of a problem in the House than in the Senate, but in the latter a system of legislative norms or folkways made possible dominance of the proceedings by leading members of the Senate inner club or establishment. In 1963 Senator Joseph Clark of Pennsylvania said, 'The Senate establishment . . . is almost the antithesis of democracy. It is not selected by any democratic process. It appears to be quite unresponsive to the caucuses of the two parties, be they Republican or Democratic. It is what might be called a self-perpetuating oligarchy with mild, but only mild overtones of plutocracy.'[23]

Clark's analysis was confirmed by eminent observers of the Senate such as William S. White and Donald R. Matthews.[24] They argued that the Senate was in the hands of a mainly southern élite, armed with a self-serving code of legislative norms. Senators who entertained thoughts of becoming effective members were obliged to serve a lengthy period of apprenticeship; they had to be dedicated to their work as senators; they were also expected to specialize and, in turn, to respect the specialization of others. In debate they had to be elaborately courteous towards their colleagues and non-ideological in their comments. And, above all else, members were obliged to display a total commitment to the Senate as an institution. Senators who refused to conform to these inherently conservative norms were condemned to ineffectiveness. Some of these arguments were overstated; nevertheless, power in the Senate in that era was, without doubt, highly centralized with most leading positions held by senior conservatives, or by those who made themselves acceptable to the ruling élite.

In both Houses of Congress in this earlier period the mechanisms of party possessed little meaning. The Democrats had ostensibly been in control of Congress for some time, but the real power lay with a conservative coalition embracing, on the one hand, southern Democrats, and Republicans on the other. This cross party informal alliance had a stranglehold on key committees such as the Rules and Ways and Means committees in the House and the Finance and Judiciary committees in the Senate.

Presidents in their dealings with congress had to cope with some extraordinarily powerful leaders. Smith and Mills in the House had their counterparts in the Senate – leaders of the 'inner club', such as Richard Russell of Georgia and Robert Kerr of Oklahoma. There were also occasionally outstanding party leaders like Speaker Sam Rayburn in the House and Senate Democratic leader Lyndon Johnson. However, these were leaders whose strength rested not so much on their control of the machinery of party as on their skill as exceptional political manipulators.

A 'new' Congress began to emerge in the early 1970s following changes in its regional composition, Congressional reform, developments in campaign practices and the new importance of television in legislative politics. In the first place Democratic representation from the South declined. In 1960, 94 per cent of House seats in the South were held by the Democrats, a figure that declined to 68 per cent by 1972. In the Senate, meanwhile, the Democrats held all the seats in the South in 1960 but only 68 per cent by 1972. As late as 1967, 50 per cent of all standing committee chairmanships in the House and 56 per cent in the Senate were held by southerners. By 1971, however, the number of house standing committees chaired by southerners had fallen to 38 per cent and to 23 per cent by 1979; meanwhile the comparable figures in the Senate were 53 per cent in 1971 and 27 per cent in 1979. In the 1970s in other words, the influence of the South in Congress declined dramatically.[25]

The 1970s was also an era of Congressional reform. Pressures for change had been building up within the legislature for some time and these were to be given added impetus by the events surrounding the resignation of President Nixon. In 1970 the first Congressional reform bill for more than two decades was passed – the Legislative Reorganization Act. Among other things, this bill strengthened the position of rank-and-file committee members *vis à vis* chairmen. Thus, in the absence of the chairman the ranking majority member of a committee would preside. There was also an attempt to ensure full and free participation in committee hearings by all members and restraints were imposed on the use of proxy votes by chairmen; in addition, all votes in committee and on the floor were now to be recorded and open to public scrutiny.[26]

In the same period the power of standing committee chairmen was further eroded by the institutionalization and proliferation of sub-committees. Hitherto such bodies had been under the sway of the main committee chairman, but now they began to acquire a life of their own. The Democratic caucus in the House decided in 1971 that members should be limited to one sub-committee chairmanship thereby making it possible for many more congressmen to hold these coveted posts. Two years later the so-called sub-committee bill of rights

> declared that full committees should respect the jurisdiction of each of their sub-committees. All legislation referred to a full committee was to be parceled out to the appropriate sub committee within two weeks. Sub-committees were empowered to elect their own leaders; write their own rules; employ their own staffs; and meet, hold hearings, and act on legislation. Each committee was entitled to its own budget. The 'bill of rights' was a declaration of independence from the full committee and its chairperson.[27]

In 1974 the Democratic caucus further decided that all standing committees with more than 20 members should have at least 4 sub-committees. The effect of all these changes concerning sub-committees was dramatic. Twenty years previously there had been only 83 sub-committees of standing committees in the House, but by 1976 there were 151; during the same period the number of sub-committees in the Senate increased from 88 to 140.[28] There were now large numbers of sub-committee chairmen and within the narrow policy area covered by that sub-committee they were highly influential political actors. Power in Congress, in other words, was even more diffused and scattered than it had been before.

The distribution of power in the legislature was also fundamentally altered by the dilution of the seniority principle in the early 1970s.

Seniority had been a bulwark of power and independence for chairmen in the past, but now both parties in both houses began to edge towards change. In December 1974 the Democratic caucus in the House took the momentous step of agreeing to an automatic secret ballot election for all committee chairmen and went on to remove W. R. Poage, the chairman of the Agriculture Committee, F. Edward Hebert, chairman of the Armed Services Committee, and Wright Patman of the Banking Committee .

Committee chairmen generally continue to be selected on the basis of seniority and, indeed, only one other sitting standing committee chairman, Mel Price of Armed Services in 1985, has actually been deposed since in either house. There have also been a few cases where junior members have successfuly challenged senior colleagues in contests for sub committee chairmanships. Nevertheless there is no denying that the threat of removal has radically altered the relationship between chairmen and committee members. Judge Smith formerly chairman of the Rules Committee was a man greatly feared by his colleagues, but no chairman would dare follow his example in the congress of today. As Representative Mo Udall has colourfully put it, 'It used to be that when you met a chairman in the hall you bowed low and said, hello Mr Chairman; now when you meet a chairman in the hall *he* bows low.'[29]

Modification of the seniority system grew out of the renewed importance of the Democratic party caucus and in turn added weight to that organization. The influence of party structures had for long been curtailed by the arrangements for selecting chairmen; arrangements which made it possible for situations to arise where the president, the Congressional party leadership and a majority of the majority party could all be united on a particular issue yet might be thwarted by the whims of an all-powerful committee chairman. Seniority reform made committee chairmen more beholden to their party and its leaders and other innovations carried this process further. The speaker, the principal majority party leader, now acquired the right to nominate his party's representatives on the mighty Rules Committee, subject to ratification by the caucus. Furthermore, the Democratic members of the House Ways and Means Committee lost the power to determine committee assignments for their party. Democratic committee assignments would now be in the hands of an executive committee of the caucus, a re-styled Steering and Policy Committee chaired by the Speaker.

The Legislative Reorganization Act of 1970, the sub committee bill of rights and seniority reform all helped to break the power of committee chairmen in the House of Representatives while other changes, including public and recorded voting, plus new rules decreeing open committee meetings, except in special circumstances, had the effect of making the House more open and accessible than it had ever been before. Parallel procedural changes occurred at the same time in the Senate, but other factors were at work there too.

By the early 1970s the Senate was no longer controlled by an oligarchy. The norms of good legislative behaviour had lost the potency they once had, as former Senate Majority Leader Mike Mansfield said on his retirement in 1976:

> There is no longer an inner club dictating the Senate's affairs. No senators are more equal than others. Assignments are made on the basis of geography and philosophy. Seniority is still a factor but in a declining sense. There is no such thing now as a super senator or a second rate senator. They all participate. They don't go through a wallflower period or a silent period. [30]

The democratization of the Senate proceeded further after Mansfield left. It became even more individualistic and displayed few signs of the closely knit and hierarchically organized structure of the previous era.[31] The balance of power shifted sharply in favour of rank-and-file members; deference towards seniors and courtesy towards all of one's colleagues became less common, and specialization was no longer essential. The norm of institutional patriotism lost its force with senators no longer speaking as if a seat in the Senate was the very height of their ambition.

The increasing irrelevance of legislative norms, the disappearance of the inner club and the triumph of individualism in the Senate are partly accounted for by the decline of the influence of the South in the chamber, although changing leadership styles have also had an effect. Lyndon Johnson led the Democrats in the Senate when the club was at its height in the 1950s; however, his all-encompassing, domineering style contrasted sharply with that of later leaders. Mansfield, Robert Byrd, Howard Baker and Robert Dole have adopted lower profile leadership styles and accepted that junior colleagues should be allowed to play a full part in the proceedings of the Senate.

The further extension of democracy in Congress and a strengthening of the legislature in relation to the executive followed the rapid growth in congressional staff in the 1970s. In a complex modern society, information and expertise are major political resources. If committee chairmen have a monopoly over such resources their colleagues will be badly disadvantaged. Similarly the executive will almost certainly have superior access to these resources when compared to the legislature. Deficiencies in information and expertise can, however, be overcome by the employment of staff. Individual members can be strengthened by the acquisition of personal and committee staff, whereas the legislature as a whole can, by employing its own bureaucracy, better compete with the vast bureaucracy of the executive branch.

Congress has always been better staffed than its counterparts elswhere in the world and by 1979 it had a total staff of 23,056. In other words, there were approximately 43 members of staff for every national legislator divided between personal, committee, leadership and support agency staff. The number of personal staff per member increased in the House from 9 in 1967 to 16 in 1979 and from 17 to 35 in the Senate during the same period. Committee staff in 1965 numbered 571 in the House and 509 in the Senate, whereas by 1979 there were 1,909 such staff in the House and 1,269 in the Senate. The staff in congressional support agencies working for members of congress grew from approximately 1,514 in 1965 to approximately 2,790 in 1979.[32]

Not all the consequences of this explosion of congressional staff have been beneficial. There are, for instance, adverse implications for democracy – in some situations the bureaucrats rather than the elected officials are likely to be found taking decisions. The proliferation of staff has also damaged collegial relationships in Congress. Inevitably there is less face-to-face contact between members and communication must often take place via staff.[33] Nevertheless, the large and rapid growth in staff assistance has undoubtedly made Congress not only more democratic internally, but also more formidable to the chief executive.

CAMPAIGNING FOR CONGRESS

Individualism in Congress arising from internal factors has been reinforced by external change, most notably in electoral campaigns. Congressional elections have, in the last twenty years, become increasingly personal. Success turns on the ability of candidates, first, to attract financial contributions as tokens of personal support; second, to construct an effective personal organization; and, third, to establish a good personal relationship with the voters.

The costs of electioneering rose sharply in the 1970s. Between 1967 and 1980 the Consumer Price Index rose by 67 per cent, whereas during the same period campaign expenditures for House elections rose by 163 per cent and by 150 per cent for elections to the Senate. The total cost of congressional elections in 1980 was $210.6 million and the overwhelming proportion of that amount was raised through personal rather than institutional means. In the House only 6 per cent of election funds were raised by the parties, whereas 66 per cent came via individual contributions and 28 per cent through political action committees, i.e. organizations that make contributions on an individual basis. In the Senate in the same year 9 per cent of funding came through the parties, 62 per cent from individual contributions and 19 per cent through political action committees. Closer examination of these figures show that the proportion of party funds tends to be higher for Republicans than for Democrats, but it is clear that parties in general contribute only relatively small amounts to Congressional election funds. [34] Consequently, parties have little by way of financial sanctions to bring against undisciplined members of congress.

State and local parties have also become significantly less important as campaign organizations for Congressional elections. Candidates must now set up personal machines manned by workers attracted to them by their individual qualities and stands on the issues with little or no reference to party loyalty. Parties, moreover, have lost some of their functions to television. Voters depend much less on the cues and guidance given them by party workers and rely instead on television. Voting decisions tend to be shaped by perceptions derived from television coverage of campaigns. Political commercials might not be as persuasive as is commonly thought, but there are few doubts as to the importance of candidate appearances on 'free' news broadcasts. Television is, of course, a relentlessly personalizing medium. Candidates are required to sell themselves to the voters not so much on the strength of their stands on the issues as on their personal qualities. A candidate's ability to project an image of an agreeable and concerned legislator who will carefully protect and advance the interests of his consituents is crucial.

Close attention to constituent needs has always been an indispensable condition for success in elections to the US congress, but in the 1970s it assumed a new significance. Members of congress increasingly came to believe that they could insulate themselves against electoral defeat by assiduous attention to constituency casework. [35] In an increasingly complex world and confronted by a vast impersonal federal bureaucracy Americans have more and more tended to turn to their Representative or Senator for help with important electoral pay-offs for legislators responsive to these needs. In the words of one congressman, 'A near idiot who has competent casework can stay in congress as long as he wants, while a genius who flubs it can be bounced very quickly.'[36]

Incumbent members of Congress have always been difficult to defeat and too much may have been made of the advantages of incumbency in the modern legislature. What is of greater significance for our analysis is the heavily personal nature of campaigning for today's congress. Members now believe that their success at the polls depends, ultimately, almost entirely on their own efforts. They must raise the large amounts of money needed themselves; recruit an effective personal staff; perform adequately before the TV cameras and maintain a satisfactory personal service for constituents. Given these conditions of campaigning it is not surprising that when they get to Washington legislators are even more inclined towards individualistic behaviour than before, and even less responsive to the appeals of party leaders and presidents.

By the middle of the 1970s a markedly different, and, according to some observers at least, much improved congress had come into being. It was less passive and more assertive, determined to hold on to the powers it had reclaimed from the executive in both foreign and domestic policy. This new Congress was more democratic in its structure with committee chairmen in the House no longer all-powerful barons and the Senate no longer controlled by an oligarchy. A career in congress had now become more meaningful with openings for committee or sub-committee chairmanships widespread. The national legislature was also now more representative and accessible and in closer touch with the world outside. In additon it was a more professional institution aided in the work of government by an expert staff and impressive resources.

There were, however, drawbacks in this new congress, particularly as viewed from the White House. Congressional reassertion from that end of Pennsylvania Avenue became belligerent bloody-mindedness, and congressional reform had created an amorphous and leaderless legislature. As a former aide to President Johnson told Paul Light in early 1979:

> In 1965, there were maybe ten or twelve people who you needed to corral in the House and Senate. Without those people you were in for a tough time. Now, I'd put that figure upwards of one hundred. Believe it, there are so many people who have a shot at derailing a bill that the President has to double his effort for even routine decisions.[37]

From the president's perspective Congress had become impossibly formless in structure. There were no effective leaders with whom he

could deal and, at this point, Congressional parties were of little h
to a chief executive trying to meet his responsibility to govern. T
Congressional reformers had hoped that, by modifying the senior
system, strengthening the party caucuses and other changes, part
would be made more viable, but their efforts were offset by ot
developments, most notably in the realm of campaigning.

The exercise of presidential power is never easy, but Rich
Nixon's successors in the 1970s faced especially difficult problems.
contrast to the boundless optimism of the 1960s the country was s
recovering from the traumas of Vietnam and Watergate and under
ing a crisis of confidence in both political leaders and institutions. T
office of president had been discredited and the balance of power in
political system had shifted in favour of a revived and even m
inchoate congress. In addition, the massive increase in the price of
1973–74 precipitated a period of recession with double-digit inflatic
high unemployment, falling industrial output and collapsing wo
trade. All of these factors taken together helped to bring abou
national sense of economic and political malaise. Yet, if Ford a
Carter were, to a significant extent, in the age of the 'post-imper
presidency victims of circumstances beyond their control, th
failures were also due, in part, to inadequacies in their approaches
the problems of presidential leadership.

GERALD FORD: MAN OF CONGRESS

The accession of Gerald Ford to the presidency in 1974 was a relief
many Americans. Watergate and other traumas could now be
behind them and in place of the paranoid, embittered and beleaguer
Richard Nixon there was now a decent and agreeable man in
White House who just might be able to heal America's wounds a
restore faith in the political system.

Nixon had gone to war with Congress, but there was reason
believe that the new president's relationship with the legislatu
would be more amicable and constructive. Ford, after all, had, un
very recently, been a member of Congress. He had served twent
four years in the US House of Representatives, including nine
Minority Leader of the Republicans, and it was Ford's popularity
both sides of the aisle that had brought him to the presidency. Wh
Spiro Agnew had been forced to resign in 1973, President Nix
would have preferred to appoint as vice-president the renega

Democrat, John Connally. Nixon's advisers impressed upon him that such a controversial figure could not be confirmed by an overwhelmingly Democratic congress. Ford , on the other hand, was one of Congress's own as well as an uncontroversial and innocuous figure acceptable even to Democrats.

When he eventually succeeded Nixon, Ford immediately made reassuring noises to his former colleagues in the legislature. There was no question of his denying the legitimacy of the role of Congress as Nixon had done. Ford signalled his intention to treat legislators as allies rather than adversaries. He assured congress, 'I do not want a honeymoon with you. I want a good marriage. As President I intend to listen.' His relationship with Congress, Ford said, would be marked by 'communication, conciliation, compromise and cooperation'.[38]

Notwithstanding these comforting words, Gerald Ford never succeeded in establishing a productive relationship with the legislative branch. According to Thomas Cronin:

> Congress did give Ford a hard time. Having shaken off years of inertia, Congress took advantage of an appointed president to regain some of its own lost authority. Thus they rejected some of his nominations; they took four months to confirm Nelson Rockefeller(as Vice President); they rejected Ford's foreign aid bill, trimmed his defense appropriations, curtailed military aid to Turkey, denied him the means to conduct open or covert operations in Angola, and so on.[39]

As Cronin and others suggest, Ford was constantly rebuffed and disappointed by Congress; his positive achievements in both foreign and domestic policy were few and in any history of presidential congressional relations he is likely to be best remembered for the most extensive use of the negative power of the veto in modern times.[40] Overall, the presidency of Gerald Ford was not a success. He proved incapable of imposing his leadership on the political system and he failed to bring about significant public policy change.

By no means can Ford's failure be wholly attributed to his personal inadequacies. The success or failure of any president is dependent upon circumstantial variables such as the mood of the country, the size of the chief executive's electoral mandate and the constellation of party forces in Congress. In some respects the popular mood was, initially, rather favourable to Ford; Gallup recorded 71 per cent approval of his presidency. To set against that, however, Ford entered office at a moment when confidence in political leaders had collapsed catastrophically and when the anti-authority tradition embedded in the American political culture had resurfaced. Ford did not possess an electoral mandate of his own at all and in both houses of congress the Republicans were in the minority by large margins – in the Senate there were 56 Democrats and 42 Republicans whereas in the House there were 242 Democrats and 192 Republicans.

Within a short period, Ford's already weak position worsened. His standing in the public opinion polls plummeted as a result of his pardon of Nixon, and the 1974 congressional elections led to further decimation of Republican party representation – the Democrats gaining 49 seats in the House and 4 in the Senate. Given these crushing disadvantages and a term of less than two and a half years, it is perhaps not surprising that Ford's presidency was a failure. As a member of his staff not unreasonably put it:

> We began the term, such as it was, under the worst possible circumstances. We weren't elected; we had only two years left before the 1976 elections; the staff was in shock; the policy process was on the skids; and we faced a basically hostile congress. The 'in' baskets were full, and nothing was going out. Then Ford granted the pardon. We just didn't have enough political *push*.[40]

Ford's own reflections several years after he left the White House are also pertinent to an understanding of the difficulties he faced whilst in office. Writing in 1980, Ford bemoaned the fact that 'the presidency does not operate effectively' and went on to identify two principal areas of difficulty – the Congress and the bureaucracy. In regard to the latter, Ford deplored 'the inability of the White House to maintain control over the large federal bureaucracy. There is nothing more frustrating for a President to issue an order to a Cabinet officer , and then find that, when the order gets out in the field, it is totally mutilated.'

The former president noted that the relationship between the legislature and the executive was no longer what it had been: 'Immediately after World War II the presidency was at a peak; the Congress was very responsive, especially in foreign policy. Today a President really does not have the kind of clout with the Congress that he had thirty years ago, even in matters that affect national security.' Ford suggested that three developments had brought about this weakening of the president's position. First, Congress lacked leaders of consequence and influence like Sam Rayburn, Lyndon Johnson and Everett Dirksen. Second, Congressional reform had made matters worse; it had 'really messed up the way the Congress effectively works. You could run down a list of things that have been done under the title of reform, and they all look good, but the net result is that the Congress has really lost its capability to respond.' The third factor pinpointed by Ford was the decline in party responsibility, 'The parties today are really more or less impotent, and if you do not have party responsibility, the system does not work.'[41]

Ford's survey of the new and more difficult circumstances for chief executives in the late twentieth century was very much to the point. Controlling the bureaucracy poses problems for all presidents and Ford was undeniably correct in arguing that presidents had been deprived of the sort of 'clout' they once had in matters of national security. The new congress did lack consequential leaders and congressional reform and the further weakening of political parties had brought about a variety of undesirable developments.

These considerations, however, do not fully account for the failure of Ford's presidency. Some commentators have found his leadership badly wanting. Richard Reeves, for instance, is quite savagely critical, presenting Ford as a rather vain, ignorant and vacuous man with no attachment to goals or principles, but a great talent for ingratiation. Ford, according to Reeves, had built a career, become a congressional leader and eventually reached the White House not on the strength of any real ability, but because of his extraordinary skill at making himself acceptable to others. He succeeded, in other words, 'by finding and being the least objectionable alternative'. On the other hand, Ford possessed few of the qualities required of a real leader: 'conditioned not to offend, [he] did not know how to inspire, persuade or force people to go anyplace. He did not have the skills and when he tried to imitate them, as he did in pushing the WIN program, all he could offer was a parody of leadership.'[42]

The above rather uncharitable analysis probably takes insufficient account of the deep affection that Ford evidently inspired amongst hard-headed and intelligent congressional colleagues. Nevertheless, Reeves' view is broadly confirmed by Barbara Kellerman's revealing case study of Ford's efforts to obtain a tax cut from congress.[43] On taking office in August 1974, Ford declared that his first priority would be to deal with the ailing American economy. Shortly afterwards he identified inflation as, 'Public Enemy Number One' and urged a tax increase upon congress as a way of damping down consumer spending. It swiftly became apparent that congress would not go along with such an increase, especially after the big Democratic gains in the 1974 elections. By late December, however, the president had, in any case, reversed his position and now took the view that rather than a tax increase a tax cut was required to stimulate the economy. This remarkable *volte face* did little for the president's public reputation, was the cause of much scathing comment in the media and, not surprisingly, a poll revealed that 86 per cent of Americans, 'had no confidence in the ability of the President to manage the economy'.[44]

At the beginning of 1975, Ford sought a tax cut of $16 billion from congress, but once again the portents for approval were not good. Conservatives worried about the budget deficit implications of the proposed cut while the many liberals in congress were convinced that the cut did not go far enough. President Ford threw himself into an extensive programme of consultation with members of congress on behalf of his new policy, but his performance in this acid test of presidential leadership was unimpressive. His earlier complete reversal of his position had done little for his credibility and now as he went after a tax cut his touch was decidedly uncertain.

The real point at issue between the president and the big Democratic majority in congress was the size of the tax cut, but Ford showed weakness by revealing, at an early stage, a willingness to give ground on size while insisting that the most important requirement was that the legislature should act quickly. This was to avoid the difficult and genuinely contentious question and to focus instead on a secondary matter. As Kellerman says,

> In [Ford], more perhaps than with a leader with a reputation for being less nice and more forceful, a premature willingness to compromise could too easily be construed as a reluctance to engage in two-way influence relationships with the gloves off. Indeed, President Ford's failure to indicate in no uncertain terms that size mattered a great deal to him appears to have been interpreted by those who should have been playing the part of followers as a sign that defiance on this issue would be almost cost-free.[45]

Eventually, faced by a less than resolute and tactically naive president, congress agreed a tax-cutting package of nearly $7 billion more than Ford had requested. For a few days the president agonized over whether to exercise his veto, but, in the end reluctantly signed what was now a Congressional rather than a presidential bill.

This lack-lustre performance by Ford, at the beginning of his presidency, in the most crucial area of domestic policy-making, set the tone for his administration. It revealed a chief executive who lacked a clear sense of direction, who compromised too early and too readily, and was insufficiently determined in pursuit of his objectives. Ford was unwilling to apply such sanctions as were available to him, and 'showed no proclivity for arm twisting, or for that matter for doing anything that was likely to incur the wrath or even displeasure of another.'[46] All in all President Ford faced many disadvantages, but he also appears to have lacked the mettle, the tactical know-how, the commitment to goals and the persuasive skills required for effective presidential leadership.

JIMMY CARTER: AN OUTSIDER IN THE WHITE HOUSE

Jimmy Carter's presidency, like that of Gerald Ford, began on an optimistic note with commentators deriving satisfaction from the fact that for the first time for eight years president and Congress would be in the hands of the same party. One journalist went so far as to assert, 'Carter should have little trouble with Congress', while Professor Ross Baker noted that 'the basic elements are in place for a highly satisfactory relationship between Carter and Congress . . . there is no reason to forecast discord between the White House and Capitol Hill. Indeed, should serious strife occur, it would imply an extraordinary erosion of some very auspicious omens.'[47] These rosy expectations were not, however, to be fulfilled and even allowing for a degree of misfortune, Carter's record of achievement as president was slim. Like his predecessor, Carter never really mastered 'that maze of personalities and institutions called the government of the United States', and did not accomplish significant public policy change.[48]

Jimmy Carter's status as an outsider is central to an understanding of his career in national politics. It was crucial to his remarkable success in winning the nomination of his party; without that asset it is most unlikely that he would have secured his narrow victory over Gerald Ford, but it was his insistence on remaining an outsider in spirit that limited his accomplishments in office.

As the 1976 national elections approached the Democrats were still smarting from the humiliations of 1972 when a badly divided party had nominated George McGovern and seen him overwhelmed by a landslide victory for Richard Nixon. Democratic leaders were anxious to avoid a repetition of the damaging splits of 1972; they hoped to nominate a candidate acceptable to all the major elements in the party. The ability of party leaders to manipulate the nomination process had been substantially undercut, however, by party reform. Nominating procedures were now more open and participatory than they had ever been before. Rules changes had transformed the Democratic National Convention into a body much more representative of minorities and the rank-and-file. And, most important of all, the number of states using primary elections to select delegates to the covention had risen from 17 in 1968 to 29 in 1976, with the number of votes cast by delegates chosen or bound by primaries increasing from 37.5 per cent to 72.6 per cent.[49]

In these new circumstances of 'open parties' and 'participatory politics' it became possible for outsiders to seize nominations irrespective of the wishes of party leaders, and Jimmy Carter proved to be just such a candidate. A former governor of Georgia with no national reputation to speak of and, unlike other candidates, unencumbered by office at the time, Carter began his campaign in December 1974, spending the next two years criss-crossing the country seeking name familiarity and the approbation of local and state party officials. By vigorous and confident campaigning Carter first succeeded in the Iowa caucuses and followed this by winning the New Hampshire primary of his party. On the strength of this scanty victory (23,000 votes, i.e. 28 per cent of the total number cast) this largely unknown candidate was now treated by the media as 'the front runner' and 'the man to beat', allowing him to gather the momentum that finally brought him the Democratic nomination.

Carter's success in obtaining the nomination rested on three strengths: first, a long, energetic and assiduous campaign aided by media hype; second, his position as a centrist candidate able to unite the liberal and conservative wings of the party; third, his position as a Washington outsider untainted by the current collapse of confidence in political leaders.

In the general election campaign Carter continued to harp on the need to clear up the 'mess' in Washington, constantly re-echoing the theme of his acceptance speech: 'We want to have faith again! We want to be proud again! We *just* want the truth again. . . . We can have an American government that's turned away from scandal and corruption and official cynicism and is once again as decent and competent as our people.'[50] Given the widespread feelings of disillusionment abroad in 1976, Carter's strategy of offering himself as a new broom was electorally well-judged, but if he impressed the voters, his relentless and sanctimonious moralizing irritated and alienated legislators whose support he would eventually need.

> Carter ran for the White House as a Mr Clean, a Mr Integrity, and a Mr Outsider. He sold himself almost like a detergent who would go to Washington and clean things up. That only bred resentment. His campaign slogans were seen as a 'put down' to Congress. He talked too much of the mess in Washington to win friends there.[51]

When the 1976 election returns were in, Jimmy Carter was found to have won a narrow victory over Gerald Ford. The latter had the important advantage of incumbency, but, as we have seen, was handicapped by a poor record as president and had stumbled badly during the campaign; nevertheless he ran Carter close – 49 to 51 per cent in the popular vote and 240–297 in the Electoral College. As a result of the congressional elections meanwhile, the Democrats retained their crushing margin of superiority, returning 292 candidates in the House (as against 143 Republicans) and in the Senate finishing up with 62 seats (compared with 38 for the Republicans). These majorities in the legislature were only marginally less favourable to the president than those enjoyed by Lyndon Johnson after the 1964 election. However, while Johnson's coat-tails had carried in a sizeable number of members of congress this was not true of Carter who, in fact, ran behind no less than 270 successful Democratic candidates for the House.[52]

The circumstantial variables that prevailed when Carter held office were mixed with some favouring the president and others not. Ford had had a measure of success in restoring confidence, but the national mood remained generally pessimistic and unresponsive to political leadership. 'The historical moment is confused, uncertain, unpredictable. The enthusiastic liberal solutions of a decade ago seem to have failed; the rise of passionate single-issue politics, the decline of party loyalty and the new brittleness that resists compromises make the tasks of leadership more difficult.'[53] Carter had done his best in his campaign to capitalize on this negative mood, yet the margin of his success at the polls had been small.

The chief executive's position *vis à vis* congress was, at first sight, far better than that of most other modern presidents. In contrast to the plight of every Republican incumbent, both the House and Senate were held by the president's party, and by big majorities at that. Other Democratic presidents, Harry Truman and John Kennedy, had been less well favoured in terms of congressional support and had been much troubled by the deep divisions in the party between northern liberals and southern conservatives. Carter, on the other hand, not only had big majorities, but was a centrist ideologically – a self-proclaimed fiscal conservative who was also a liberal on civil rights, the environment and education, making it possible for him to straddle the historical division in the Democratic party. Nevertheless, when it came to seeking allies in Congress, Carter's position was much weakened, first, by the fact that so few members had any reason to be grateful to the president for their election and, second, because he had so conspicuously run against the existing political order which included, of course, Congress.

The demanding business of running for the presidency had shown Carter to be an exceptionally energetic, ambitious and intelligent politician and it was to be expected that he would want to be an activist in the White House – a president who left his mark and fulfilled the commitments he had entered into during the campaign. In fact Carter's performance in office fell far short of his and other people's expectations.

The formulation and implementation of a national energy policy was the first priority of the new president in domestic politics, and, as he saw it, some sort of test both of the governability of the United States and of his exercise of leadership, 'Our decision about energy will test the character of the American people and the ability of the President and the Congress to govern this nation.'[54] An energy policy was, however, not surprisingly not quickly agreed; it passed only after a long and bitter struggle that extended through most of Carter's term of office and the package of measures finally agreed was inevitably different and weaker than the one the White House had originally requested.

If the development of an energy policy was a test of presidential leadership, it was not one that Jimmy Carter passed with distinction. To the chagrin of congressional leaders, his policy proposals were prepared in secret without consultation with them. In general, the attitude of the administration towards congress was disdainful and unsympathetic. The president's lobbying on behalf of his programme was uneven and spasmodic. He had begun by characterizing the struggle for an energy policy as the 'moral equivalent of war', but then, for long periods, his enthusiasm for this cause appeared to wane while his proposals floundered in the legislative maze.[55]

Incredible though it seems for such an intelligent man, Carter's principal error at the beginning was to assume that once the underlying rationale of his energy programme had been explained to, and absorbed by the public, opposition would melt away. The crassness of this assumption was forcibly put to the president by the speaker, Tip O'Neill, following the former's televised address to the nation on the energy problem on 18 April 1977. According to O'Neill:

> After the speech, I went up to congratulate him. 'That was a fine speech, Mr President,' I said. 'Now here's a list of members you should call to keep the pressure on, because we'll need their votes.' 'No,' he replied, 'I described the problem to the American people in a rational way. I'm sure they'll realize that I'm right.' I could have slugged him. Did he still think he was dealing with the Georgia legislature? 'Look,' I

said, trying to control my frustration. 'This is politics we are talking about here, not physics. We need you to push this bill through.' 'It's *not* politics,' he replied. 'Not to me. It's simply the right thing, the rational thing. It's what needs to be done.'[56]

Given this remarkable posture it is not surprising that Carter's record of policy-making in other fields was unimpressive. Thus, in the key area of economic policy, despite an occasional victory, Carter achieved little. Tax reform had been a major campaign commitment in 1976, but four years later very little progress had been made on this matter. Similarly, few of the president's counter-inflation measures became law and, indeed, the inflation rate rose to 18.2 per cent during his tenure. As the *Congressional Quarterly* commented in 1980, 'on the economic front the administration has little to crow about. Most of the programs Carter proposed either were never passed or were drastically rewritten by Congress.'[57]

Major reform of the welfare system was one of Carter's most important objectives, but that too fell by the wayside. Likewise, after a long and acrimonious struggle with congress the president's plan for containing hospital costs was defeated. The introduction of a national health care system had been a major plank in Carter's programme in 1976, but his proposals failed to become law. As the president himself said later, 'The fight for equitable health care was one of my major efforts and one of my great disappointments.'[58]

In the realm of foreign policy, Carter had two notable successes, the negotiation and ratification of the Panama Canal treaties and the negotiation of the Eygptian-Israeli Peace Treaty. On the other hand, his presidency, in its last year, was crippled by the Iran hostage crisis. Carter also suffered a devastating setback when the invasion of Afghanistan by the Soviet Union made necessary the withdrawal of SALT II from the Senate, a treaty that had been the centrepiece of his defence policy.

Obviously these latter disasters were largely outside the President's control, but the generally poor state of his relations with congress was not inevitable. Carter himself, however, has been reluctant to accept that his record in dealing with congress was particularly bad. In 1980, for instance, he claimed, 'There's not been a president in modern history, including Franklin Delano Roosevelt and including Lyndon Baines Johnson, who has a better record of support from the Democratic Congress than has Jimmy Carter.'[59] In his memoirs, Carter is more restrained, but even there he makes much of *Congressional Quarterly* presidential support scores to support his claim that he 'did reasonably well in (his) overall relationship with congress'. It is true that his average support score during his presidency was 76 per cent (Johnson's was 83 per cent, and no figures are available for Roosevelt), but such scores are of only limited value as a measure of a president's relationship with the legislature. Presidential support scores are compiled by calculating the number of times members of Congress vote in a way preferred by the president, even though he may not have proposed the measure in question. There is no attempt to weight the votes – a vote on whether the marigold should be the national flower counts as much as a vote on an arms limitation treaty. These scores also combine Congress's support for the president's proposals with the president's support for bills and resolutions emanating from Capitol Hill not sponsored by him. Presidential support scores are so inadequate and so subject to misinterpretation by students and others (including presidents!) that it is time for *Congressional Quarterly* to consider abandoning them.

President Carter, in his 1976 campaign, referred to the 'present disharmony and total separation' between president and congress and pledged to remedy the situation. In the long run he learned some hard lessons and improved his grasp of what good executive legislative relations require in the American pluralist system. Nevertheless, taking his presidency as a whole, harmony between the two branches was not realized and many important goals remained unfulfilled.

In attempting to understand why yet another presidency in the 1970s failed, it is necessary first to return to some of the earlier analyses. Carter, like Ford before him, was handicapped by the circumstances of the time-conditions that were particularly unfavourable to the exercise of presidential leadership. In the summer of 1979, well before the Iran hostage crisis, Carter's approval rating, as measured by an ABC-Harris poll, had slumped to 25 per cent and in commenting on the crisis of national leadership Lance Morrow wrote:

> Americans have been historically disorderly in their response to leadership. (Parties had contributed a modicum of order but) today the parties seem to be approaching merely decorative or ceremonial status. In an age of direct contact through television, more and more candidates avoid party labels to function mainly as independents. Congress used to operate through party discipline enforced by powerful leaders like Sam Rayburn who in turn responded to leads from the White House. Now Congress has become a catfight of centrifugal energies, a fractured, independent crew that in its less disciplined moments approaches the opera buffa standards of the Italian Chamber of Deputies.[60]

This is to state in moderately colourful terms some of the points raised in previous pages and also addressed by Jimmy Carter himself in his memoirs:

> I learned the hard way that there was no party loyalty or discipline when a complicated or controversial issue was at stake – none. Each legislator had to be wooed and won individually. It was every member for himself, and devil take the hindmost! Well-intended reforms in the organization of Congress and of the Democratic party had undermined the power of party leaders. The situation was completely different from the time of Lyndon Johnson's presidency, when he, the Speaker of the House, and the Chairman of the House Ways and Means Committee could agree on a tax or welfare proposal and be certain the the House of Representatives would ratify their decision.[61]

It is difficult to quarrel with the main thrust of Carter's observations, although indiscipline within the Democratic party was hardly a new development. It is also the case that the president's unfalteringly outsider style of leadership tended to make worse an already difficult predicament. It is difficult to think of any twentieth-century president who was a more complete outsider. That role made possible his nomination; he was elected as an outsider and, by his own admission, he never ceased being one whilst in office. 'We came to Washington as outsiders and never appreciably changed that status.'[62]

Carter was an outsider to an extent even greater than he was prepared to admit. He was not just antithetical to the way national politics had developed in the United States in the 1970s, he was totally out of sympathy with the very foundations of the political system. His occasional genuflections in the direction of the Constitution, in his memoirs and elsewhere, are not to be taken seriously. The separation of powers, one of the two central principles upon which the Constitution is based, was for Carter a flaw that prevented presidents from governing rationally in the best interests of the nation at large. Outwardly Carter was more polite towards Congress than Nixon had been, but he shared the latter's contempt for the legislature and was no less shocked by its disorderly, undisciplined ways and its vulnerability to special interests.

President Carter's background and philosophy of life made him ill suited to the demands of presidential government. It was not just that he was unversed in Washington mores; he was also a deeply religious man with a highly developed moral sense. Moralists are, by definition, inclined to deal in absolutes and to be uncomfortable with pragmatic accommodation, but political leadership in the United States requires bargaining skills and, 'calls for actions such as compromise, renunciation, face saving of oneself, which are morally ambiguous or even downright immoral to people with morally rigorous standards.'[63]

Before entering Georgia politics Carter had been an engineer in the navy, but that did not provide very suitable preparation for his political career. As William Pfaff has argued, engineers and scientists typically assume that, given the requisite amount of research and application of the relevant expertise, objective answers to particular problems are possible. Agreement on solutions will follow, provided that the channels of communication are working properly. Carter, accordingly, seemed to believe that if he studied the energy problem in sufficient detail and drew on the views of the appropriate experts his administration could develop an adequate policy. Once the policy had been formulated, its acceptance by the American people would turn on communication, on whether the president and his staff were sufficently adept as communicators. However, scientifc problem-solving and public policy-making are not the same thing, and Carter as a policy-maker was 'a scientific man searching for certitude in an area of human experience, that of political conflict, which lacks mathematical or material certitude.'[64] Politicians rarely deal in objective answers; in the real world of politics, they are often obliged to steer a course between incompatible interests; they are required to bargain and accommodate and must always settle for less than ideal policies.

Jimmy Carter's limited experience in politics had not given him adequate preparation for the demands of the White House. He had served in the Georgia legislature and been elected governor of the state in 1970. As governor, Carter had to deal with a one-party, part-time legislature quite unlike that found in larger, more populous states, to say nothing of the United States Congress. As Speaker O'Neill forcibly pointed out to the newly elected President Carter, tactics that had worked in the relatively sedate politics of Georgia were unlikely to be effective in Washington.[65]

The inappropriateness of Carter's background and experience was reflected in the insensitivity of his handling of Congress. In September 1976, he evinced some good intentions:

> I think just a few personal moves on my part – treating Congress members as though they were presidents themselves, returning their phone calls, letting my staff members respect them thoroughly, dealing with the problems that they present to me, making my own presence felt in the Capitol building itself on occasion – would be contributions that might alleviate the present disharmony and total separation of the White House on the one hand and the Congress on the other.[66]

In practice, however, Carter failed miserably to live up to these sentiments. At the beginning there was the ritual flurry of meetings and consulations with members of Congress, but these soon tapered off and there was, in any case, little real meeting of minds. Very quickly, complaints about the president and his staff began surfacing on Capitol Hill. Members complained that their phone calls were not being answered; federal appointments were being made without reference to them; legislative proposals were emerging without prior consultation with congress and senior presidential staff were accused of not treating Congressional leaders with sufficient respect. Congressmen and senators did not like being bombarded with an estimated eighty legislative proposals in Carter's first year and were unimpressed by his resistance to compromise, his aversion to bargaining and his threats to go over their heads directly to the people.[67]

The president's efforts, early in 1977, to eliminate arbitrarily some public works water projects dear to the hearts and the constituent interests of members caused uproar in Congress and legislators were heavily critical of the quality of Carter's legislative liaison operation. An effective legislative liaison office had, since the days of President Eisenhower, been seen as essential to a good relationship between the chief executive and Congress. Typically, Carter appointed as head of legislative liaison Frank Moore, a Georgia associate and professional management specialist with no experience of Washington politics. The staff recruited were young and inexperienced and the structure of the operation was seriously flawed.[68]

As outsiders, Carter and his staff seem not to have fully appreciated that,

> congressional politics is coalition politics and that members of Congress will not automatically jump to the support of White House programs, even if they come from a Democratic White House and reflect the work of the best experts in the field. . . . Carter basically won the nomination without having to build a coalition. He did not have to make side payments to any of the major groupings within the Democratic Party. . . . (And he and his assistants concluded that) since they did not have to engage in bargaining to get the nomination or to win the election, they would not have to engage in bargaining or exchange to get their programs passed on Capitol Hill.[69]

Of the other presidents who had served in his lifetime, Carter admired Harry Truman the most – an unlikely choice in a number of respects. In fact Carter's style as president was probably closest to that of Woodrow Wilson who, as it happens, died a few months before Carter was born in 1924. Both were deeply religious, highly intelligent, moralistic southerners who went to the White House as amateurs and outsiders. Carter was a president in the progressive mould that Wilson had helped to fashion; both were self-righteous and sanctimonious in their attiudes towards politics as commonly practised; they shared a powerful distaste for special interests and demonstrated a comparable insensitivity in dealing with the legislature. Neither seemed willing to accept that lobbying on behalf of special interests and trading in order to build coalitions in congress are both necessary and entirely legitimate activities in the context of the American pluralist system. Wilson, unlike Carter, sufficiently overcame his lack of sympathy with the system to compile an impressive record of legislative achievment early in his first term.

Carter's saving grace was that he was probably one of the most honest, honourable and hard-working presidents to have graced the White House. Unfortunately, virtue alone is not enough; possibly Carter would have been more successful and might have won a second term if he had been less intense, more flexible, less immersed in the detail of government and a little more willing to dissemble occasionally. His presidency, in other words, might have ended less ingloriously if he had been more like his successor in the White House.

NOTES AND REFERENCES.

1. *Time* (10 Nov. 1980), p. 30.
2. 'The Fatal Arrogance of Power', *New York Times*, Sunday Magazine (15 May 1966), p. 104.
3. Arthur M. Schlesinger Jr, *The Imperial Presidency*. Popular Library, New York 1973, p. 139.
4. Ibid., p. 136.
5. Arthur M. Schlesinger Jr, *The Cycles of American History*. Andre Deutsch, London 1986, p. 277.
6. Clinton Rossiter, *The American Presidency*. Harcourt Brace and World, New York 1956, *passim*.
7. Schlesinger, *The Imperial Presidency*. op. cit., p. 131.
8. *The Memoirs of Richard Nixon*. Arrow Books, London 1979, p. 771.
9. According to H.R. Haldeman, Presidents Franklin Roosevelt, Lyndon Johnson and John Kennedy had all taped conversations in the Oval Office. *The Ends of Power*. Book Club Associates, London 1978, pp. 191–194.
10. Op. cit., p. 761.
11. Richard Nathan, *The Plot that Failed: Nixon and the Administrative Presidency*. John Wiley and Sons, New York 1975, p. 8.

12. *Memoirs*, op. cit., p. 770.
13. *Witness to Power: The Nixon Years*. Pocket Books, New York 1982, Ch. 12.
14. C.O. Jones, 'Congress and the Presidency' in T. Mann and N. Ornstein (eds), *The New Congress*. American Enterprise Institute, Washington 1981, pp. 223–249.
15. Gabriel Almond and Sidney Verba, *The Civic Culture*. Princeton University Press, Princeton 1963, p. 102.
16. Gabriel Almond and Sidney Verba, *The Civic Culture Revisited*. Littel Brown, Boston 1980, p. 189.
17. Richard Neustadt, *Presidential Power*. John Wiley and Sons, New York 1976 edition, p. 16.
18. Schlesinger, *The Imperial Presidency* op. cit., p. 300.
19. Harvey Mansfield Sr, *Congress Against the President*. Praeger, New York 1975, pp. 61–2.
20. Hedrick Smith, *The Power Game*. Random House, New York 1988, p. 23.
21. The best example among the academics was Arthur Schlesinger.
22. Samuel Huntington, 'Congressional Responses to the Twentieth Century' in David Truman (ed.), *The Congress and America's Future*. Prentice Hall, Englewood Cliffs, New Jersey 1973.
23. *The Senate Establishment*. Hill and Wang, New York 1963, p. 22.
24. *Citadel: the Story of the US Senate*. Harper and Brothers, New York 1956; *US Senators and their World*. Vintage Books, New York 1960.
25. Norman Ornstein *et al.*, *Vital Statistics on Congress, 1984–85 Edition*. American Enterprise Institute, Washington 1984, pp. 10, 14 and 114.
26. The intricacies of these and other congressional reforms are discussed fully in Leroy Rieselbach, *Congressional Reform*. Congressional Quarterly Press, Washington 1986.
27. Ibid., p. 50.
28. Ornstein *et al.*, op. cit., pp. 109–10.
29. Quoted in Mark Green, *Who Runs Congress?* Dell Books, New York 1984, p. 135.
30. 'Senate More Democratic Now, Mansfield Claims', *Wisconsin State Journal* (17 Sept. 1976), Section 1, p. 15.
31. See 'The Individualist Senate', *Congressional Quarterly Weekly Report* (4 Sept. 1982).
32. Ornstein *et al.*, op. cit., pp. 120,121, 124.
33. Michael Malbin, 'Delegation, Deliberation and the New Role of Congressional Staff' in Mann and Ornstein, *The New Congress*, op. cit., pp. 134–77.
34. Ornstein *et al.*, op. cit., pp. 78–9.
35. See Morris Fiorina, *Congress: Keystone of the Washington Establishment*. Yale University Press, New Haven 1977, especially Ch. 6.
36. Quoted in Joseph Cooper and G.Calvin Mackenzie (eds), *The House at Work*. University of Texas Press, Austin 1981, p. 66.
37. Paul Light, *The President's Agenda*. The Johns Hopkins University Press, Baltimore 1982, p. 211.
38. Thomas Cronin, 'A Resurgent Congress and the Imperial Presidency', *Political Science Quarterly* **95**, No. 2 (Summer 1980), p. 226.

39. Ibid.
40. Light, *The President's Agenda*, op. cit., p. 114.
41. *Time*, op. cit.
42. *A Ford Not A Lincoln*. Harcourt Brace and Jovanovich, New York 1975, pp. 187–8.
43. Barbara Kellerman, *The Political Presidency: Practice of Leadership*. Oxford University Press, New York 1984, Ch. 9.
44. Ibid., p. 164.
45. Ibid., p. 183.
46. Ibid., p. 184.
47. Frank Aukhofer, 'Carter, Congress Apt to Mesh', *Milwaukee Journal* (3 Nov. 1976); Ross K. Baker, 'The Outlook for the Carter Administration' in Gerald Pomper (ed.), *The Election of 1976*. David McKay Co., New York 1977, p. 137.
48. Neustadt, *Presidential Power*, op. cit., 'Preface to Original Edition'.
49. Austin Ranney, 'The Political Parties Reform and Decline' in Anthony King (ed.), *The New American Political System*. American Enterprise Institute, Washington 1976, p. 218.
50. Pomper, *The Election of 1976*, op. cit., p. 11.
51. Cronin, op. cit., p. 57.
52. Ornstein, *et al.*, op. cit., p. 57.
53. *Time* (5 Feb. 1979), p. 28.
54. Jimmy Carter, *Keeping Faith*. Collins, London 1982, p. 91.
55. See Barbara Kellerman, op. cit., Ch. 10.
56. Tip O'Neill, *Man of the House*. Random House, New York 1987, p. 320.
57. Irwin B. Arieff, 'Carter – Congress Relations Still Strained Despite Gains', *Congressional Quarterly Weekly Report* (11 Oct. 1980), pp. 3095–102.
58. Carter, op. cit., p. 87.
59. Arieff, op. cit., p. 3098.
60. 'A Cry for Leadership', *Time*, (6 Aug. 1979), p. 4.
61. Carter, op. cit., p. 80.
62. Ibid., p. 127.
63. Robert Dahl and Charles Lindblom, *Politics, Economics and Welfare*. Harper and Row, New York 1953, p. 334.
64. 'Carter's Science of Politics', *International Herald Tribune* (9–10 June 1979).
65. O'Neill, op. cit., p.302.
66. 'Carter and Congress Strangers to the End', *Congressional Quarterly Almanac 1980*. CQ Press, Washington 1981, p. 3.
67. See, for example, O'Neill, op. cit.
68. Eric Davis, 'Legislative Liaison in the Carter Administration', *Political Science Quarterly* **94**, No 2 (Summer 1979), pp. 287–301.
69. Ibid.

CHAPTER FOUR

A Presidential Candidate for the 1980s

The 1980 presidential election provoked much critical comment. In Europe and the United States observers were scathing about the lack of qualifications for the presidency of both Jimmy Carter and Ronald Reagan. In comparing the procedures for electing party leaders in Britain and the United States, Anthony King concluded that, 'recent developments in the American presidential nominating system have greatly increased the probability that men will be nominated who lack relevant experience and have no evident aptitude for one of the most demanding and powerful jobs on earth'.[1] The discussion in the previous chapter provides a degree of support for such a conclusion. In 1976, earlier changes in the nominating process had made it possible for an outsider to seize the Democratic nomination, but in office, Carter's lack of 'relevant experience' and 'aptitude' had proven to be a serious liability. The example of Ronald Reagan is, however notably less supportive of King's thesis.

PRESIDENTS AND PRIME MINISTERS

In his discussion, King brings out major differences between the selection of party leaders in the UK as compared to the US. Both Margaret Thatcher and James Callaghan, for instance, had worked their way up through the structure of party; they had spent a lifetime in politics and had served long periods of apprenticeship, first as backbenchers and then as junior ministers, ministers and shadow cabinet members. They had then been elected as party leaders by their colleagues, by fellow members of the political élite with no popular participation. In other words, party leaders in the UK are selected from experienced national politicians whose competence and party loyalty have been regularly tried and tested, who have been subject to a careful process of peer review and have come to the fore not as a result of their electoral appeal, but because they have won the confidence of the people with whom they would have to work in government.

Carter and Reagan, by contrast, had come into politics relatively late in life, had no prior experience of national politics and had become party leaders after long and expensive electoral campaigns. These were leaders who had not been subject to party screening or peer review and had succeeded almost exclusively on the strength of their appeal to mass electorates. Both candidates for the presidency in 1980 were short of relevant experience and had shown no great aptitude for working with other political leaders.

One problem with King's line of argument is that several modern presidents, apparently long on relevant experience, have not done well in the White House. Richard Nixon had been in the House and the Senate and vice-president for eight years, but ultimately he proved to be a disastrous president. His successor displayed no great competence for the job even though he had been a member of the House for twenty-four years and had successfully met the demands of peer review to achieve major leadership posts in the legislature. Franklin Roosevelt, generally agreed to have been the most successful of modern presidents, had, by contrast, no national legislative experience and had held only very junior office in Woodrow Wilson's administration.

There are also difficulties arising from cross national comparison in these matters. By British standards Ronald Reagan was apallingly ill-qualified for a party leadership position. We can hypothesize that he would not have survived the rigorous processes of peer review in the British system and it is exceedingly difficult to envisage him negotiating the hazards of leading a party from the dispatch box in the House of Commons. Similarly, it is inconceivable that Mrs Thatcher would have succeeded in the American context. A leadership style that has made her a remarkably effective prime minister would be a crippling liability in the White House. This brings us back to some of the points raised at the beginning of this book. The political systems and the political cultures of the United States and the United Kingdom are very different and the demands and expectations that face British prime ministers are quite unlike those encountered by American presidents.

Presidents are tribunes of the people in a way that prime ministers are not, and British general elections – notwithstanding some recent increase in the importance of the personality of leaders – continue to be overwhelmingly party-based affairs. Politics in the US is less structured, less ideological and less dominated by party. Presidential elections turn on the personality of the candidate to a far greater extent; those who seek the presidency must communicate effectively with a mass electorate at a personal level. It was Franklin Roosevelt's extraordinary skill as a communicator that made possible his legendary success; he campaigned superbly, handled the press deftly and brilliantly exploited the new medium of radio. Half a century later, given the further demise of party and the massive presence of television in American life, it is even more imperative that presidents should be good communicators.

THE GREAT COMMUNICATOR IN TRAINING

In considering Ronald Reagan's pre-political experience, therefore, we must take account of his long training in the communications industry. As Laurence Barrett puts it, 'by the time he got to the White House he had spent more than fifty years using every communications medium save Morse code and smoke signals. He had been a successful stage actor in high school and college, a pioneer in the young radio business, a journeyman screen performer, a television personality, a speechmaker to audiences of all description, author of a syndicated newspaper column.'[2]

The starting place for Reagan was the small midwestern town of Tampico, Illinois, where he was born on 6 Febuary 1911. His father was of Irish descent and his mother's parents were of Scottish and English origin. The Reagan family, while not impoverished, was of modest circumstances. 'Our family didn't exactly come from the wrong side of the tracks, but we were certainly always within sound of the train whistles.'[3] Reagan's formative years were spent in a series of small Illinois towns – Tampico, Monmouth, Dixon and finally Eureka where he attended the small church-related Eureka College from 1928 until 1932. Like many students the world over, the young Reagan was not overly committed to academic work; both at school and college his grades were mediocre and his principal preoccupations were sport and drama.

On graduation Reagan opted for a career in show business. At first he believed Hollywood and Broadway to be out of reach, and decided to try his luck in another branch of the industry, radio, centred in nearby Chicago. Initially rebuffed by NBC in Chicago, Reagan found work as a sports announcer for a small radio station in Davenport, Iowa. Moving on to a major NBC station WHO in Des Moines, Iowa, Reagan, during the next four years, acquired considerable broadcasting experience. 'I did possibly forty-five football games from virtually every major press box in the Midwest. I covered by telegraph more than six hundred big league baseball games, plus swimming meets (and) track meets. . . . Those were wonderful days. I was one of a profession just becoming popular and common – the visualiser for the armchair quarterback.'[4] Reagan was obviously rather good at his job, rapidly becoming something of a celebrity in Des Moines and, 'one of the best sportscasters in his region'.[5]

In June 1937 Reagan took up residence in Hollywood and quickly established himself as a promising film actor, performing in eight films in his first eleven months and going on to make more than fifty films altogether. Few of these were memorable, but in a fiercely competitive profession Reagan was a notable success even if never a star of the front rank. By the age of thirty he had proven himself in the communications industry. He had emerged as a consistent and capable performer and had acquired a range of skills essential to his later success in politics.

Ronald Reagan's serious interest in politics dates at least as far back as his early days in Hollywood and, given the later doubts about his intelligence, it is interesting to note that, at this stage, he hardly lived up to the image of an empty-headed film actor. Indeed, according to Lawrence Williams, who appeared in five films with him, Reagan in those days was a surprisingly intense, well-informed and thoughtful man to be avoided in the studio canteen by colleagues likely to be somewhat less interested in the world about them. On the set Reagan was liable to use the long, slow periods that abound in film making as opportunities to

> express his animated views on an infinite variety of subjects to us, his fellow actor-captives on the set trapped as we all were for ten hour working days. . . ..Statistical information of all sorts was a commodity Ronnie always had in extraordinary supplies, carried either in his pockets or in his head. Not only was this information abundant, it was stunning in its catholicity. There seemed to be absolutely no subject, however recondite, without its immediately accessible file. Ron had the dope on just about everything: this quarter's up-or-down figures on GNP growth, V.I. Lenin's grandfather's occupation, all history's

baseball pitchers' ERAs, the optimistic outlook for California sugar-beet production in the year 2000, the recent diminution of the rainfall level causing everything to go to hell in summer [in] Kansas and so on. One could not help be impressed.[6]

Admittedly not everyone was impressed. Some found Reagan to be rather shallow; the formidable Bette Davis, for instance, marked him down initially as a 'silly boy'. Other sources confirm that he was a voracious reader and Jane Wyman, a notably intelligent actress, not only married Reagan, but is also said to have 'admired his mind'. Similarly, June Allyson, 'thought it was wonderful that Ronnie was vitally interested in everything and was always studying a new subject . . . he showed the same thoroughness in matters other than politics and he was . . . always studying'.[7] In this phase of his life, at least, Reagan was regarded by many who knew him well, not as an 'amiable dunce' but as a lively, intelligent man with an obsessive interest in politics.

It was this interest in politics no doubt that caused Reagan to become an active trade unionist. He joined the Screen Actors Guild in 1937 and was appointed to its board in 1941. After World War II industrial relations in Hollywood were in a turmoil and the SAG became

> an obsession with Reagan. He spoke of almost nothing else. (Jane) Wyman found it difficult to discuss with him her own concerns, which seemed lightweight against such heavy issues as the strike, violence at the studios, gangsterism in the unions, talk of Communist infiltration in the industry, or the negotiations on the producers' contract. At home, he was either on the telephone in conference calls, working with various members of the Emergency Committee or writing speeches.[8]

Reagan became president of the SAG in 1947 and was subsequently elected to a further five one-year terms as president. It was also during this period that his political ideas began moving sharply to the right. In the past he had been, by his own admission, 'a near-hopeless hemophilic liberal' and a devout follower of Franklin Roosevelt, but by the late forties he was rabidly anti-communist, an FBI informer and a Republican in all but name. Reagan remained a major trade union leader in the film industry until 1960 and there can be no doubt that during this phase of his career he gained much experience relevant to his later career in politics. As Oliver Wright has remarked, 'to be the president of a trade union is to gain an apprenticeship in negotiating, to develop an instinct for when to "hang tough" and when to "cut a deal".'[9]

By the middle of the 1950s Reagan was no longer in great demand as a film actor, but new opportunities became available to him in television. In 1954 he was contracted to host a television programme, General Electric Theater (he also acted in some of the plays presented). This popular prime-time, Sunday evening CBS network show provided Reagan for eight years with 'a vehicle for becoming familiar to a whole new generation of young people who would later vote for him. They were the first television generation, being introduced to the man who would use television better than any other politician.'[10]

No less important to Reagan's political future was the other part of his contract with General Electric which required him to spend 16 weeks a year touring GE plants around the country. The purpose of these tours was to boost morale and encourage a sense of identity amongst the company's 700,000 employees. Over a period of eight years, Reagan visited 135 plants in more than forty states, met 250,000 people and stood before a microphone for an estimated 250,000 minutes. On some days he delivered as many as fourteen speeches and on one occasion shook 2,000 hands in a receiving line. According to Reagan himself, when he appeared on the factory floor

> Machines went untended or ground to a halt; the aisles filled with men and women bearing their children's autograph books. I walked signing, answering questions, asking a few of my own, and generally having a hell of a good time getting acquainted. . . . (In some plants) we varied the hike by shutting down sections of the assembly line and getting the people in an open space where for twenty minutes or so I'd talk to them. . . . The trips were murderously difficult. . . . *But I enjoyed every whizzing minute of it.* (Reagan's italics) It was one of the most rewarding experiences of my life. . . . No barnstorming politician ever met the people on such a common footing.[11]

In assessing Reagan's qualifications for the presidency his experience before he ran for elective office cannot be discounted. There is more to his background than the dismissive labels of 'retired film actor and professional after-dinner speaker' would suggest.[12] Although he was paid a handsome salary by GE to be a morale booster and public relations spokesman, it should not be assumed that his role was merely that of a glad hander, a retired film star capitalizing on a fading reputation. There was something of that to be sure, but his tours were soon extended to include speeches to more discriminating audiences. Speaking before business, civic and other groups Reagan was an impressive performer according to the former newspaperman who organized his early GE tours. On one occasion when Reagan, at short notice, addressed an audience of between three and four thousand teachers

> he got up there and gave a speech on education that just dropped them
> in the aisles. He got a good ten-minute standing applause afterward.
> This is when I began to realize the depth and breadth of his
> knowledgeability . . . everything that went into that mind stayed there.
> He could quote it out like a computer any time you wanted. He did
> read widely, and he remembered what he read. He tended to mesh
> everything in together to get a pattern out of things . It was an amazing
> *tour de force*. It really was.[13]

As a GE spokesman Reagan had the opportunity to hone his oratorical skills, and develop his political ideas. He spoke increasingly less about Hollywood and more on the political issues of the day. In particular, he began to harp on the conservative themes that would provide the centrepiece of his campaigns for the governorship of California and which he would eventually carry with him into the White House.

By 1966 when Reagan ran for the governorship of California, he was not simply a novice with little to offer except an agreeable manner and celebrity status; he was rather a widely experienced and articulate political animal with many of the attributes necessary for success in American politics in the late twentieth century. Since his youth he had been perceived as a likeable man. Physically attractive and possessed of considerable personal charm, his demeanour was self-effacing, gracious and polite. In maturity Reagan was undoubtedly politically ambitious, but continued to project an unassuming and non-threatening image and to display the great political gift of making others feel comfortable in his presence.

As a young radio announcer he had shown a talent for communication that he had subsequently built on during his years in Hollywood and it was also during this period that politics became a consuming interest. The GE phase of Reagan's working life was to act as a bridge between his declining film career and public life. In his relentless meeting, greeting and speaking on behalf of GE he gained experience directly relevant to politics. At the same time he moved into television, thereby acquiring knowledge and understanding of a medium destined to become of supreme importance in American political life.

Presidents must be good communicators and, in the modern age, television is *the* medium of communication. Reagan's aptitude in front of the television camera, his ability to project a positive image, has been a priceless political asset. And such talents, it should be emphasized, are necessary not just for campaigning, but also for governing; presidents unable to master television are unlikely to be effective in office. As Joseph Califano observes, 'Television is critical to the president, initially in his attempt to reach office, then in the exercise of his power as he presents to the people his policies, programs and interpretations of events.'[14] Reagan's command of television was a vital qualification for the presidency in the 1980s.

RUNNING FOR GOVERNOR

Ronald Reagan has made a career out of being underestimated and the same mistake was made in 1980 when his critics wrote him off as an amiable, ex-movie actor ill-qualified for the presidency. In fact, by then Reagan had served a valuable apprenticeship in the communications industry and had completed two terms as governor of the most populous state in the union with a GNP comparable to that of Canada and exceeded by only six national economies. California in the 1960s was not only a big and important state, it was also a political forcing ground where developments were occurring in microcosm that would eventually take on national dimensions. It is possible, for instance, to see in California at this time the beginnings of a national swing to the right. It was here that disenchantment with the liberalism of the New Deal and its successor the Great Society began setting in, which eventually culminated in the landslide victories for Ronald Reagan in the 1980s. More specifically it was in southern California, Reagan's home territory, that political issues began to surface that were to play a major part in national politics in the years that followed. It was in this region that James Wilson writing in 1967, found evidence of a new conservative political culture amongst the children of those who had emigrated to southern California from small mainly midwestern towns. In this culture, business values were preeminent and, 'business values are here meant in the widest sense – a desire for expansion and growth, a high rate of increase in property values, finding and developing mass markets, and keeping capital moving and labor productive'. Such people believed that the principal purpose of government was not to protect gains already made, but to facilitate further growth in the economy. These largely working class conservatives wanted 'limited government, personal responsibility, "basic" education, a resurgence of patriotism, an end to "chiselling", and a more restrained Supreme Court'.[15]

It was by appealing to such sentiments that Goldwater had defeated the liberal Nelson Rockefeller in the crucial Republican primary in California in 1964. In the general election, Lyndon Johnson took the state by a landslide, but his majorities were notably slim in southern counties. Goldwater, in any case, fought an inept campaign and was ruthlessly outmanoeuvred, but, in retrospect, his candidacy was a harbinger of the future. One of the bright spots in that black year for Republicans was an inspired television address on behalf of Goldwater by a rising star in the party and one of southern California's own, Ronald Reagan. Goldwater's enemies presented the Senator as a harsh, uncompromising ideologue, a threatening figure likely to abolish social security and to get the United States involved in a nuclear war. Reagan, by contrast, appeared to be a much more reassuring figure. His views were no less radical than those of Goldwater, but his mild, self-deprecating smiling manner was, in the long run, to make him a far more formidable advocate of conservatism.

Reagan's campaign for governor in 1966 was a response to the same shifts in public opinion that Goldwater had attempted to exploit, but it was not only in political attitudes that southern California was ahead of its time. By the end of the 1970s, the increasing weakness of American political parties had become the subject of comment and concern across the country. In California there was nothing new about enfeebled parties. Progressive reforms dating from the beginning of the twentieth century such as the presidential preference primary, the direct primary, cross filing, the initiative and the referendum had long since destroyed party machines and undermined the power of party bosses. Party leaders in California possessed few of the powers available to their counterparts elsewhere. The early introduction of merit systems deprived them of patronage, and nominations for public office were outside their control.

In the absence of significant parties, nominations could be won by charismatic self-starters who could project an acceptable image. Successful candidates were those who were good at selling themselves personally to the voters. The politics of party, in other words, was replaced by a politics of personality in California many years before such trends became widespread elsewhere. According to Lou Cannon, 'Most importantly the near destruction of the parties had created a star system of personality politics long before television had arrived. At a time when most other states favored candidates who had advanced through the ranks California selected office holders on the basis of real or supposed charismatic appeal.'[16] Well before such things had become commonplace elsewhere, campaigning for office in California was a personal rather than a party matter, depending on the candidate's ability to attract funds, to put together a personal following and to master the available means of communication. By the 1960s parties in California had relatively little to do with campaigning:

> Campaigns are today waged largely through the media of mass communication – the press, radio, television, billboard, and direct mail. With this change in the form of campaigning and with the breakdown of party functions has come a corresponding change in the location of political power in the state. Candidates no longer owe their election to the efforts of political organizations, but rather to personal campaign organizations. No longer are they elected because of effective precinct work, but rather through well publicized campaigns.[17]

The state of California in the 1960s thus offered a singularly appropriate training ground for an aspirant national politician. It was here that attitudes and issues began emerging that were later to assume national significance and where parties were being transformed into empty shells, the eventual fate of parties at both the national and state levels.

It was the chronic condition of parties in the state that allowed Reagan, despite his novice status, to obtain the Republican nomination for governor in 1966. He entered the primary at the urging of a group of wealthy backers including Holmes Tuttle a car dealer, Henry Salvatori and Cy Rubell, both oil magnates, and Stuart Spencer, a political consultant. As Cannon comments, 'in no other populous state of the nation at this time could a handful of millionaires and a political consultant so early have decided on their own to run an aging actor for governor without consulting party leaders.'[18] Reagan's opponent in the primary was George Christopher, a Republican moderate and former mayor of San Francisco. In their campaign speeches, the Republican candidates refrained from attacking one another and Reagan concentrated his fire on the incumbent Democratic governor, Pat Brown. Reagan hammered away at themes which he had been developing for some years and which would be wheeled out every time he ran for public office. Government had become too big and too expensive. Taxes were too high and the state bureaucracy too large and too much power had become centralized in Washington at the expense of the states. A Reagan administration in Sacramento, the voters were led to believe, would do something about the rising tide of crime in the state, would take people off welfare and put them to work and, above all else, it would get the government off the people's back.

Reagan throughout his political career had more than his share of good fortune and he had the luck to begin by facing a weak and inept opponent; Christopher was ill equipped to meet the demands of appearing on television, and, according to one authority, he 'conducted one of the most ineffective campaigns in California's political history'.[19] Reagan, on the other hand, soon showed himself to be an effective campaigner who projected an attractive and reassuring image on television. When the votes were counted the novice in politics had routed the experienced professional, taking 65 per cent of the votes cast and amassing large majorities in southern counties in particular.

In the general election, the incumbent, Brown had two strategies, neither of which seems to have worked very well. Reagan was presented first of all as a hopelessly unqualified candidate and, secondly, as an extremist of the Goldwater stripe. As a way of emphasizing the first charge, TV commercials were run, including clips from old Reagan films embellished with slogans such as 'Vote for a real governor, not an acting one', or 'Over the years Ronald Reagan has played many roles. This year he wants to play governor. Are you willing to pay the price of admission?'[20] To offset the charge of inexperience, Reagan's sponsors arranged for him to be briefed on state issues by specialist advisers. They also sought to turn the criticism on its head by offering Reagan as a 'citizen' candidate running against a seasoned and, by implication, tainted professional politician. The attempt to portray Reagan as an extremist, meanwhile, failed in the face of his likeability. 'He did not come across to people as an inflexible ideologue, but as a sensible sincere man with a good sense of humor and a friendly interest in other people's concerns. In short, he had a warm, human quality that defied the stereotype of the evangelist or extremist set on an unrealistic return to the past.'[21]

The strength of Reagan's appeal in combination with the rightwards shift in the thinking of many Californians was reflected in a landslide victory for Reagan and successes for other Republican candidates in 1966. Reagan secured 57.5 per cent of the vote as compared to Brown's 42.5 per cent and the Republicans gained seven seats in the State Assembly plus six seats in the Senate.

GOVERNOR OF CALIFORNIA

When Reagan first became governor the worst fears of those who had questioned his suitability as a candidate for public office appeared to be confirmed. He went to Sacramento with no readymade staff; he had no understanding of how the political system worked and had no strategy for translating the goals he had espoused during the campaign into a programme of practical proposals. Two and a half months after his inauguration, journalists asked the governor what his legislative programme was and were stunned by his reply. Glancing towards his staff he said, 'I could take some coaching from the sidelines, if anyone can recall my legislative program.'[22] Reagan, however, throughout his life displayed a quality that other, more egotistical or less self-assured political leaders have lacked: the ability to learn from past errors. Gradually, he discovered what he needed to do in order to meet his responsibilities as governor.

The Reagan forces claimed that the previous administration, anxious to avoid a tax increase in an election year, had left behind a sizeable budgetary deficit thereby forcing on the new governor the need to introduce legislation substantially raising some forms of taxation. The obvious contradiction that this created between Reagan as campaigner and as governor was partly offset by compensatory reductions in property taxes. In addition, Reagan introduced a number of economies in line with his pledge at his inauguration 'to squeeze and cut and trim until we reduce the cost of government'. An across the board budgetary cut of 10 per cent for all state departments was proposed; there was to be a freeze on the hiring of state employees, a large reduction in the staffing of state mental hospitals and various other cost cutting measures. Within a short time, however, most of Reagan's proposed changes had foundered either because they were inherently unworkable or because of his failure to consult with those who would have to approve the necessary changes in the law, i.e. members of the state legislature. As a reform candidate Reagan had made clear his low view of legislators, presenting them as the tools of special interests, primarily concerned with feathering their own nests. According to one moderate Republican leader in the Assembly, 'The first year or two of Reagan's administration in California was a disaster. The Reagan crowd ran against the government and against Sacramento and they came in on their white horses and railed against the Legislature. The people around the Governor didn't like us. In their view, we were the hacks he'd run against and we didn't like being treated that way.'[23]

During his first term, Reagan and his staff eventually developed a better appreciation of the merits and responsibilities of legislators and came to realize that the making of policy required the executive branch to 'bargain with, cajole and otherwise court the legislative branch'.[24] Reagan's capacity to learn from past mistakes and to make the adjustments necessary to achieve at least part of his declared purpose can be seen in his second term and in the passage of welfare reform legislation. This was the most impressive accomplishment of the Reagan administration and was made possible by a *modus vivendi* worked out between the Governor and Robert Moretti, the Democratic Speaker of the Assembly. After long and difficult negotiations a 'classical political compromise' was reached which allowed Reagan to meet one of his main objectives, a narrowing of the criteria for receiving welfare.[25] In return the Democrats obtained improved benefits for those who remained on welfare. Even Reagan's critics concede that welfare reform was a significant achievement, but more than that it was an important turning point in the education of a chief executive.

Reagan absorbed many other valuable lessons from his experience as governor of California and it is possible to see in this period the evolution of a style of executive leadership that he was to take with him to the White House. In Sacramento he began as an unworldly ideologue, but went on to become a pragmatist. He came to understand the need to settle for half a loaf rather than nothing at all; he recognized the need to negotiate with legislators while he also discovered how to bring them into line by going over their heads to the people. He experimented with a chairman of the board management style, delegating details to others without surrendering overall control. Most importantly of all, he acquired an understanding of the realities of decision making without losing his sense of direction, or his commitment to a set of simple conservative beliefs. This is attested to by Moretti, a key Reagan opponent in Californian politics, yet one who came to realize that, despite his failings, the governor also had some strengths.

> He had certain assets. He had a philosophy he was willing to pursue to enunciate that he was willing to attempt to push. Even if you disagreed with that philosophy, the fact that he had one and that he stood up for it was something. And he was a strong personality. . . . He had an enduring desire to leave something behind that was really material which he could point to as a change. He wanted to improve where he had been.[26]

Just how successful Reagan was as governor of California has, not surprisingly, been the subject of dispute, with his supporters exaggerating his achievements and his opponents giving him less than his due. The beginning of his first term was unimpressive, but, after an initial learning period, the governor and his staff improved their performance considerably. Even a harsh Reagan critic like Garry Wills concedes that he governed California, 'competently, popularly, routinely'.[27] It goes without saying that his accomplishments did not match his campaign rhetoric – taxes were increased, the state budget more than doubled while he was in office and there were no significant reductions in the size of the state workforce yet his 'record in Sacramento is generally regarded as favorable'.[28] And this, it should be remembered, was in a large important state with many difficult problems and a notoriously fractious and undisciplined legislature that, for six of Reagan's eight years, was under Democratic control.

We must surely conclude that when Reagan ran for national office in 1980 he was hardly the amateur in politics that his critics suggested. To be sure, he lacked the background appropriate to a British prime minister and even in American terms his credentials were open to question. He had not worked his way up through his party in the manner of a Franklin Roosevelt and unlike, say, Nixon, Kennedy, Johnson and Ford he was totally without legislative experience. Yet for all that, Reagan was not without experience highly relevant to the demands of executive leadership in the 1980s. Natural aptitude and a career in radio, film and television had helped him become an outstanding communicator – a strength that not only made him a formidable campaigner, but also equipped him for the business of government in the television age. Then, in Sacramento, he underwent a lengthy apprenticeship in the art of executive leadership and was, ultimately, reasonably successful as the governor of a major state.

THE ROAD TO THE WHITE HOUSE

Anyone elected governor of a major state immediately becomes, in the eyes of the media, a possible candidate for the presidency and Reagan, in 1966, was no exception. Even as governor-elect he was obliged to disavow any interest in the 1968 nomination; however, it seems that his wealthy backers from the beginning had the White House in mind. Henry Salvatori, Goldwater's finance chairman in California, came to realize that Reagan had strengths that the Arizona senator lacked. No less conservative, Reagan presented his ideas far more skilfully, 'People criticize Ronnie for having no political experience. But he has a great image, a way to get through to people. Look at the Goldwater experience. His philosophy was sound, but he didn't articulate it moderately. The Governor has a similar philosophy but he can express his thought.'[29]

Reagan's half-hearted bid for the Republican nomination in 1968 had little hope of success against an extremely well-prepared Richard

Nixon. Despite his humbling defeat for the governorship of California in 1962, the latter had made a remarkable comeback. He had campaigned assiduously for Goldwater in 1964 and worked hard for Republican candidates in the difficult year of 1966. Consequently, Reagan, in looking for support from conservative Republicans, ran up against the reality that many of those same people felt bound by obligations to Nixon, who duly won the nomination on the first ballot at the Convention. When it came to 1972, Reagan had no chance of wresting the nomination from a well-entrenched incumbent, but in 1976 Watergate and President Ford's misplaced decision to pardon Nixon raised the possibility of an incumbent president being deprived of the nomination. In the end, Reagan came very close to defeating Ford, obtaining more popular votes in the primaries than the president and only losing on the ballot for the nomination in the Convention by 111 votes out of a total cast of 2,257.

Reagan's strong showing against Ford is accounted for by several factors; the continued reaction to Watergate compounded by the pardon of Nixon; campaign finance reforms that had improved the chances of outsider candidates; new apportionment rules in the Republican convention that strengthened the Sunbelt states of the South, the Southwest and the West and, finally, the increase in the number of primary elections. 'The spread of presidential primaries . . . favoured Reagan. Party leaders became less influential in the choice of delegates. Instead, an effective campaigner like Reagan could make a direct, popular appeal, and actually outpoll the President in these contests.'[30]

By a slim margin Ford defeated Reagan in the 1976 Convention, but the former governor had run surprisingly well and the conservative wing of the Republican party had substantially strengthened its position. The ground was well prepared for another bid for the nomination by Reagan in 1980. On the other hand, many commentators believed that it would be disastrous for the Republicans to nominate Reagan encumbered as he supposedly was by three disadvantages: his lack of experience of national office, his age and, most importantly, his identification with the extreme right of his party. According to the conventional wisdom, successful presidential candidates had to come from the middle of the political spectrum. Parties committed electoral suicide by nominating extremist candidates like George McGovern and Barry Goldwater. Reagan, however, was no Goldwater. The former's adherence to conservatism was tempered by an easy and agreeable manner that disarmed public, politicians and the press alike. Furthermore, he did not make the mistake of insisting on ideological purity during his nomination campaign; there was to be no 'extremism in the defence of liberty is no vice' or 'moderation in the pursuit of justice is no virtue' rhetoric from Reagan and no abrasive assaults on the liberals in the party as had occurred in 1964.

Reagan possessed other strengths as well. Prior to the 1970s, delegates to national conventions had been selected by a mixed system of state conventions, caucus gatherings and primary elections; under these arrangements nominations remained largely under the control of party leaders with a limited degree of popular participation. But now there was in place a plebiscitary system; the total number of presidential primaries had risen sharply, thereby substantially increasing popular participation in the selection of delegates and further weakening the power of party leaders. Under this system

> . . . the key actors are the people and the individual aspirants. Along with the emergence of this new institutional form has come a new method of generating support in presidential campaigns: 'popular leadership', or the attempt by individual aspirants to carve out a personal mass constituency by their own programmatic and personality appeals and by the use of large personal campaign organizations of their own creation.[31]

These were conditions tailormade for a candidate like Reagan. After the completion of his second term as governor in 1975, he was unemployed and had the opportunity to trail back and forth across the country making contact with local and state party leaders, raising financial support and fashioning a personal organization.

The increase in the number of primary elections and other assaults on the power of parties during the 1970s were enthusiastically welcomed by the Reagan forces. Over many years in California they had acquired the know-how required to exploit a weak party situation. They were years ahead of their rivals in the use of political consultants, computers, direct mailing systems and polling techniques. And in Reagan they had an exceptionally gifted and professional campaigner. He was, however, prone to gaffes, and doubts were repeatedly raised about how much substance lay behind the impressive campaign style. Reagan had a better grasp of the complexities of politics than sometimes appeared to be the case, but regrettable though it may be, primary elections turn on superficial impressions. In introducing primaries at the turn of the century, progressive reformers had naively thought that such arrangements would allow an enlightened electorate to make considered, responsible choices. Unfortunately, despite advances in education such hopes have not been realized. Like the citizens of other advanced industrial countries, Americans in general have only a slight and spasmodic interest in politics. Most voters have neither the time nor the inclination to scrutinize position papers or to weigh judiciously the qualities of those who offer themselves in primary elections.

Such contests have always been likely to degenerate into personality or 'beauty contests'. Ronald Reagan was well equipped to succeed in such situations. By 1980 he had a well-established track record as a campaigner. He was physically attractive and highly photogenic; on the television screen he came across as a man of warmth and charm. It should be added that Reagan was not all style and no substance. He was not an intellectual; he made constant use of anecdotal evidence and some of his views bordered on the banal, but one of his great strengths has always been his resolute attachment to a few simple conservative themes. This gave his candidacy a clear sense of direction that others have lacked. Voters may not have agreed with Reagan, but they had no doubt where he stood.

Television, which had become a major force in American political life, was essential to Reagan's success in obtaining the Republican nomination in 1980. Whereas in the past voters had looked to parties and party workers to help them make sense of politics, this function was now largely given up to television news broadcasts. The major network evening news programmes were being watched by an estimated 50–60 million people and 65 per cent of people were said to be getting 100 per cent of their news from such programmes.[32] Primary elections are very popular with the television industry; they make for good visuals, and they allow producers to focus *ad infinitum* on personalities rather than getting bogged down in the boring complexities of issues. Such contests permit 'horse race journalism'; they make possible endless speculation about who the front runner is, who the dark horses are and who has fallen at what fence, all of which helps to make television news broadcasts more exciting and enter- taining than they would otherwise be.[33]

Reagan stormed through the Republican primaries in 1980 winning 29 of the 34 held, aided by an experienced professional staff fully aware of the significance of television and of the need to shape a campaign around the exigencies of those responsible for television news. Many of the latter looked on politics and politicians with a jaundiced eye and held in their hands the means of destroying ill-prepared, amateurish candidates. A good staff manoeuvred to avoid such disasters, attempting to manipulate the presentation of news. This required taking such steps as arranging the candidate's

schedule so as to ensure that he arrived at campaign stops in time for coverage on the nightly news. It was essential that the candidate's appearances were carefully staged so that he came across in a favourable light before the television cameras. Reagan's staff had the advantage of a candidate responsive to direction, a man who knew about the importance of good camera angles and could read from a teleprompter with the effortless ease of a trained, accomplished communicator.

The importance of television in US politics, it should be stressed, lies not so much in the paid media of political advertising as in the free media of news broadcasts. Much money is spent on political commercials, but students of the subject are sceptical about their benefit – a viewpoint reinforced in 1980 by the experience of John Connally, one of Reagan's most feared rivals for the nomination. Ostensibly, Connally was a very strong candidate. With a handsome face and flowing silver hair, his appearance was eminently statesmanlike; he was a former Governor of Texas and, unlike Reagan, he had had experience of national politics, as Nixon's Secretary of the Treasury. Notwithstanding these advantages and the expenditure of close to \$13m mainly on television advertising, Connally won no primaries and had only one delegate committed to him at the convention.[34]

Success in primary elections, it would seem, cannot simply be bought by political commercials however cunningly they are crafted. What is of far greater importance is that the candidate should come across well on TV news programmes and should constantly be seen in favourable settings making crisp and newsworthy remarks. It is often argued that television has contributed much to the trivialization of politics in general and to the nomination process in particular. The network news programmes provide only a 'headline service', nothing can be dealt with in any depth and everything that is covered has to be supported by good televisuals. Primary elections have always personalized politics to an excessive degree, but television has made the situation much worse.

The arrangements for selecting presidential candidates that produced Ronald Reagan in 1980 have been the subject of much criticism. Anthony King, David Broder and others have deplored the fact that candidates for the presidency are no longer subject to adequate party screening and peer review procedures. *The Economist* a few years ago conceded that the new system had some merits, but carried with it some important disadvantages; on the positive side

> It obliges the candidates to present themselves around the country and in so doing to see the different regions' problems at first hand. And its very length and arduousness provide some sort of test of character of the

candidates. Money is given undue importance, to be sure; so is television. And the system may result in the election of a president – such as Jimmy Carter – who is good at getting himself elected and bad at running the country.[35]

The nomination process is certainly very costly, yet trying to engage the attention of a mass electorate scattered across a huge and diverse country is bound to be expensive. In spite of its pernicious effects television has made possible a degree of political education and communication between politicians and voters that was not possible years ago. The voting decisions of most Americans in the past will have been very uninformed. Even the sight of a national candidate must have been a rare and unusual occasion. Few voters could have obtained a real grasp of the issues at stake and hardly any would have been in a position to assess the leadership qualities of the candidates on offer. Citizens in an earlier age got their voting cues from friends and relations, from newspapers and party workers and it is doubtful whether their decisions today are any less soundly based.

It is also possible to make too much of the argument that the present procedures produce candidates good at running for office but not qualified to run the country. The processes of governing and campaigning are not unrelated and both require mastery of the principal means of communication in American life, television.

> Self-presentational skills are vital for candidates in the current nominating process – not just 'looking good on television' but being able to persuade sceptical journalists and others to accept one's interpretation of the complex reality of the campaign. If it does nothing else, the endless contest, which carries candidates from place to place for months and months in settings that range from living rooms to stadiums, probably sensitizes candidates to citizens in ways that uniquely facilitate the choice of a president who has a strong strategic sense of his time.[36]

Once in office this sensitivity to the thinking of the people is an invaluable resource and the skills of self-presentation are not irrelevant to the task of government. To be an effective leader, to get bureaucrats and legislators to do what he wants them to do a president must retain the support of the public and, in the modern age, that is hardly possible without consistent command of television.

THE 1980 GENERAL ELECTION

Reagan's victory in the 1980 General Election was of landslide proportions. He won 51 per cent of the popular vote against 41 per cent for Jimmy Carter and in the Electoral College led by 489 to 49. At the same election the Republicans gained twelve seats in the Senate and won control of that chamber for the first time in twenty-five years. In elections to the House of Representatives the Republicans made a gain of 33 seats and managed to defeat four incumbent committee chairmen. For Republicans this was a particularly rewarding set of results; in recent decades they had enjoyed considerable success in presidential elections, but the victories of Eisenhower and Nixon had not, with the fleeting exception of 1953–55, been flanked by success in Congressional elections. However 1980, it seemed, just might represent a genuine national shift towards conservatism thereby providing the underpinning for a new alignment of electoral forces to replace the Democratic coalition founded by Franklin Roosevelt.

There are no simple explanations for complicated events like general elections, but we shall take as our starting point V. O. Key's learned view that elections are determined largely by retrospective considerations.[37] The 1980 election, in other words, is to be seen primarily as a referendum on Jimmy Carter's stewardship during the previous four years. For most voters, evaluations of Carter's record turned primarily on economic matters. For many years prior to 1976, foreign policy questions had headed Gallup polls as the most important issues in presidential campaigns, but all this had changed by 1980. Economic issues had loomed large in the primaries and continued to be the most important concerns of voters in the General Election. Unfortunately for Carter public perceptions of his record in economic affairs were overwhelmingly unfavourable whereas, by comparison, Reagan appeared to many voters to have something to offer in this key area. In September 1980 when Gallup asked which of the three main candidates would best deal with 'improving the economy' 44 per cent said Reagan, 30 per cent Carter and 12 per cent Anderson; on 'reducing inflation' the figures were 44 per cent for Reagan, Carter 29 per cent and Anderson 13 per cent.[38]

When it came to the television debate between Carter and Reagan, the latter brilliantly exploited his advantage on economic questions by asking the voters to consider 'Are you better off than you were four years ago?' When the voters went to the polls, of those who believed they were worse off, 64 per cent voted for Reagan and 25 per cent for Carter. Even among blue-collar workers, traditionally strong supporters of Democratic candidates, 62 per cent of those who thought they were worse off than four years previously voted for Reagan and 30 per cent for Carter.[39]

In the field of foreign policy, Carter was also weak although less disastrously so. He had the advantage of being seen as a man of peace, whereas Reagan made many voters nervous. When asked which candidate would do a better job at 'Keeping the United States out of war', 50 per cent of those polled said Carter while 25 per cent opted for Ronald Reagan. On the other hand, polls measuring public approval/ disapproval of Carter's handling of foreign policy generally were highly unfavourable. When asked which candidate would do better in 'strengthening national defence', 55 per cent of those polled said Reagan as against 28 per cent for Carter. On the matter of 'Increasing respect for the United States overseas', 42 per cent believed that Reagan would do the better job as compared to 31 per cent for Carter.[40]

The question of international respect for the US was clearly at issue in the Iran hostage crisis, and over the long term this matter had a relentlessly negative effect on Carter's chances of re-election. Initially his management of this crisis had met with high levels of popular approval, but as the conflict dragged on it became a damaging symbol of American weakness and presidential ineptitude with polls clearly revealing the public's dissatisfaction with Carter's performance. Taken together, Carter's handling of economic affairs, the hostage crisis and foreign policy in general combined to give him 'the lowest job approval ratings of any president since Gallup began taking these measurements in the 1940s'.[41]

Ronald Reagan was not without handicaps and dissatisfaction with both of the party's standard bearers in this election was unusually widespread. In the case of Reagan many had doubts about his age, his competence, his inexperience and his tendency towards extremism. If elected he would be almost seventy as he took office; some spectacular gaffes during the campaign did not inspire confidence. He described the Vietnam war as a 'noble cause', charged that Carter's economic policy had caused a 'severe depression' and raised doubts about the theory of evolution.[42] Reagan, furthermore, notwithstanding executive experience as a two-term governor of California, was totally without national political experience and was a complete novice in foreign affairs. In addition, despite a disarmingly pleasant manner, Reagan was widely considered to harbour views that placed him outside the mainstream of American politics; there was a possibility that he might tamper with social security or lead his country into war.

This perception of Reagan as an ideologue had its beneficial side for 'the strong beliefs that made many voters fearful of Reagan also attracted voters to him, since they suggested leadership and decisiveness – qualities widely felt to be lacking in the Carter presidency'.[43]

The issue of leadership was crucial in this election; Carter came across to the voters as a decent man of high moral principles, sympathetic to the underprivileged and of moderate views, but he was not perceived as a strong positive leader. In front of the all-seeing eye of the TV camera, he did not appear to have a firm grasp of America's problems or a clear understanding of where he wanted to go. As Elizabeth Drew remarked, 'Carter does not have a commanding presence, and his efforts to appear to take charge have flopped. . . . History, if it is fair, will probably say of Carter that he was able to get some things done but that he wasn't able to lead, that he wasn't able to get the confidence of the people.'[44]

There were many reservations about Reagan, too, but these were offset by some notable strengths. Reagan was perceived by many to possess the leadership qualities that his opponent lacked. Gallup in September 1980 asked voters to indicate which of various descriptions best suited the two candidates and Reagan was placed well ahead of Carter on several leadership questions: 'Has strong leadership qualities', 65 per cent–31 per cent; 'Decisive sure of himself', 69 per cent–37 per cent; 'Has a well defined progam for moving the country ahead', 53 per cent–27 per cent; 'You know where he stands on the issues', 54 per cent–33 per cent.[45] In a rather confused, uncertain, period Reagan stood out as an upbeat, optimistic candidate who, despite his failings, had an easily understood programme and a clear sense of the direction in which he would take his country, if given the opportunity.

How is the 1980 election to be interpreted? Did it represent a significant move to the right by the people of the United States presaging a deep rooted realignment of electoral forces favouring the Republican party? Or was the 1980 result merely a personal victory for Reagan? The Republicans drew comfort from the fact that trends of opinion had, for some time, been moving in their direction. Disillusionment with the 'big' government philosophy of the New Deal and the Great Society had been growing during the 1970s – even Carter had been fairly conservative in domestic policy. More and more Americans were coming to the conclusion that government itself was a problem – a belief that 'clearly squares with established Republican doctrine and thus contributes positively to the fortunes of the GOP'.[46] To set against this trend, however, there was much evidence to support the view that the public continued to look to government for assistance. Thus, by overwhelming margins voters, in 1980, believed that 'too little, or about the right amount' of public money was being spent on various problems: halting crime (94 per cent); drug addiction (92 per cent); health (92 per cent); education (89 per cent). The voters, in other words, had not moved solidly to the right, their position was one of ambivalence; they had become deeply sceptical about the role of government and yet they still expected government to aid them as they tried to meet the pressing problems of modern life.[47]

With the benefit of hindsight it can be seen that the 1980 breakthrough for the Republicans did not herald a realignment. To be sure, many core groups from the old Democratic coalition voted in large numbers for Reagan, including Catholics, Jews, southerners, blue-collar workers, union members, the poor and even a third of the unemployed. However, despite holding on to the Senate for a total of six years and securing further landslides in the 1984 and 1988 presidential elections, the Republicans have not been able to bring about a real realignment – a fundamental reordering of political loyalties extending down through all levels of the political system. The Democrats in the 1980s have continued to dominate congressional, gubernatorial and state legislative elections. As a party, the Republicans, in electoral terms, remain weak below the presidential level and Reagan's victory in 1980 can now be seen as largely a personal rather than an ideological or party triumph.

By the end of the 1970s the American electorate was in a fluid, dealigned state with parties no longer able to provide the degree of structure that they had contributed in the past. Parties, in many respects, were no longer taken seriously by the voters; many more people now disavowed parties altogether and declared themselves to be independents. Few looked upon parties in a favourable light and majorities even of party identifiers were unable to perceive any important differences between what the Republican and Democratic parties stood for.[48] Other evidence of the amorphous state of the electorate in 1980 was to be found in poll data revealing rapidly shifting tides of support for various candidates. Thus, a survey in November 1979 showed that 69 per cent preferred Edward Kennedy as the Democratic candidate for the presidency as compared to 31 per cent for Jimmy Carter. By early January 1980, 58 per cent preferred Carter while 42 per cent went for Kennedy and when, in the same poll Carter was matched with Ronald Reagan he outpolled the Californian 65 per cent–35 per cent. Another poll in July 1980 had Reagan leading Carter 55 per cent–27 per cent and then in September public opinion swung back to Carter again giving him 44 per cent to Reagan's 40 per cent. Finally, in the election itself Reagan led Carter by ten percentage points. To add to these impressions of an electorate in a constant state of flux there were other polls showing that many voters only decided at the last minute how to vote. Gallup, for example, claimed that 37 per cent of voters made up their minds in the last week and 10 per cent decided on the day of the election.[49]

The American electorate for much of 1980 was in an uncertain state of mind. Parties no longer provided the signposts that citizens had earlier relied upon to guide them in their voting decisions. Such situations favoured effective personal campaigners – candidates with the ability to master the available means of communication and to make favourable personal impressions. Carter had been no mean personal campaigner himself in the past, but by 1980 his situation had changed fundamentally. He was now encumbered with a record that the voters generally regarded in an unfavourable light. He was personally held responsible for the failures of his economic stewardship. Throughout the campaign he was deeply absorbed with the plight of the hostages in Teheran and when they were not released it was seen as a personal failure.

During the second half of his presidency, Carter's image on the television screen was unfavourable. He came across as a weak, indecisive leader wracked by doubt and in danger of drowning in the complexities of the problems that faced him. Reagan had no record to defend and had spent years perfecting the skills required to project an effective personal image. Instead of gloom and despair, he offered optimism and reassurance. In place of agonizing doubt and uncertainty, he appeared to have a clear sense of direction. To voters who had lost their party moorings, who focused on political matters only spasmodically and relied on fleeting impressions derived from television, Ronald Reagan proved to have exceptional appeal. He was in that sense truly a presidential candidate for the 1980s.

NOTES AND REFERENCES

1. Anthony King, 'How Not to Select Presidential Candidates: A View From Europe' in Austin Ranney (ed.) *The American Elections of 1980*. American Enterprise Institute, Washington 1981, pp. 303–28.
2. *Gambling with History: Reagan in the White House*. Penguin Books, London 1984, p. 33.
3. Ronald Reagan (with Richard Hubler), *My Early Life or Where's the Rest of Me?* Sidgwick and Jackson, London 1981, p. 40.
4. Ibid., pp. 58–9.
5. Lou Cannon, *Reagan*. G. P. Putnam's Sons, New York 1982, p. 139.

6. Anne Edwards, *Early Reagan: The Rise of an American Hero*. Hodder and Stoughton, London 1987, p. 171.
7. Ibid., pp. 172, 205, 228–30.
8. Ibid., p. 320.
9. Op. cit.
10. Garry Wills, *Reagan's America*. Doubleday and Co., New York 1987, p. 268.
11. Reagan, op. cit., p. 258.
12. King, op. cit., p. 314.
13. Edwards, op. cit., p. 455.
14. Joseph Califano, *A Presidential Nation*. W. W. Norton and Co, New York 1975, p. 103.
15. 'A Guide to Reagan Country: The Political Culture of Southern California' in Daniel Elazar and Joseph Zikmund III (eds), *The Ecology of American Political Culture*. Thomas Y. Crowell, New York 1975, pp. 228–44.
16. Cannon, op. cit., p. 105.
17. Joseph Harris, *California Politics*. Chandler Publishing Co., San Francisco 1967, p. 38.
18. Cannon, op. cit., p. 104.
19. Harris, op. cit., p. 27.
20. Stephen Salmore and Barbara Salmore, *Candidates, Parties and Campaigning*. Congressional Quarterly Press, Washington 1985, p. 130.
21. Robert Dallek, *Ronald Reagan: The Politics of Symbolism*. Harvard University Press, Cambridge, Mass. 1984, p. 37.
22. Cannon, op. cit., p. 119.
23. Hedrick Smith, 'Mr Reagan Goes to Washington' in Hedrick Smith *et al*, *Reagan the Man, the President*. Macmillan Publishing Co., New York 1980, pp. 147–75.
24. Robert Lindsey, 'California Rehearsal'. Ibid., pp. 35–51.
25. Ibid.
26. Quoted in Cannon, op. cit., p. 186.
27. Wills, op. cit., p. 312.
28. Lindsey, op. cit., p. 41.
29. Wills, op. cit., p. 291.
30. Gerald Pomper, *The Election of 1976*. David Mckay, New York 1977, p. 19.
31. James W. Ceaser, *Presidential Selection: Theory and Development*. Princeton University Press, Princeton 1979, p. 5.
32. Theodore White, *America in Search of Itself* (1982), p. 174.
33. See Austin Ranney, *Channels of Power: The Impact of Television on American Politics*. Basic Books, New York 1982, p. 55.
34. Michael Robinson, 'The Media in 1980: Was the Message the Message?' in Ranney, *The American Elections of 1980*, op. cit., pp. 177–212.
35. *The Economist*, 31 March 1984, p. 15.
36. Michael Nelson, 'The Case For the Current Nominating Process' in George Grassmuck (ed.) *Before Nomination*. American Enterprise Institute, Washington 1985, p. 31.
37. *The Responsible Electorate*. Vintage Books, New York 1966, p. 61.
38. William Schneider, 'The November 4 Vote for President: What did it Mean?' in Ranney, *The American Elections of 1980*, op. cit., pp. 212–63.

39. CBS/New York Times figures cited in Everett Ladd, 'The Brittle Mandate: Electoral Dealignment and the 1980 Election', *Political Science Quarterly* (Spring 1981), pp. 1–25.

40. Gallup figures cited in Schneider, op. cit., p. 231.

41. Ibid., p. 241.

42. Albert Hunt, 'The Campaign and the Issues' in Ranney, *The American Elections of 1980*, op. cit., p. 142–77.

43. Schneider, op. cit., p. 243.

44. *Portrait of An Election*. Simon and Schuster, New York 1981, p. 300.

45. Schneider, op. cit., p. 242.

46. Ladd, op. cit., p. 22.

47. Ibid.

48. Ibid., p. 5.

49. Ibid., p. 9.

CHAPTER FIVE

Changing the Terms of Debate

Presidents of the United States rarely accomplish very much. They enter office clutching sheaves of policy intentions, but the translation of those expressions of intent into realities is another matter. The president has to operate within an inert political system. one which is monumentally difficult to galvanize into action outside of crisis situations. In the modern age he is expected to lead and the people look to him for solutions to their problems, but the chances of his being allowed to do what he needs to do are negligible.

This built-in tendency towards stalemate is accounted for in a number of ways. For instance, embedded in the American political culture is an antipathy towards government in all its forms and an almost paranoid suspicion of leaders. The constitutional framework reflects and sustains that political culture by providing an almost paralysed political system that sets one branch against another and hamstrings those who aspire to lead. If a president is to break out of this situation, if he is to become a leader rather than a mere presider, he requires a reasonably united administrative branch, yet that minimum requirement is not easily come by. The loyalty of cabinet members and other political appointees is likely to weaken in the face of intense cross pressures, and senior career officers in the bureaucracy, from the beginning, may not share the president's policy preferences.

Assuming that a president can overcome these difficulties sufficiently to establish some discipline within the executive branch, he must also obtain the agreement of congress to his legislative proposals. But congress is not easily brought to order, it is a legislature with teeth and a fractured distribution of power well capable of preventing a president from governing. In the 1970s the odds had lengthened against effective leadership from the White House; there had been a

Table 1. Presidential Capital

President	Year	Senate seats	House seats	Electoral margin %	Public approval* %
Kennedy	1961	65	261	50	72
Johnson	1965	67	295	61	80
Nixon I	1969	43	192	43	59
Nixon II	1973	42	192	61	65
Carter	1977	61	292	50	66
Reagan	1981	53	192	51	51

* Gallup figures: first approval rating of the year.
Adapted from Paul Light, Table 1.

succession of failed presidencies, public confidence in political institutions had slumped disastrously and congress had become even more difficult to deal with.

In 1980, it seemed unlikely that the elderly Ronald Reagan, lacking in Washington experience and with an insubstantial mandate, would be able to impose his will and his policy preferences on the political system. Few grounds for optimism in these matters could be derived from the analysis of Paul Light who argued in *The President's Agenda* that a chief executive's success in getting his domestic policy agenda accepted would depend on his command of internal and external resources. The internal resources are time, information, expertise and energy, but they alone are insufficient; however skilled, resourceful and energetic a president and his staff may be, policy change will not occur without adequate external resources, in other words, political capital. Capital is an amalgam of party support in Congress, public approval as expressed in public opinion polls, and the margin of the president's victory at the election. The principal element in capital is party support for public approval, and presidential electoral success will count for little if the seats in Congress are not there.[1] Ronald Reagan's stock of capital as he began his presidency was comparatively low, as Table 1 shows. By comparison with recent predecessors (apart from Richard Nixon in 1969), Reagan's situation as he embarked on the 'honeymoon' period of his first term was not especially favourable. John Kennedy, despite a narrow popular vote margin, had large majorites in both houses of the legislature and a high level of public approval. Lyndon Johnson had massive support in all forms of political capital, and even Jimmy Carter had commenced with big majorities in Congress and a level of popular approval far higher than Reagan's.

In early 1981, Reagan and his aides spoke confidently of his having received an impressive mandate at the recent elections, and many in Congress and the media seemed to find the argument convincing. On closer inspection, however, that mandate appears to be distinctly fragile. In the Electoral College, Reagan's victory had been of landslide proportions, but the popular vote told a different story. In a three way contest almost as many people had voted against Reagan as for him and in only a few states, mainly in the South, had he performed significantly better than Gerald Ford in 1976. Of those who voted for Reagan many did so without great enthusiasm and a 'large, if indeterminate, proportion of Reagan's support came from people who went to the polls to vote *against* President Carter'.[2] Reagan's party had won control of the Senate, which was most unusual for a Republican president, by 53–47 and this was an undeniably important material and psychological gain. On the other hand, the margin of seats in the Senate was slim and in the House, despite an impressive surge by the Republicans, the Democrats were still ahead by 51 seats.[3]

All in all, as Reagan prepared to take office the omens for a successful presidency did not look particularly good. According to one authority, 'Most close observers of the Washington scene and system saw Reagan as a media success who would be overwhelmed by the immense substantive and managerial demands of the presidency.'[4] Others anticipated that Reagan would 'be a fairly passive president, a throwback to the conservative, pro-business quietism of Warren G. Harding and William Howard Taft'.[5] In the event, these gloomy prognostications proved to be unfounded. Against the odds, Reagan and his staff were not overwhelmed by the demands of the office; indeed, they established sufficient mastery over the machinery of government to bring about major changes in the direction of public policy.

> The American political system, during the presidency of Ronald Reagan, has been transformed to an extent unknown since the days of Franklin Delano Roosevelt. The terms of political debate, the course of domestic and foreign policy, and the dominant line of partisan cleavage have all been fundamentally changed. Only rarely in American history has the political system broken as sharply with governing customs to address festering national problems or to confront social and economic issues head-on.[6]

REAGANISM

In his first term Ronald Reagan was spectacularly successful in bringing about a fundamental change in the 'terms of political debate'. His principal objectives as expressed in the 1980 campaign, were to reduce the size and role of the government, to revive the economy and to strengthen the nation's defences.[7] In pursuit of these aims the president and his staff proposed bold innovations in economic policy, the introduction of which became their first priority.

For years before becoming president, Reagan had harped on conservative economic themes. He had constantly called for reductions in the burdens of taxation on both corporations and individuals and regularly denounced the federal government for being too big, too meddlesome and too wasteful of the taxpayers' money. As the 1980 election approached, advisers like Martin Anderson set about incorporating Reagan's idea into a coherent economic strategy. The essentials of that strategy, of Reaganomics, were put together in an economic policy memorandum agreed seventeen months before Reagan took office.[8]

This blueprint challenged the assumptions of Keynesian theory that had provided the basis of economic policy in the United States for close to half a century. It had long been argued that the maintenance of a low level of unemployment should be the guiding principle of a government's economic policy. According to the Keynesians, unemployment rose when demand was too low, but fortunately demand could be stimulated by lowering taxes or increasing public expenditure. When full employment was reached and demand exceeded supply, inflation was likely to follow, but this could be counteracted by reducing demand so that it came back into line with supply.

Previous administrations had tried to manage the economy principally by 'fine tuning' demand. Obsessed by the need to keep unemployment low they had, according to their conservative critics, pushed up levels of public expenditure and recklessly run up budget deficits without regard to inflation and the difficulties it created. The Reaganites argued that the 'stagflation' of the 1970s demonstrated that there was no evidence of a trade-off between unemployment and inflation, and heaped scorn on policies aimed at managing demand or artficially controlling wages and prices. With the right policies they believed it was possible to reduce inflation without incurring excessive levels of unemployment – to keep prices down and to sustain economic growth at the same time.

Many of the economic advisers in the Reagan camp were influenced by the 'supply side' theory. They argued that the Keynesian obsession with the demand side of the economy was misplaced; the real focus of attention should be the supply side. Policy-makers should stop fretting about unemployment and the provision of welfare state safety nets and should concentrate on doing whatever was necessary to achieve inflation free economic growth. This required, above all, substantial tax cuts to foster hard work, enterprise and saving. Public expenditure must be savagely reduced, business had to be liberated from the web of state and federal regulations and stability brought about in the monetary system. The capitalist system had to be unchained and the conditions created that would allow it to flourish. Market forces should, as far as possible, reign supreme and welfare state arrangements should be minimized or eliminated altogether, except for those in dire need.

Reagan rarely used the term 'supply side' himself and in the long run shrank from the full implications of the theory. Nevertheless, supply-side doctrine provided a theoretical underpinning for the main thrust of his economic strategy. There were to be four principal elements to that strategy: (1) a substantial reduction in taxes; (2) heavy cuts in the rate of growth of public spending; (3) deregulation reform; and (4) the establishment of a sound monetary policy. Before attempting to introduce the legislation this strategy required, the Reagan forces prepared the ground by taking unprecedented steps to ensure that those appointed to the new administration were fully committed to the president's aims.

ADMINISTRATIVE STRATEGY

Effective presidents, according to the criteria used in this book, are those who succeed in translating the proposals they have advanced on the campaign trail into policy action. In trying to accomplish these ends, a president is dependent on the services of senior White House staff and the agencies that fall within the Executive Office of the President. In the normal course of events, such agencies can be relied upon to pursue conscientiously the president's programme. However, the loyalty of political appointees and career civil servants in the federal administration at large is much more open to question. As Clinton Rossiter maintained, for some presidents the chief executive's most difficult task 'is not to persuade Congress to support a policy dear to his political heart, but to persuade the pertinent bureau or agency or mission, even when headed by men of his own choosing, to follow his direction faithfully and transform the shadow of the policy into the substance of a program'.[9]

Conservative Republican presidents are especially vulnerable in this regard. 'Big' government is anathema to them, and bureaucrats are their natural enemies. Senior career civil servants invariably identify with the Democratic party.[10] The dangers inherent in the situation had been brought home to senior figures in the Reagan camp who had served in the Nixon administration. In his first term, Nixon had devoted relatively little attention to the selection of those who would be responsible for the administration of his programme. Reasonably careful consideration was given to cabinet appointments, and appointments at the sub-cabinet level were also subject to vetting, but responsibility for selecting the remaining 2,000 political appointees was delegated to cabinet members. Furthermore, President Nixon misguidedly instructed his cabinet to appoint on the basis of ability first and loyalty second.[11] The adverse consequences of such loose rein appointment procedures were not lost on one White House aide who served both Nixon and Reagan

> The US Government is so large and so complex that it takes thousands of dedicated, competent, loyal people to turn campaign promises into national policy . . . (but during the Nixon years) the departments were staffed primarily with people with an agenda different from that of the White House. . . . We argued over what to do rather than about how to do it. The departments and agencies were full of people who basically disagreed with many of Nixon's policies. They were nice people, competent people, but we wasted a great deal of time arguing with them, cajoling them, persuading them. I recall going to policy meetings with a dozen or more people where I would be the *only* person in the room supporting President Nixon's policy position.[12]

During the transition the Reagan forces took a number of steps designed to deal with the sort of problems over appointments that Nixon had encountered. The first appointments were made by Reagan himself. His chief advisers were to be Edwin Meese, James Baker and Michael Deaver and Meese, as Counsellor to the President, took on the major responsibility for selecting and indoctrinating political appointees. Meese was well qualified to be the keeper of the Reaganite grail. He had been a friend and ally of the president for many years and had served as chief of staff when Reagan was governor of California. Meese was also something of a hard-line conservative, ever alert to any dilution of the faith or any hint of disloyalty to the president. Meese was closely involved in the appointment of cabinet members and worked with Pendleton James, the White House personnel director, to ensure that not only sub-cabinet appointments but also the 2,000 lower level political positions went, as far as possible, to candidates who were both competent and ideologically sound. It was quite unheard of for the White House to be so intimately involved in the appointment process so far down the administrative hierarchy.

Elaborate precautions were also taken to guard against the danger of senior members of the administration becoming, in Reagan's own words, 'captives of the bureaus or special interests in the departments they are supposed to direct'.[13] Richard Nixon had been plagued by the phenomenon of political appointees 'going native', a process that began immediately with career civil servants initiating their newly appointed political superiors into the mores, values, policy preferences and interest group connections of the department. In part to prevent such developments, the Reaganites established transition task forces comprised mainly of conservative ideologues who were commissioned to scrutinize and prepare detailed reports on the workings of agencies and departments. When these investigations were concluded, the task forces briefed cabinet members on their responsibilities, suggested where funding cuts might be made and which bureaus might be closed while also advising on the hiring, firing and movement of personnel. Cabinet members and other senior administrators were also obliged to attend indoctrination sessions where major figures, from the president down, lectured them on the virtues of teamwork and exhorted them to remain faithful to the principles of Reaganism.

Economic policy was the core of Reagan's programme and especial care was taken to ensure that those primarily responsible for economic matters were fully conversant with and totally committed to the president's position. There was to be no debate about which direction to take in economic policy; the essentials of supply-side theory were to be taken as given and the criteria for appointment to the major economic policy posts were to be, 'competence, experience, and absolute, complete loyalty to Reagan's economic policies. . . . Every key player in the decision-making process was carefully chosen and fully indoctrinated.'[14]

Some interesting reactions from a cabinet member on the receiving end of the doctrinal ministrations of Meese and other Reaganite hawks are to be found in the reflections of Terrell Bell, a Republican moderate and Secretary of Education in Reagan's first administration.

The Department of Education had been established by Jimmy Carter and during the 1980 campaign Reagan had declared his intention to abolish the department if elected. Bell was appointed to preside over an abolition which, in the event, proved imposssible. At the first meeting of the new cabinet, Bell was surprised and mildly irritated to be repeatedly told, first by Meese and then by the president, of the need for teamwork. 'It seemed redundant to me to tell us we were "part of the president's team". We were his cabinet so this was obvious.'[15] This was a rather naïve reaction on the part of Bell; as the senior presidential advisers knew only too well, there is always a danger that cabinet members will develop a relationship with their department that takes precedence over their loyalty to the president and his programme.

Bell also took exception to the briefing provided by the task force assigned to his department. 'My meeting with the transition team was a testy one. I was not prepared to do much of the aggressive abolishing and slashing proposed in its reports.'[16] In addition, the secretary had grave difficulty in reaching agreement with the White House on senior appointments in his department. Bell vigorously resisted the attempts by Meese and others to foist on him people he regarded as unqualified ideologues; he was convinced that movement conservatives wanted to infiltrate his department with appointees who shared their extreme views: 'They wanted to be able to monitor deliberations about proposed actions and have early warning of what might be brewing in suspect agencies. (The Education Department) was high on that list of departments.'[17]

It is difficult not to sympathize with the frustrations of an obviously sincere cabinet member trying to remain loyal to the president while, at the same time, protecting the education service from the depredations of conservative extremists. Bell, however, had the misfortune to be a moderate serving in a conservative administration and he was bound to be regarded with suspicion. Looked at from a White House perspective, it is clear that if a president is to be effective in achieving his objectives he needs unity and discipline within the executive branch. This is not easily accomplished in a vast and amorphous federal bureaucracy, but Meese and his colleagues were more successful than most presidential staffs in bringing it about.

Cohesion in the administration was also facilitated by a system of cabinet councils, introduced at the suggestion of Meese and a major feature of Reagan's administrative strategy in his first term. Initially five cabinet councils were established; one on economic affairs, one on commerce and trade, one on human resources, one on natural resources and the environment and finally, one on agriculture and food. As their names suggest, these councils covered broad policy areas affecting several departments; they brought together senior White House staff with cabinet members at the highest level of decision-making.[18] This countered the tendency towards antagonism between presidential advisers and departmental secretaries that had weakened other administrations, and it also reduced the chances of cabinet members 'going native'.

All cabinet council meetings took place in the west wing of the White House within a few feet of the Oval Office. This enabled the president to attend a large number of these gatherings, thereby delivering on his promises to work closely with his cabinet in the formulation of policy. The symbolic importance of cabinet members being regularly drawn into the White House ambit was stressed by one participant. 'Just the act of having to leave their fiefdoms, get into a car, and be driven to the White House was a powerful reminder to every member of the cabinet that it was the president's business they were about, not theirs or their department's constituents.'[19] White House control was further strengthened by the staffing arrangements for cabinet councils. Each council was staffed by a secretariat made up of one representative from each cabinet member with its work directed by an executive secretary from the staff of the Office of Policy Development within the White House. This apparatus provided a 'superb control and monitoring instrument' allowing presidential advisers to keep a tight grip on the domestic policy agenda and to guard against any dilution or deviation.

DEREGULATION

The Reagan forces were also alert to the possibilities of using administrative discretion as a means of policy change. They recognized that some of their objectives could be reached by administrative action without running the gauntlet of the legislative process. Regulatory reform, for example, was a major item on Reagan's agenda. In common with other supply-side enthusiasts, he was convinced that sundry federal agencies had put in place a web of unnecessarily restrictive regulations that distorted market forces and inhibited the spirit of free enterprise. Carter had advocated deregulation , but he approached reform via legislation whereas his successor sought the same end primarily through administrative action.

Reagan, at the beginning of his first term, appointed Vice-President Bush as chairman of a Presidential Task Force on Regulatory Relief which was made up largely of cabinet members and staffed by the Office of Management and Budget. Most of the actual work was done by staff rather than the high powered task force members. Nevertheless, in April 1982 the OMB was able to claim that the size of *The Federal Register* listing regulations had been reduced by a third. A few months later OMB also claimed that deregulation had brought about savings of $9 billion to $11 billion in once-only costs and $6 billion in annual recurring costs.[20]

The deregulation effort eventually petered out, but the Reaganites continued to use administrative discretion in their efforts to lighten the burden of regulation on industry and business. Cutting back on the staff of regulatory agencies was one ploy used, and, according to figures provided by one source, in eleven selected agencies there was an average 29 per cent decline in permanent staff positions during Reagan's first term; including falls of 53 per cent in the Federal Grain Inspection Service, 41 per cent in the Interstate Commerce Commission, 38 per cent in the Consumer Product Safety Commission, 32 per cent in the Federal Trade Commission and 21 per cent in the Environmental Protection Agency.[21] The work of regulatory agencies was also undermined by budget cuts and a concerted unwillingness to enforce existing regulations. Thus, in Reagan's first term the overall budget of the EPA was cut by 35 per cent, there was a 62 per cent drop in enforcement actions against strip mine violations and a 50 per cent fall in hazardous waste prosecutions.[22] The Reagan administration weakened the enforcement of anti-trust laws and, where possible, held back from implementing in full civil rights and affirmative action legislation. The decisions of bodies like the Occupational Safety and Health Administration tilted towards business and against labour and Reagan used the appointment power to bring about similar results at the National Labor Relations Board. The percentage of decisions by the NLRB in unfair labour practice cases favouring employers increased sharply.[23]

The Reagan example illustrates the advantages that a president may derive from an effective administrative strategy. By carefully vetting and indoctrinating appointees, he can bring some order and direction to a mammoth, unruly bureaucracy and progress towards policy change can be made by administrative action. On both counts, it would seem, the White House was unusually successful and this is important to an understanding of President Reagan's effectiveness.

If one strand of Reagan's economic strategy – deregulation – was pursued principally by administrative means, a second – the establishment of a sound monetary policy – was, in the main, beyond the executive branch's sphere of influence. Monetary policy is, in fact, the responsibility of the Federal Reserve Board, an independent agency that may be influenced by the executive but is not subject to its direction. The two remaining elements of Reaganomics – tax cutting and reductions in the rate of growth of public spending – would require the agreement of the US Congress.

AN ECONOMIC POLICY COUP

In a well-known biography of Franklin Roosevelt, it is asserted, that 'the classic test of greatness in the White House has been the chief executive's capacity to lead Congress.'[24] This is hardly less true in the 1980s than it was in the 1930s. To govern rather than merely preside, to bring about meaningful policy change as distinct from tinkering with the status quo, a president must establish a productive relationship with congress. In other words, he needs a successful legislative strategy to place alongside his administrative strategy.

In the 1970s neither Nixon nor Ford nor Carter could be said to have passed the 'classic test'. Nixon had tried to govern without congress and Ford had been pathetically inconsequential; Carter, in his memoirs, claimed to have had a reasonably good relationship with the legislature, but this was not a widely shared view. Ronald Reagan, on the other hand, stunned observers by his early success in getting the legislature to accept a fundamental reordering of national priorities. At the end of the first session of the 97th Congress, Helen Dewar reported in the *Washington Post*:

> [Congress] ended yesterday, as it began: dominated by President Reagan and his crusade to cut taxes, strengthen the military, and reverse half a century of growth in social programs. The Republican Senate and Democratic House, although split along party lines, came under the Reagan spell to make more history in a few months than most Congresses have made in two full years.[25]

Even one of Reagan's severest critics, Tip O'Neill, the former Speaker of the House of Representatives, does not underestimate Reagan's early achievements: '(He) pushed through the greatest increase in defense spending in American history together with the greatest cutbacks in domestic programs and the largest tax cuts the country has ever seen.'[26] The magnitude of these accomplishments should be fully recognized. Irrespective of whether Reagan's economic policy was correct or not, or whether it achieved the objectives sought, the fact that the policy was put into place at all is remarkable in itself. This provides a classic instance of a president taking on the legislature in the most important of policy areas and succeeding in imposing his will.

THE BUDGETARY PROCESS

The principal instrument for this economic policy coup was to be the budgetary process.In the United Kingdom the legislature has effectively long since surrendered the power of the purse to the executive, but that is far from being the case in the United States. At Westminster, the government annually presents a package of spending and revenue-raising measures which parliament, after a relatively brief period of ritual debate, duly ratifies. The executive branch in Britain is firmly in charge of the budgetary process with the legislature, in the normal course of events, little more than a cypher. There is some tendency to assume that in Washington, too, budget-making is largely an executive function. Reference is constantly made to the president's budget and the chief executive is held responsible for the consequences of budgetary policy, especially by members of the opposition party in Congress. In truth, however, Congress is a full partner in the business of budget-making as Donald Regan, Reagan's first Secretary of the Treasury, made clear:

> The budget is not controlled by the Executive Branch but by the Congress. What goes up the Hill in the form of the President's budget has little meaning. What comes down the Hill represents the fiscal reality of the federal government, and it is invariably a command to spend according to the whim and the myriad political debts of Congress.[27]

This is an executive branch viewpoint, but hardly an excessive overstatement. The initiative in budgetary matters rests mainly with the president, but, once he has submitted his proposals, they cannot become law until they have obtained Congressional approval. In all probability, his budget will be substantially rewritten as it trails through the Congressional maze and the eventual outcome may be quite at odds with the president's original intention. Even in 1981 this occurred, to some extent, with the president's budgetary plans being modified to a degree that a British prime minister would regard as wholly intolerable. However, relatively speaking, Reagan and his staff, in the first year of his presidency, were brilliantly successful in maintaining control over the budgetary process and were able to ensure that the budget that eventually emerged was reasonably close to their original blueprint.

In approaching the legislature, the Reagan forces were determined to avoid the mistakes of Jimmy Carter; the new administration would have a clear sense of direction and a well-defined order of priorities. Thus, for the moment, foreign policy and other issues were to be neglected while economic policy took precedence. '[The Reaganites] put only one legislative ball in play at a time, and they kept their eye on it all the way through. Shortly after the inauguration, for example, when Secretary of State Haig tried to raise the issue of Central America, the White House told him to leave it alone. There was to be only one issue on the agenda – the economy.'[28] It was essential, moreover, that the executive should, as far as possible, remain in charge of the budgetary process to ensure that the final product, as far as possible, reflected the president's economic policy preferences rather than those of the legislature. To that end Stockman, the director of the OMB and the principal architect of Reagan's first budget, set about reducing the role of Congress to something not far removed from that of the House of Commons. 'The constitutional prerogatives of the legislative branch would have to be, in effect suspended. Enacting the Reagan administration's economic program meant rubber stamp approval, nothing less. The world's so-called greatest deliberative body would have to be reduced to the status of a ministerial arm of the White House.'[29] As with so many of Stockman's ambitions, this one did not come close to full realization; nevertheless, in the early months of Reagan's first term, the legislature was repeatedly upstaged and out-manoeuvred by the White House.

Constructing the federal budget is a protracted and complex matter, not easily described in brief. The first stage of a process taking, roughly a total of eighteen months to complete, occurs within the federal administration. Over a period of approximately nine months, departments and agencies of the federal government engage in detailed discussions with the White House prior to the presentation of the president's budget proposals to the legislature shortly after Congress convenes in January. On receipt by congress, the budget is dealt with first by a variety of committees. Before the expenditure of any money can be approved, authorization is required and this is a matter for the specialist, standing committees. Assuming authorization has been agreed, actual expenditures, or appropriations, are considered by the appropriation committees. Proposed revenue changes are dealt with by the Ways and Means Committee in the House and the Finance Committee in the Senate.

Prior to 1974 these various activities took place in an uncoordinated manner, but, since then, budget committees have been set up in both houses. These committees are responsible for drafting resolutions that must eventually be agreed by Congress as a whole. The first such resolution is designed to provide coordination and guidance to the specialist, appropriations and tax-writing committees. It includes aggregate estimates of government spending and revenue while also providing target figures for expenditures broken down into functional categories. After the initial, concurrent budget resolution has been agreed, the committees go to work considering the president's budget proposals in minute detail. At the end of these deliberations there are likely to be discrepancies between committee recommendations and the target guidelines. These have to be settled, if necessary, by a process of reconciliation whereby the budget committees impose specific ceilings. Eventually a further final, concurrent budget resolution has to be voted on and submitted for the president's signature, theoretically in time for the beginning of the financial year on 1 October.

CUTTING THE BUDGET

Throughout his campaign, Reagan had made clear his intention to cut government expenditure, to lower taxes and to increase defence spending, and he and his staff now moved to make a reality of those promises. In his first State of the Union message, Reagan reiterated the essentials of his programme and went on to call for an increase in defence spending of $7.2 billion and cuts in excess of $40 billion from the proposed 1982 budget of $740 billion. Agreement on this package within the administration had not occurred without a struggle. Despite the care taken in selecting cabinet members to ensure that only men and women loyal to Reagan were appointed, there were inevitable attempts to break ranks when budget-cutting proposals were under discussion.

As director of the OMB, David Stockman's responsibility was, first, to keep the cabinet in line and then to mastermind the passage of the president's proposals through Congress. Stockman got most of the cuts he wanted from the cabinet and then turned his attention to the legislature. As a former congressman himself, he was well acquainted with the dangers facing the executive's proposals when they reached Capitol Hill. Without close supervision the suggested cuts, in particular, would fall victim to the machinations of interest groups and the pork barrel orientations of members of Congress.

In other words, if precedent was followed, the package of budget cuts would be attacked piecemeal when it disappeared into the congressional maze; even though there might be general agreement on the need to cut the budget, vested interests operating through sympathetic members could, one by one, weaken or restore specific cuts. It was to counter such developments that the Reaganites and their allies in Congress resorted to a reconciliation strategy. The reconciliation procedure was designed for use at the end of the budgetary process, but the Reaganites manoeuvred to attach reconciliation instructions to budget resolutions at the beginning.

The effect of this profoundly important innovation was that members of Congress were required to vote up or down the administration's complete package of cuts at the beginning of the congressional phase of the budgetary process. In addition, the relevant committees, when they began their work, would be obliged to operate not with fairly loose guidelines and a relaxed timetable but with specific ceilings and a tight schedule. Effectively, the legislature agreed to forego the extended debate and process of negotiation over appropriations that normally occurred. In institutional terms these procedural manoeuvres were of great significance; the executive was strengthened while the legislature, to some extent, was reduced to the rubber stamp status craved by Stockman. It was hardly a parliamentary situation with the executive totally dominant, but it was a striking change from what had gone before.

With good reason the Reagan administration began the fight for the budget in the Senate where there was a Republican majority. The Senate Budget Committee duly reported out reconciliation instructions on 23 March 1981 requiring fourteen Senate authorizing committees to alter programmes so as to cut $36 billion from the fiscal year 1982 budget.[30] Ten days later, the Senate as a whole approved this bill by an overwhelming majority before going on in May to embrace a budget resolution that 'contained nearly one hundred per cent of the administration's entire economic program, by a vote of 72–20. The politicians had flinched. They had rubber stamped the Reagan Revolution.'[31]

The House of Representatives presented an infinitely more daunting challenge; in that chamber there were only 190 Republicans, against

242 Democrats. Of the Republicans, Stockman estimated that perhaps fifty were not enamoured with budget-cutting; these were the so-called 'Gypsy Moths', liberal Republicans from the Northeast and the Midwest. On the other hand, there were around sixty southern Democrats, potential 'Boll Weevils', some of whom might be induced to vote with the administration. But both of these key groups, in Stockman's view, were made up of unreliable allies. Even the conservatives in the House could not be entirely depended on, for all but a few of them were no more than 'Hooverites' to use Stockman's contemptuous label; they were keen on budget-cutting only up to a point and were anxious that the budget should be balanced, but they had no stomach for swingeing tax cuts – the main article of the supply-side faith.

Despite these unpromising signs, there were reasons for the Reaganites to hope that they might be able to succeed in the House. For a start, the Democratic leadership capitulated rather easily; the 1980 election results appeared to frighten them into cooperation with the president. According to a member of the Speaker's staff, the Democrats felt that they should 'recognize the cataclysmic nature of the 1980 election results. The American public wanted this new President to be given a chance to try out his programs. We weren't going to come across as being obstructionists.'[32] This defeatism, unwarranted either by the fragility of Reagan's mandate or by the public opinion polls, led the Speaker meekly to surrender his control over the legislative schedule by agreeing to an accelerated timetable allowing for final votes on the president's programme by mid-summer. In his memoirs, O'Neill offers an unconvincing explanation for this major concession; 'I was fully aware of the advantage I was giving the Republicans as all the votes would take place well within the new president's honeymoon period. But my strategy was to keep in mind the long-term situation. . . . I was convinced that if the Democrats were perceived as stalling in the midst of a national economic crisis, there would be hell to pay in the midterm elections.'[33] By conceding on the timetable, O'Neill gifted the Republicans an important advantage, helping them by drastically curtailing the protracted and damaging interplay of pluralist forces that would have otherwise taken place over the budget.

Other evidence of the Democrats in the House surrendering the initiative to the White House is to be seen in the actions of the Budget Committee. The chairman of the committee was Representative Jim Jones of Oklahoma, a conservative Democrat who agreed with the main thrust of Reagan's economic policy – the need for budget cuts and for a reduction in taxation. Under Jones' leadership, the Democratic majority on the committee was prepared to give the president much of what he wanted. 'They disagreed with him on the size of the tax reduction. But they acceded to his request for an overall cutback in government spending and accepted to the letter a majority of the budget drafted by the OMB.'[34] By conceding a large part of Reagan's requests in both budget cuts and tax reductions, Jones hoped that compromise with the White House would be possible, but he was to be bitterly disappointed. Stockman, Regan and the president all made it clear that compromise was not on offer – a position that Jones rightly interpreted as an assault on congressional prerogatives. 'The administration says it can accept no amendments; that its budget is untouchable. No administration has ever made such demands; and no congress has ever accepted such demands. It is not the job of Congress not to think.'[35]

In the end, however, Reagan won this crucial skirmish with the legislature. On 16 April the House Budget Committee reported out a budget resolution that incorporated $15.8 billion in cuts – $20 billion less than the administration had requested – and the battle was now joined for the votes of those who could make or break the president's programme, the Gypsy Moths and the Boll Weevils. The chances of the Democrats succeeding in this crucial struggle were not helped by the Speaker who, after a trip abroad, gave a 'dispirited news conference' where he said, 'I can read Congress. They go with the will of the people and the will of the people is to go along with the President. I've been in politics a long time. I know when you fight and when you don't.'[36] The president, meanwhile, stood high in the public opinion polls after the attempt to assassinate him at the end of March. He and his staff had also been busy cultivating the swing voters in the House and on 28 April he capped his effort with a triumphant televised address to Congress.

In this speech, Reagan again made clear his determination not to compromise with the House Budget Committee and threw his support behind a bipartisan resolution fostered by Stockman and dubbed Gramm-Latta after its co sponsors. This resolution was offered as a substitute for that reported out by the Budget Committee, and if accepted would give the president virtually all the cuts he had asked for. The stage was set for a critical vote where members would be asked to decide whether they were for or against Reagan's economic programme. In Stockman's words this 'decisive battle for the Reagan Revolution got reduced to an image contest between the Speaker and the President, a question of hope versus nostalgia. Would you go with the President's brave new gamble or stick with the Speaker's failed tax-and-spend policies of the past?'[37]

On 7 May 1981 the House of Representatives opted heavily for Reagan in accepting by a vote of 253–176 the Gramm-Latta programme of cuts. This was followed eventually by the adoption by congress, as a whole, of a concurrent budget resolution including reconciliation instructions requiring the authorizing committees to cut approximately $36 billion from the financial year 1982 budget. During June the administration successfully fended off Democratic attempts to recoup their losses earlier in the year, allowing the president, on 13 August, to sign 'into law the deepest and farthest-reaching package of budget cuts that Congress had ever approved.'[38]

THE TAX CUT

The administration's success in cutting the budget was an impressive accomplishment, but for supply-side hawks like David Stockman, it was only a means to an end, an essential first step, for the real heart of the Reagan Revolution lay in the massive tax cut needed to unfetter the capitalist system and to revive the American economy. In the late 1970s, Congressman Jack Kemp and Senator William Roth had put forward the idea of an across-the-board income tax cut of 10 per cent in each of three successive years, a proposal taken up enthusiastically by supply-side advocates like Stockman and warmly embraced by Ronald Reagan. Stockman portrays himself as being almost alone amongst the Reaganites in having 'an actual passion for a supply-side tax cut. To me the issue was meta-numerical. It was critical to my view of the world. As I saw it, supply siders were dedicated to capitalist wealth distribution, whereas the politicians were dedicated to socialist wealth redistribution.'[39] The majority of Democrats in congress were opposed to Kemp–Roth, the Boll Weevils were not enthusiastic and this was also true of many traditional Republicans. Republican congressional leaders like Howard Baker and Robert Dole in the Senate and Robert Michel in the House were, at best, lukewarm in their support and 'all in all, the Congress of early 1981 was exceedingly inhospitable terrain upon which to champion a supply-side oriented tax cut'.[40]

Even in the White House itself, Stockman detected ideological fainthearts. James Baker, the Chief of Staff, was a natural compro-miser happy to settle for half a loaf as long as it could be made to look like a victory for the president. Donald Regan, the Secretary of the Treasury, had no personal commitment to Kemp–Roth and only worked for it out of blind loyalty to the chief executive. Given these circumstances it seems remarkable that the proposed tax cut made any significant headway at all, but it had one enormously important advantage – the whole hearted support of Ronald Reagan.

> The tax cut was one of the few things Ronald Reagan deeply wanted from his presidency. It was the only thing behind which he threw the full force of his broad political shoulders. Getting the tax cut passed was one of the few episodes involving domestic policy and legislative bargaining in which he firmly called the shots. By intimidating and overpowering the whole lot of the nation's politicians, he got what he wanted. It was at once awesome and tragic.[41]

In a book generally very critical of Reagan, this comes as a rather surprising encomium to his effectiveness in office, although Stockman also makes it clear that the president did not get all that he had asked for in tax cuts. With great reluctance, Reagan bowed to pressure from his advisers and compromised the Kemp–Roth principle somewhat by agreeing that the first cut should be delayed for a few months and reduced to 5 per cent in the first year with 10 per cent cuts in years two and three. Reagan had also hoped for a 'clean' bill, one that was not adorned with 'ornaments' – in other words, concessions made to facilitate passage. However, only by accepting the inclusion of a number of such 'sweeteners ' was Reagan able to prevent his bill being replaced by a one-year tax cut proposal offered by the chairman of the House Ways and Means Committee, Dan Rostenkowski.

The president refused any further compromise on the Kemp–Roth principle before launching another masterly televised appeal for support on 27 July that produced an avalanche of mail and telephone calls to members of congress. Reagan's success in the Senate was never in doubt, and on 29 July a package of tax cuts virtually identical to those asked for by the president was approved by 89–11. On the same day, the House voted on whether to adopt an administration-backed bill in place of that sponsored by Ways and Means with Rostenkowski warning: 'If we accept the President's substitute, we accept his dominance of our house for the months ahead. We surrender to the political and economic whim of his White House.'[42] On this crucial vote, 48 Democrats voted with the president while all Republicans, with one exception, stayed loyal and the House voted 238–195 in Reagan's favour. In early August, Congress formally ratified both parts of the administration's economic programme, the budget cuts and the tax cut, and at this point few could doubt that Ronald Reagan had passed with distinction the classic test of presidential greatness.

The weakness, if not incompetence, of the opposition would appear to have been an important contributory factor in Ronald Reagan's astonishing early success in seizing control of the agenda in the manner of a Roosevelt or a Johnson, even almost of a prime minister. In the Senate the Democrats acted as if shell-shocked by the experience of losing overall control, and a non-charismatic, unimaginative leader like Robert Byrd was no match for White House strategists and men like Howard Baker and Robert Dole on the Republican side. In the House, Speaker O'Neill's leadership, as we have seen , was not impressive. In his memoirs he rightly insists that the 1980 election 'did *not* represent a revolution in American values. And, despite what the media claimed, Reagan was not elected because people were fed up with the huge federal deficit and were clamoring for budget cuts. . . . I didn't buy the idea of a Reagan mandate then, and I certainly don't buy it now.'[43] This is brave talk after the event, but in 1981 the speaker certainly acted as if the president had a mandate, meekly conceding control over the timetable and repeatedly running up the white flag before crucial votes. Thus, at the end of April, as the battle over budget-cutting came to a head in the House with members asked to choose between the Democratic-controlled Budget Committtee package and the administration-sponsored Gramm-Latta substitute, O'Neill, 'threw in the towel two days before the actual vote.'[44] Similarly, as the debate on the president's tax reform bill was about to get underway in the House the speaker 'all but conceded the battle was lost – largely as a result of heavy lobbying by the president, his aides and voters mobilized by Reagan's television appeal'.[45]

It is difficult to understand why the Democratic leadership should have been quite so defeatist in 1981. To be sure, Reagan had a number of strengths. There was much disenchantment with the policies of the past; he had won by a landslide in the Electoral College; his party controlled the Senate; he had run ahead of quite a few southern Democrats in the House and he was clearly an exceptional performer on television. On the other hand, the Democrats still held the House and the 1980 election result was at best ambiguous, representing neither a vote for conservatism nor for liberalism. Public opinion polls, furthermore, provided additional evidence of that ambiguity, showing that many Americans had negative attitudes towards big government, but by large majorities wished to preserve, if not extend, the 'service state'.

> The popular sense of government as a 'problem' squared clearly with
> established Republican doctrine and thus contributed positively to the
> fortunes of the GOP. But at the same time, people had not stopped
> looking to government for solutions and assistance. Americans of all
> classes expected high levels of performance by government. This

Table 2. Presidential Approval (in percentages)

President	First approval score	After fourth month	After fifth month	First year average
Truman	87	–	–	81
Eisenhower	68	74	69	
Kennedy	72	76	74	76
Johnson	78	73	77	76
Nixon	59	65	63	61
Ford	71	42	39	54
Carter	66	64	63	62
Reagan	51	68	58	58

Gallup figures.
Sources: Public Opinion (Sept./Oct. 1987), p. 40 and Wayne Shannon, 'Ronald Reagan's Unique Pattern of Public Approval', Paper prepared for Conference of the American Politics Group (Jan. 1987), Birkbeck College, University of London.

commitment conformed with traditional Democratic doctrine and was of electoral benefit to the Democratic party, although the presidency was lost.[46]

The sight of Ronald Reagan on television clearly terrified the Boll Weevils and the Democratic leadership, but, in fact, it is not the case that Reagan, *in 1981*, enjoyed high levels of popular approval. Reagan actually began his first term with an approval rating lower than that of any other president for whom records are available. In answer to the question 'Do you approve or disapprove of the way . . . is handling his job as President?' the respondents answers are given in Table 2, which also shows that after the fourth month of Reagan's first term, and in the wake of the assassination attempt on 30 March, his approval rating rose to 68 per cent. But even that was inferior to Eisenhower, Kennedy and Johnson and hardly better than Nixon and Carter at the comparable stage in their presidencies. By the following month, furthermore, Reagan's rating had dropped ten points, where it broadly stayed during the next three months while the administration successfully defended its budget-cutting package and won a stunning endorsement of the tax reduction measure.

LEGISLATIVE LIAISON

Whether soundly based or not, it is clear that congressional perceptions of Reagan's popularity were important in influencing votes in the legislature; and the defection of Boll Weevils, in particular, was essential to the president's success on key votes. This support, however, did not fall into the president's lap; David Stockman regarded both Republicans and conservative Democrats as very suspect allies, unreliable when it came to budget cuts and with little stomach for serious tax reduction.

> There wasn't a semblance of a Reagan ideological coalition in Congress to support the revolution. The Republicans and conservative Democrats amounted to a frail, faction-ridden, and unstable political gang, saturated with fierce sectional and parochial cross- pressures. The latent GOP–Boll Weevil parliamentary majority, in terms of gross vote numbers was nearly meaningless. An actual majority for any specific bill had to be reconstructed from scratch every time. [47]

The Reagan administration's success in building a series of ad hoc coalitions in support of key economic policy votes owed much to the brilliance of the White House staff with special responsibility for dealing with legislature.

Reagan's notoriously detached style of management made high-quality staff essential, and in his first term he appears to have been particularly well served by those responsible for ushering his economic policy proposals through congress. Stockman was obviously a key figure; a supply-side zealot with an impressive grasp of the complexities of the budgetary process, he dazzled both colleagues and adversaries. 'If Reagan provided the soul of the Administration's program, Stockman provided the intellect. He seemed to have all the answers, all the zeal . . . (he was) the structural engineer of Reaganomics.'[48]

Responsibility for Reagan's legislative strategy in general rested with the Legislative Strategy Group chaired by the president's Chief of Staff, James Baker. Baker an urbane, Princeton-educated Texan was a close friend of Vice-President George Bush and had been Bush's campaign manager during the 1980 primaries. As his effortless glide from the staff of the liberal Bush to the conservative Reagan suggests, Baker was a skilful operator – a man with no strong political convictions, fascinated by the machinery of politics and deriving satisfaction from getting the system to work. Above all else, Baker understood the essential role of compromise in executive–legislative relations and it was the LSG that prevailed upon Reagan to give ground on the tax cut by accepting reductions of 5 per cent–10 per cent–10 per cent in three successive years in place of the 10 per cent–10 per cent–10 per cent of Kemp–Roth.

Baker's part in such compromises angered conservatives in the country who saw him as a closet liberal subverting the president's conservative instincts. Martin Anderson is one conservative insider who believes this to be a misconception. In his view, Baker and the LSG loyally pursued the president's agenda and it was Reagan himself who decided whether to compromise, and when: 'It was Reagan, and Reagan alone, who decided that four fifths of a loaf, especially a loaf that was perhaps too large to begin with, was better than no loaf.'[49] It is also possible to see Baker as a 'lightning rod' for the president, protecting him from the ire of conservative ideologues who, by definition, would never be satisfied with less than the whole loaf.

Baker's principal lieutenant on Capitol Hill was Max Friedersdorf the first head of the new administration's Congressional liaison office. Legislative liaison in the Carter administration had been notably weak; Frank Moore, a fellow Georgian whom Carter placed in charge of the operation, had no previous congressional experience and proved inept and insensitive in his dealings with members of congress in the crucial early months. Friedersdorf, by contrast, was an old hand in the field of congressional liaison, having worked in the area for Nixon and been Ford's chief of legislative liaison. 'Quiet and distinguished, Friedersdorf had a reputation for honesty and integrity and was highly regarded by senators and Congressmen of both parties. He was indispensable to Reagan's extraordinary success with Congress in the first year.'[50]

As the architects of the president's legislative strategy, Baker and Friedersdorf moved first to gain control of the legislative agenda. They were mindful of Carter's mistake at the beginning of his term in setting off too many policy hares at the cost of a focused programme with a clear sense of priorities. For the Reaganites, economic policy was *the* legislative priority; first came budget cuts and then tax reduction and it was essential that these should be in place within a few months, before the end of the honeymoon period. According to Friedersdorf, 'We knew we had to get our bills enacted before the Labor Day recess.'[51]

Again in contrast to the Carter administration, the Reagan legislative liaison office mounted an efficient operation. According to Mark Siegel, who worked in the Carter White House,

> It doesn't take much in the White House to pick up the phone and say, 'Is there anything I can do for you in the next two or three months?' In the Carter White House that was regarded as treason. Congress was the enemy. The Democratic party was the enemy. The Washington establishment was the enemy. Tip O'Neill wanted to help a Democratic president enact a democratic agenda, but the Carter people didn't understand Tip O'Neill. They regarded him as a horse's ass, and if you call someone a horse's ass in the White House, do you know how fast that gets back to that someone?[52]

With Reagan in the executive mansion the atmosphere was different; members of congress were pleased to have their telephone calls returned; where possible they were provided with assistance and they were carefully plyed with the 'small potatoes' of presidential patronage. Tip O'Neill is instructive on the differences between the two administrations in these matters:

> . . . during the Carter years, congressional Democrats often had the feeling that the White House was actually working against us. Once when the city of Boston applied for a government grant for some new roads, I called the Carter people to try to speed it along. Instead of assisting me, however, they did everything possible to block my way. When it came to helping out my district, I actually received more cooperation from Reagan's staff than from Carter's.[53]

Being 'helped out' in one's district was a matter of the greatest importance to members of the House of Representatives, the forum where Reagan's legislative strategists would face their severest test. Not only were the Republicans in a minority, in recent years the House had become a less disciplined and more individualistic legislative body. Party leaders and committee chairmen no longer carried the weight they once had and ordinary members now assumed that the secret of holding one's seat in perpetuity depended on their success in cultivating their district.

It was clear to the LSG that their success in getting Reagan's radical programme adopted would require careful coalition building. They would need to hold together their Republican support while detaching sufficient numbers of conservative Democrats to fashion the succession of majorities required. Coalition-building was to be approached on two fronts; the first involved horse-trading, the striking of deals or bargains in order to win support. The second approach was to bring pressure to bear on Congressmen indirectly, by working through conservative sympathizers and contributors in their districts.

Carter, certainly at the beginning, had been reluctant to engage in conventional trading for support, but the Reaganites were significantly less inhibited. When, for instance, the president's programme of budget cuts was in danger of being subverted in the summer, a rash of horse-trading took place as Stockman reveals. As the moment approached for a key procedural vote that would make or break Reagan's programme, Stockman received an agitated telephone call from Bill Thomas, a conservative Republican from California and an agent of the administration on Capitol Hill:

> 'We ain't gonna make it' (Thomas) said. "Not unless you open the soup kitchen". In the Congress the "soup kitchen" is what you throw open in

the last hours before a vote to get people off the fence. At this point democracy becomes not a discussion of the ideals of Jefferson or the vision of Madison. It becomes a $200,000 feasibility study of a water project; the appointment of a regional director of the Farmers' Home Administration in western Montana. Bill Thomas had spent some time practising this art in the California state legislature, and he was now the official cook of the GOP soup kitchen. And he was good at it. If someone came at him and started talking about the plight of the elderly or an end to hunger on the planet, Thomas would hold up his hand and say, "Don't give me all that bullshit . . ." And of course it had *nothing* to do with the plight of the elderly or an end to hunger on the planet Earth. It had to do with re-election. The deals that were dished out in the soup kitchen were the irreducible minimum, the quarks of politics.[54]

This extended quotation provides a fascinating picture of the American pluralist system in operation while helping us to understand why the Reaganites were successful in fashioning the coalitions they required in the House of Representatives.

That success, as Hedrick Smith shows, also turned on the ability of the Reagan administration to play 'outside politics'.[55] They understood that the modern congress with its emphasis on constituency service provided new opportunities for influencing members of congress. The president's television addresses activated grass-roots support in members' districts, but administration strategists were not content to leave the matter there. Lyn Nofziger and Lee Atwater took responsibility for stimulating outside pressure on congressmen from fifty-four swing districts – areas of the country where there were likely to be many conservative activists and where the president had run strongly in 1980. These districts were treated almost as if a presidential campaign was underway; radio and television advertising time was bought; mail and telephone blitzes were organized; administration speakers appeared and organizations like the National Association of Manufacturers, the US Chamber of Commerce, the American Medical Association and other organizations supportive of Reagan's programme were mobilized. According to Atwater, at the time

> The premise of the whole operation is that political reforms and the impact of the media have made it so that a congressman's behavior on legislation can be affected more by pressure from within his own district than by lobbying here in Washington. The way we operate, within forty-eight hours any congressman will know he has had a major strike in his district. All of a sudden, Vice President Bush is in your district; Congressman Jack Kemp is in your district. Ten of your top contributors are calling you, the head of the local AMA, the head of the local realtors' group, local officials. Twenty letters come in. Within

117

forty-eight hours, you're hit by paid media, free media, mail, phone calls, all asking you to support the president.[56]

There was nothing new as such about grass roots lobbying, but the sophistication and skill brought to this tactic by the Reaganites in the new conditions of the 1980s was a development of great significance.

THE CHIEF LEGISLATOR

Reagan was supported by an exceptionally talented staff in his first term and it might be said that his legislative triumphs can best be explained by the quality of the team around him. Presumably the ability to attract good staff is, in itself, the mark of a good leader, but beyond that it can be said that Reagan himself was an indispensable part of the team.

In 1981 Reagan was at his best, at the height of his powers. He had learned valuable lessons from his experience as governor of California and illness and old age had yet to take their toll. Like most presidents, he began with earnest expressions of intent to work harmoniously with congress, but unusually, he followed through on the promise. In the early months, Reagan was meticulously attentive to the legislature. He met frequently with the Congressional leaders of both parties; and he made considerable use of the telephone in seeking the votes of rank-and-file members while also inviting them to the White House in groups. To cite O'Neill again, 'Some House members said they saw more of (Reagan) during his first four months in office than they saw of Jimmy Carter during his entire four years. . . . Reagan took Congress very seriously and was always coming over to the Capitol for meetings.'[57] In his meetings with legislators Reagan's personal qualities proved invaluable; his relaxed and affable manner, his warmth, humour and charm all helped him to establish an unusual rapport with both Republicans and Democrats.

Unlike, say, Lyndon Johnson, there was no chance of Reagan overwhelming or brow-beating legislators into submission; nor was he likely to intimidate them as Jimmy Carter often did by dazzling but discomfiting displays of his mastery of the detail of policy-making. The contrast between Reagan and his predecessor in these situations has been pointed up by one Democratic congressman. He recalled an unsatisfactory meeting with President Carter, 'We had hardly got seated and Carter started lecturing us about the problems he had with one of the sections of the bill. He knew the details better than most of us, but somehow that caused more resentment than if he had left the specifics to us.' The contrast with a meeting that took place with Reagan was considerable. No details were discussed: 'I wasn't there more than a couple of minutes, but I didn't feel rushed and I am not quite sure how I was shown the door. The photographer shot the usual roll of pictures; the President gave me a firm, friendly handshake. He patted me on the back and told me how much he needed and appreciated my support. He said I should call if I needed help on anything. That was it.'[58]

Reagan's low-key, laid-back, non-specific approach clearly went down well with legislators who, for once, could feel they were being treated as genuine co-partners in the policy-making process. It is also evident that, unlike Carter, Reagan had no inhibitions about tending to the needs of congressmen in return for their support. That is to say, he was perfectly willing to make deals where necessary, although he was careful to leave the details to his staff. However, if many members found Reagan personally impressive, there were others who were disconcerted by his folksy, anecdotal style and alarmed by his insecure grasp of detail. Some clearly shared David Stockman's notoriously low estimate of Reagan's intellect and were not convinced that he had an adequate understanding of the intricacies of economic policy-making.

I shall return to these reservations in a later chapter, but for the moment it should be noted that well-qualified observers such as Martin Anderson and Donald Regan take a different view. They insist that the president did understand the rudiments of economic theory and, despite an unusual propensity to delegate detail, made the crucial decisions himself. Thus Regan, in memoirs not noted for their kindness to the president, says, '[Reagan's] grasp of economic theory as it had been taught in his time (Eureka College, class of 1932) was excellent, and he kept abreast of later theory. He had no trouble understanding the leading ideas of the day, or in making reasonable judgements about the effects produced by policies based on Keynesian theory, of which he was deeply suspicious.'[59] Meanwhile, Anderson says of the president, 'Over the years he made all the key decisions on the economic strategies he finally embraced. He always felt comfortable with his knowledge of the field and he was in command all the way.[60]

Reagan's reluctance to dabble in detail may have contributed to one of his undoubted strengths, his sense of direction. Again, unlike Carter, he left no one in any doubt as to where he wanted to go in policy terms. His ideas on economic policy, as on other matters, may have been overly simplistic or even fundamentally erroneous, but the fact that he had a vision of the America he wished to bring about was a strength he possessed, one that many other presidents and presidential candidates have lacked. Reagan also met one of the crucial tests of leadership in a pluralist system – the capacity to be both firm and flexible. He did not compromise easily, but was willing to accept less than he had hoped for rather than to make no gain at all.

Finally, in considering Reagan's personal contribution to the triumphs of his first term, we must obviously take into account the consequences of his appearances on television . No administration has been more conscious of the political power of TV or, Kennedy apart, been blessed with a more gifted exploiter of the medium as president. In 1981 Reagan appeared regularly on television to advance the claims of his economic policy, and several of these were impressive performances with the president drawing on the skills acquired during many years in the business of communications. Reagan's television appearances furthermore were carefully scheduled to take place just prior to critical votes on his budgetary and tax policy. Carter had used television in a somewhat haphazard fashion, but Reagan 'marshaled his television appearances to promote his policies. Each was dramatic and each was followed only a short time later by a key Congressional vote.'[61]

One of Reagan's most spellbinding TV performances came on 27 July, two days before both houses were to vote on his tax cut proposal. It generated a large volume of mail and telephone calls and frightened enough members into believing that the electoral consequences would be dire if they failed to support the president. In reaction to Reagan's performance, one southern Democrat said, 'I sure hope he doesn't go on television to promote the elimination of fucking', while another, more politely, said, 'The constituents broke our doors down. It wasn't very subtle.'[62] The picture that these comments conjure up of a president made massively popular by his command of TV is not confirmed by public opinion poll statistics. After the seventh month of his presidency (July), Reagan's popular approval rating, according to Gallup, was 60 per cent which compares with 66 per cent for Carter, 62 per cent for Nixon and 73 per cent for Kennedy at the comparable point in their first terms. And a month later, Reagan's rating fell to 52 per cent.[63] Even if such statistics belie the myth of an enormously popular president, the fact is that he and his staff managed to convince sufficient members of congress that he and his programme enjoyed overwhelming public support.

Thus, Reagan's early successes can be variously accounted for. The Democratic leadership was inadequate. This mattered less in the Senate, but in the House, where the battle was really joined, the unwarranted defeatism of the speaker played into Reagan's hands. The defection of southern Democrats was essential, but it should not be assumed that this came about automatically, As Stockman makes clear, a whole series of ad hoc coalitions involving many unreliable allies had to be painstakingly constructed. The high quality of White House staff with special responsibility for legislative–executive relations – notably Baker, Stockman and Friedersdorf – was another major factor. From the beginning they established control over the legislative agenda, obliging congress to focus almost exclusively on economic policy and requiring the legislature to deal with these matters in a manner and a timeframe favourable to the president's programme. They mounted an especially effective legislative liaison operation that secured a high level of Republican unity while drawing in conservative Democrats. In support of this 'inside' strategy, there were other members of Reagan's staff out in the grass roots exploiting the constituency orientations of members of Congress, those who might provide the swing votes on key roll calls. Finally, there was the contribution of the president himself. He provided the essential vision; it was his power of persuasion, exercised via the telephone or in face-to-face meetings with members of congress, that brought sufficient votes to his side for the crucial roll calls. And it was his skill as a communicator, mainly through television, that created the impression of towering popular support for his programme. As the *Congressional Quarterly Almanac* concluded: 'In all, the first session of the 97th Congress was a great personal triumph for Reagan. Congressional approval of his plan was due largely to his own efforts and strengths'.[64].

The magnitude of Reagan's achievement in his first term has been subject to question on several grounds. Many have argued that the economic policy put in place in 1981 was, from the beginning, ill-conceived and wrong headed. However, this analysis is not concerned with the merits or the efficacy of policies, but with a president's success or failure in gaining acceptance of his policies by other political actors. Of more relevance here are the criticisms of those who argue that Reagan, in reality, fell far short of his declared policy purposes, or who point to the thinness of his legislative record in the remaining three years of his first term.

David Stockman ultimately proved to be one of Reagan's most trenchant critics. His book is the testimony of a disillusioned man who turns with some bitterness on his former colleagues. He chastises them for their lack of true commitment to the supply-side faith and their unwillingness to make the necessary hard choices. With the passion of a self-proclaimed 'radical ideologue' and revolutionary, Stockman called for the immediate liberation of American capitalism from the fetters of 'welfare statism'.

> Forty years worth of promises, subventions, entitlements, and safety nets issued by the federal government to every component and stratum of American society would have to be scrapped or drastically modified. A true economic policy revolution meant risky and mortal combat with all the mass constituencies of Washington's largesse: Social Security recipients, veterans, farmers, educators, state and local officials, the housing industry and many more.[65]

The 'combat' called for here would certainly have been 'risky' for it would have led inevitably to the destruction of both the Republican party and the Reagan administration. The fact is that neither congress nor the American people were ready in the early 1980s for the demolition of the welfare state, however much conservative theorists might believe that to be desirable. Stockman recognized that the sort of fundamental change he sought 'would have hurt millions of people in the short run' and involved the, 'ruthless dispensation of short run pain in the name of long term gain', but these, he believed, were the hazards that true revolutionaries faced without flinching.[66] 'Revolutions have to do with drastic, wrenching changes in an established regime. Causing such changes to happen was not Ronald Reagan's real agenda in the first place. It was mine, and that of a small cadre of supply-side intellectuals.'[67]

It is obvious that neither Reagan nor the men around him such as Meese, Baker, and Regan were revolutionaries. They held conservative views, some of them very radical in their implications, but they remained realists endeavouring to work within the existing political system. They accepted the need to formulate policies that the US congress and the American people could be induced to accept by democratic means. The politicians that Stockman so despised knew that the dismantling of the welfare state and the elimination of federal largesse were not options available to them – public opinion polls had made that very clear.

Stockman denounces Reagan for his susceptibility to hard luck stories and his economic illiteracy, but, if the president's grasp of economics was shaky, he understood politics in a way that the director of the OMB did not. Reagan was indeed a 'consensus politician, not an ideologue', but he could hardly be anything else.[68] Had the

Republican candidate in 1980 been an ideologue, he would have suffered the same fate as Barry Goldwater in 1964; if, by some fluke, he had been elected, he would have been denied cooperation by congress and would have been drummed out of office in 1984. The constraints on presidential power are formidable. Chief executives are obliged to back and fill, to accommodate, to deal and to compromise if they wish to accomplish that modicum of public policy change that, short of crisis situations, is usually the best that can be hoped for. The sort of 'sweeping, wrenching change in national economic governance' that Stockman yearned for is the stuff of utopian dreams and has little to do with the realities of American politics.[69]

It certainly is the case that the Reagan administration was never able to duplicate the domestic policy triumphs of 1981 in the remaining three years of the first term. The president's later budgets were substantially rewritten; he was obliged to accept a succession of tax increases; the legislature was unreceptive to the president's agenda of social issues, ie school bussing, abortion and prayer in public schools. Congress also declined to cooperate with Reagan in many of his more ambitious attempts to reduce the size of the federal government.[70]

The paucity of Reagan's legislative record after 1981 is reflected in *Congressional Quarterly* presidential support scores. Indeed, if taken at their face value, these measures suggest that Reagan was less successful in his dealings with the legislature than almost any other modern president. According to Charles O. Jones's calculations, the average support scores for presidents since Truman were Eisenhower 72 per cent, Kennedy–Johnson 84 per cent, Nixon–Ford 65 per cent, Carter (four years) 76 per cent and Reagan (seven years) 64 per cent.[71] As Jones acknowledges, and as was argued earlier, presidential support scores are far from adequate measures of presidential success or failure. They take no account of the lineup of party forces in congress and, most importantly, they do not weight different votes. Such calculations, therefore, fail to distinguish between important and trivial bills whereas the Reagan administration, unlike almost all others, succeeded in obtaining the adoption of landmark legislation.

The effect of the Omnibus Budget Reconciliation Act and the Economic Recovery Tax Act was to move the United States in new directions in economic policy; fundamental change of a sort that had not been seen for half a century. A new political atmosphere was created where minimal government, budget-cutting and low taxation had become the norm. The significance of these bills for domestic policy in the future far outweighed those passed by any president since Franklin Roosevelt. The budget act has been characterized by one scholar as 'the most important piece of domestic legislation since the Social Security Act of 1935 . . . (bringing about) a marked shift in the substance of domestic policy and in American federalism'.[72] In pursuing their administrative and legislative strategies, the Reaganites were not fiddling at the margin or tinkering with the status quo. They sought a change in the terms of the debate and, to a large extent, they succeeded in bringing that about in 1981.

NOTES AND REFERENCES

1. Johns Hopkins University Press, Baltimore 1982, p. 15.
2. Theodore Lowi, 'Ronald Reagan–Revolutionary?' in Lester Salamon and Michael Lund (eds), *The Reagan Presidency and the Governing of America*. The Urban Institute Press, Washington DC 1984, p. 48.
3. See also Fred Greenstein (ed.), *The Reagan Presidency: An Early Assessment*. Johns Hopkins University Press, Baltimore 1983, p. 15.
4. Richard Nathan, 'Institutional Change under Reagan' in John Palmer, *Perspectives on the Reagan Years*. The Urban Institute Press, Washington DC 1986, p. 141.
5. Hedrick Smith, *Reagan the Man, the President*. Macmillan Publishing Co., New York 1980, p. 150.
6. John Chubb and Paul Peterson, *The New Directions in American Politics*. Brookings Institute, Washington DC 1985, p. 1.
7. John Palmer and Isabel Sawhill (eds), *The Reagan Record*. The Urban Institute, Washington DC 1984, p. 2.
8. Martin Anderson, *Revolution*. Harcourt Brace and Jovanovich, New York 1988, p. 121.
9. *The American Presidency*. Harcourt, Brace and World, New York 1956, p. 59.
10. See Joel Aberbach and Bert Rockman, 'Clashing Beliefs Within the Executive Branch: The Nixon Administration Bureaucracy', *The American Political Science Review*. **LXX** (June 1976), No. 2, pp. 456–68.
11. Richard Nathan, *The Administrative Presidency*. Macmillan Publishing Co., New York 1986, p. 39.
12. Anderson, op. cit., p. 195.
13. Ronald Reagan, Televised Address (3 Nov. 1980).
14. Anderson, op. cit., p. 204.
15. *The Thirteenth Man*. The Free Press, New York 1988, p. 16.
16. Ibid., p. 21.
17. Ibid., p. 44.
18. For discussion of cabinet councils see Michael Turner, 'The Reagan White House, the Cabinet and the Bureaucracy' in J.D. Lees and Michael Turner (eds), *Reagan's First Four Years*. Manchester University Press, Manchester 1988.
19. Anderson, op. cit., p. 226.

20. Chester Newland, 'Executive Office Policy Apparatus: Enforcing the Reagan Agenda' in Salamon and Lund, op. cit., p. 163.
21. Thomas Ferguson and Joel Rogers, *Right Turn*. Hill and Wang, New York 1986, p. 131.
22. Ibid.
23. Ibid., p. 136.
24. James MacGregor Burns, *Roosevelt: The Lion and the Fox*. New York 1956, p. 186.
25. 'Dominated by Reagan, Session Makes Much History in a Hurry', (17 Dec. 1981).
26. *Man of the House*. Random House, New York 1987, p. 341.
27. *For the Record*. Harcourt, Brace and Jovanovich, New York 1988, p. 155.
28. O'Neill, op. cit., p. 342.
29. Stockman, op. cit., p. 170.
30. *Congressional Quarterly Almanac 1981*. Congressional Quarterly, Washington DC 1982, p. 257.
31. Stockman, op. cit., p. 180.
32. Laurence Barrett, *Gambling with History: Reagan in the White House*. Penguin Books, London 1984, p. 147.
33. O'Neill, op. cit., p. 342.
34. *Congressional Quarterly Almanac 1981*, op. cit., p. 248.
35. Ibid.
36. Barrett, op. cit., pp. 153–4.
37. Op. cit., p. 185.
38. *Congressional Quarterly Almanac 1981*, op. cit., p. 245.
39. Stockman, op. cit., p. 253.
40. Ibid., p. 248.
41. Ibid., p. 245.
42. *Congressional Quarterly Almanac 1981*, op. cit., p. 103.
43. Op. cit., p. 336.
44. Stockman, op. cit., p. 186.
45. *Congressional Quarterly Almanac 1981*, op. cit., p. 103.
46. Everett Carll Ladd, 'The Reagan Phenomenon and Public Attitudes Toward Government' in Salamon and Lund, op. cit., p. 225.
47. Stockman, op. cit., pp. 268–9.
48. Barrett, op. cit., pp. 188, p. 190.
49. Anderson, op. cit., p. 242.
50. Anderson, op. cit., p. 239.
51. Stephen Wayne, 'Congressional Liaison in the Reagan White House: A Preliminary Assessment of the First Year' in Norman Ornstein (ed.), *President and Congress*. American Enterprise Institute, Washington DC 1982, p. 57.
52. Hedrick Smith, *The Power Game: How Washington Works*. Random House, New York 1988, p. 461.
53. Op. cit., p. 308.
54. Stockman, op. cit., p. 237.
55. *The Power Game*, op. cit., pp. 474–6.
56. Ibid., p. 476.
57. Ibid., p. 341.

58. Allen Schick, 'How the Budget was Won and Lost' in Ornstein, op. cit., pp. 23–4.
59. Op. cit., p. 191.
60. Op. cit., p. 164.
61. Ornstein, op. cit., p. 95.
62. Barrett, op. cit., p. 170.
63. *Public Opinion* (Sept./Oct. 1987), p. 40.
64. Op. cit., p. 14.
65. Stockman, op. cit., p. 9.
66. Ibid., pp. 11–12.
67. Ibid., p. 9.
68. Ibid., p. 10.
69. Ibid., p. 11.
70. *Congressional Quarterly Almanac 1982*. Congressional Quarterly Press, Washington DC 1983, p. 10.
71. Charles O. Jones (ed.), *The Reagan Legacy*. Chatham House Publishers, Chatham, New Jersey 1988, p. 53.
72. Nathan in Palmer, op. cit., p. 127.

CHAPTER SIX

Tax Reform and the Bork Nomination

Presidential effectiveness has been a central concern of this book. In evaluating presidents, the most important measurement is the success they have had in imposing their policy preferences on the American political system. By this standard, Reagan was brilliantly successful at the beginning of his first term: he gained acceptance of his budget cuts, engineered a substantial tax reduction and obtained a marked increase in defence expenditure. These accomplishments were brought about despite a distinctly fragile mandate and a relatively low level of political 'capital'.[1]

In some respects, the prospects in 1985 for effective leadership from the White House appeared to be rather brighter than four years previously. The president had a landslide in the popular vote to match the one obtained in the Electoral College. He had won every state in the Union except that of his opponent, and many core groups of the old Democratic coalition had voted for him in large numbers. Furthermore, the public opinion polls, at the beginning of the year, recorded high levels of popular approval for the re-elected president – Gallup, for example, gave him an approval rating of 64 per cent.[2] The congressional election results had been less impressive, but for all that, the Republicans, despite a net loss of one seat, retained control of the Senate and gained sixteen seats in the House of Representatives.

In the event, however, Reagan's second term began far less promisingly than his first and so it continued, with the president never able to duplicate the mastery over congress that he had displayed in 1981. To a large extent this was unavoidable; second term presidents, even when fortified by landslide re-election victories, have suffered some crushing reverses at the hands of the legislature and there is ample historical evidence to support the claim that 'the longer a president remains in office the more difficult his relations with Congress will become'.[3] Woodrow Wilson, in his second term, suffered a devastating defeat with the Senate's rejection of the Treaty of Versailles. Franklin Roosevelt, notwithstanding a mammoth re-election victory in 1936, was rebuffed by congress over his plan to 'pack' the Supreme Court and, by the late 1930s executive–legislative relations were at a low ebb. Eisenhower had a reasonably productive relationship with congress in 1953, but this was not the case in 1957, the first year of his second term.[4] Within two years of President Johnson's 1964 landslide, his dominance of congress had disappeared.

These precedents suggest that second-term presidents typically run into serious difficulties in their dealings with the legislature, and it is at this point that the concept of the 'impossible presidency' becomes especially apposite. At the best of times, presidents face awesome restraints on their exercise of leadership and yet, if they overcome these difficulties in their first term sufficiently to secure re-election, they must then face the further problems posed by the 22nd Amendment. In his first term a president has at his disposal various resources which can be used to persuade or intimidate members of congress. He has available an impressive array of bargaining counters and his command of public opinion may offer a significant threat to a congressman's chances of re-election. Once his second term begins, however, a president's resources rapidly decline and his ability to influence the legislature is sharply diminished. The 22nd Amendment, in other words, is another daunting limitation on executive power in the United States. British prime ministers, by contrast, are secure in the knowledge that in theory at least they may, 'go on and on'.

By 1985 members of congress saw the president in a new and different light. Boll Weevils, Democratic congressional leaders and liberal Republicans were convinced in 1981 that the president had his finger on the national pulse, and saw him as an exceptionally gifted communicator well placed to wreak electoral retribution on those who defied him. Four years later the picture had changed; the president enjoyed enormous personal popularity, but the elections of 1982 and 1984 had provided little evidence of that popularity rubbing off on other candidates and there were few signs of a full-scale Reagan led electoral realignment favouring the Republican party.

As soon as the second term commenced Reagan's magic, as far as the Washington community was concerned, had begun to wear thin. His lame-duck status immediately became a subject of discussion and the jostling for the succession got underway at once.[5] Coalition-building in congress, especially in the House, became infinitely more difficult than before. The Democrats were less cowed. Their leaders had recovered their nerve, while the Republicans no longer felt as obliged to support their man in the White House as loyally as before. There was much that was inevitable about these developments, but the Reaganites also added to their own difficulties.

In the 1984 campaign, they had done little to provide a sound foundation for policy-making in the event of their candidate being re-elected. Rather than laying before the electorate a clear-cut programme of policy proposals, they had sought to exploit the well-established inclination of voters to evaluate incumbent candidates in retrospective terms – to be more interested in past records than in promises for the future. In the key area of economic management Reagan's record, by 1984, looked rather good. A rocky period in 1981–82, when the United States slid into recession, gave way to a strong economic recovery and the president's standing in the public opinion polls consequently improved dramatically. The Reagan forces accordingly mounted a 'feel good campaign, wrapped around the glow of economic recovery, low inflation, the Olympic slogan "Go for Gold" and the campaign ad "It's Morning Again in America".'[6]

In 1980 Reagan had offered the electorate a fundamental change of direction, but this was not the case this time. In 1984 there were vague assurances of more of the same. The image-makers were now firmly in the saddle and the president could get by with crass, meaningless slogans like 'You aint seen nothing yet'.

Reagan was also weakened as his second term began by changes amongst senior White House staff. Previously he had relied on the skills of the famous troika of Edwin Meese, Michael Deaver and James Baker. Meese was a long-standing friend and loyal ally. Deaver had also been close to the president for many years, was a master of image-making and a confidante of the ever important Mrs Reagan. Unlike the other two, Baker was a recent recruit to the Reaganite ranks, but he swiftly made himself indispensable. A smooth, cultivated Texan, Baker had a keen sense of the political and was especially adept at cultivating both the press and members of congress. In 1981 he played a major part in making a legislative reality of Reagan's policy aspirations and by 1984 had assumed a position of *primus inter pares* amongst the president's most senior advisers. The troika had disadvantages. No one was really in charge and uncertainty, confusion and conflict resulted. Nevertheless, the arrangement kept open lines of communication with various sections of the party and ensured that the president was surrounded by politically sensitive minders – an essential requirement for a chief executive who delegated so extensively and, on occasion, needed saving from himself.

Within a few months of Reagan's re-election, the troika had gone. Meese was seeking confirmation as Attorney General, Deaver was bent on returning to private life and Baker had exchanged jobs with Donald Regan, the first-term Secretary of the Treasury. The emergence of Regan as chief of staff was a development ultimately of great significance for Reagan's presidency. The White House chief of staff role is something of an anomaly. As the examples of Sherman Adams in the Eisenhower administration and H. R. Haldeman in that of Richard Nixon illustrate, it is potentially a position of great power and yet it is an appointive rather than an elective office, not even subject to Senate confirmation. The importance of the post varies with the management style of the president; 'hands on' chief executives like Franklin Roosevelt, Lyndon Johnson and Jimmy Carter, personally immersed in the detail of government, effectively become their own chiefs of staff. Presidents who delegate substantially, on the other hand, and assume a chairman of the board style of management create a vacuum that may be filled by an ambitious chief of staff. This explains both the rise of Adams and the importance of Donald Regan in the first half of Reagan's second term.

Regan's background was largely non-political. After his education at Harvard and service in the marine corps during World War II, he had begun his career on Wall Street which culminated in his becoming chairman and chief executive of Merrill Lynch, one of the largest and most prestigious firms of stockbrokers in the world. Regan had spent little time in the president's company before 1985, but as Secretary of the Treasury he had been a notably loyal cabinet member. He was also closer in age to the president than others around him, and the two men had similar class origins and ethnic roots. A warm, close relationship soon existed between Reagan and his new chief of staff.

The hard-driving, abrasive workaholic Regan seized the opportunity created by the withdrawal of the troika and the president's management style. He set out to bring greater order to the White House by introducing corporate management methods. This required a simplified hierarchical structure in the Executive Office of the President with the chief of staff at the apex supported by disciplined underlings. Regan also reduced the number of cabinet councils from seven to three and arranged matters so that he became *the* funnel of access to the president. 'All duties formerly exercised by Baker, Meese and Deaver devolved on me – personnel, the coordination of information, the choice of issues, the flow of paper, and the schedule that controlled the President's travel and other movements and determined who would see him and who would not.'[7] Regan met with the president at least six times each day, was a member of the cabinet and the National Security Council, sat in on meetings with congressional leaders and, in general, ensured that no decisions of significance were taken without his participation.

Not surprisingly, Regan's dominance in the White House led to allegations of megalomania, a charge that he forcefully rebutted.

> People cannot believe that I don't have my own agenda. 'What is this guy after?' they say. 'He's power mad.' I'm not power mad. I'm trying to put this President's policies into effect. They are the things I stand for and work for. Look, I'm 67. I don't want a political or a business life hereafter. I came here to carry out Ronald Reagan's policies. . . . What I want to achieve is to get Ronald Reagan's agenda translated into law.[8]

These disclaimers were not without foundation, but by no means did they entirely dispose of the charges made. The chief of staff had no personal agenda and was meticulously loyal to what he believed the President's intentions to be. He was too old to nurture political ambitions and, on the face of it, his single-minded determination to realize the president's policy purposes was precisely what was required of a chief of staff. Nevertheless, there were problems. Regan laid himself open to the allegation that he encouraged the president to delegate excessively as a way of maximizing his own power. The charge that the chief of staff was 'power mad' also gained credence from his manoeuvring to achieve a complete monopoly of access to the president. According to some sources, it was this that led to the departure of Robert McFarlane and the emergence of Regan, in effect, as chief of staff for both domestic and foreign policy – a position of pre-eminence that not even Adams had aspired to.

By his own admission Regan did not 'possess the politician's temperament' – surely a fatal weakness in the holder of such an intensely political post.[9] He was a tough-minded, egotistical and authoritarian figure who had

> seen enough of Washington to become impatient, even contemptuous of the time-consuming political process and its emphasis on negotiations and consensus. James Madison's delicate separation of powers, with its inherent inefficiencies to slow the process of change, could scarcely have been more alien to someone used to the fast pace and brute force of Wall Street.[10]

According to Senator Paul Laxalt, Regan 'thought Congress was a damn nuisance', an attitude that was swiftly communicated to legislators – always quick to take offence at executive branch snubs –

and did nothing to help the president's cause on Capitol Hill. The chief of staff's low view of the press was similarly apparent and equally damaging to the president's interests. The contrast with James Baker was, of course, considerable – the latter had a masterly touch in dealing with legislators and consistently maintained cordial relations with the press. The departure of Baker and his colleagues and their replacement by Donald Regan is an important part of the explanation for some of the disasters of President Reagan's second term.

The first Reagan administration had begun with a clear sense of direction; they had 'hit the ground running' and immediately seized control of the legislative agenda. 1985 was to be very different, as Hedrick Smith noted. 'What is striking about the start of Reagan's second term is that this extremely popular president did not repeat the successful format of his first year; have a clear game plan, claim a mandate, start fast, focus your agenda.'[11] The 'feel good' campaign of 1984 had not rallied public opinion behind specific policy proposals and the upheaval of senior staff changes delayed getting down to business. In the early months of 1985, Reagan's presidency already appeared to be in the doldrums. No clear order of priorities had been established; the president's budget had quickly run into difficulties on Capitol Hill; he failed to obtain congressional approval for aid to the contras in Nicaragua and the Bitburg affair cast a dark shadow. The latter crisis arose from Reagan's insistence on honouring a pledge he had made to Chancellor Kohl of West Germany, whereby he had agreed to participate in a reconciliation ceremony honouring Germany's war dead and timed to coincide with the 40th anniversary of the end of World War II in Europe. The revelation that the Bitburg military cemetery, the venue for the ceremony, included graves of Waffen SS troops created uproar in the US, but Reagan, typically, stuck stubbornly to the undertaking he had given Kohl despite the heavy political damage.

When tax reform finally emerged in May 1985 as Reagan's first priority in domestic policy he was showing all the signs of becoming a lame duck. Seventeen months later, to the amazement of many observers, the president signed into law a major tax overhaul measure, a legislative achievement quite different from, but hardly less astonishing than, the triumphs of 1981.

THE TAX REFORM ACT OF 1986

Decision-making in the American political system, especially in domestic policy, is ill-suited to rational problem-solving, major change or outcomes directed towards some notion of the public interest. Policy normally emerges from conflicts between the representatives of partial interests crudely resolved by accommodation and compromise – arrangements that tend to inhibit fundamental change and to favour powerful vested interests. It was not surprising, therefore, that when President Reagan, in his 1984 State of the Union address, urged tax reform on congress 'a wave of laughter rippled through the well of the House', reflecting the belief of congressmen and senators that such a proposal could be no more than a presidential 'pipedream'.[12]

Although it had been generally agreed for years that the existing tax code was in desperate need of reform, few were willing to grasp this particular nettle. Jimmy Carter, for instance, in 1976, denounced the tax system as 'a disgrace to the human race' and yet had not attempted serious reform. Reagan had, for many years, been a critic of the tax system, but hitherto it had been his strategy to pursue tax cuts while leaving the cause of tax reform to others. Donald Regan, as Secretary of the Treasury, brought home to the president the need for reform, arguing that the present tax code was excessively complicated, grossly inequitable and riddled with loopholes. He explained to the president that

> A myriad of tax dodges gave certain individual taxpayers gross advantages over their neighbors. Whole industries, such as oil and gas, real estate and agriculture, benefited from tax laws that favored their interests and gave them enormous competitive advantages. Most of these tax breaks had been justified on grounds that they were in the national interest. The accumulated weight of the inefficiency and selfishness they had created had become a burden on the economy and an affront to economic and social justice.[13]

A major obstacle to reform was the lack of enthusiasm amongst the American public for this particular cause. Public opinion surveys indicated that most Americans doubted whether real reform could ever be forthcoming from congress, suspected that, in any case, reform would lead to tax increases and gave greater priority to the need to reduce the budget deficit.[14] Tax reform was also anathema to some of the most powerful vested interests in the country. Small businesses and high tech industries were generally in favour, but old-fashioned capital-intensive industries like steel and textiles and weighty lobby groups such as the US Chamber of Commerce and the National Association of Manufacturers were opposed.

A cursory inspection of the tax reform measure eventually agreed makes it clear why so many business interests were hostile to its passage. The bill eliminated hundreds of tax shelters beneficial to the well-to-do, and substantially increased the federal income tax liabilites of corporations while reducing those of individuals. Over a period of five years it was intended to shift $120 billion in tax liability from individual Americans to corporations. In 1967 the corporate share of income tax was 35.6 per cent whereas by 1983 that had fallen to 11.4 per cent; the reform measure aimed to reverse that trend and to move the corporate share back to an estimated 24.5 per cent of the total by 1988.[15] The bill, while reducing the number of income tax brackets from fourteen to two, reduced the burden on most of those of modest means and removed six million poor people from the tax rolls altogether. The bill also eliminated investment tax credit arrangements and cut back on deductions for business expenses.[16] When a modified version of the Reagan bill was before the House of Representatives the Speaker urged its acceptance by saying, 'It is a vote for the working people of America over the special interests. It is a vote for the individual taxpayer over the well-financed corporations. It is a vote to restore the confidence of our neighbor in the tax code.'[17]

It may seem surprising to find a conservative Republican president throwing his weight behind such a bill, and certainly the Reaganites were to have difficulty in keeping Republican legislators in line on this issue. It should be remembered, however, that the Republican party is not only the party of business; it also has a progressive tradition. In an earlier era, Republicans like Robert LaFollette Sr, George Norris and Hiram Johnson had been fervent supporters of small business, bitterly opposed to the special interests and the great monopolies. They cherished American individualism and saw themselves as the champions of the little man against the plutocrats of commerce and industry. Congressman Jack Kemp and his supply-side allies could claim lineal descent from the old progressives, and even Reagan, although he had many big business friends, had been touched by the same tradition.

In addition, some Republican strategists believed that tax reform with a populist thrust just might prove to be the issue to bring about the long-awaited party realignment. Frank Fahrenkopf, for instance, chairman of the Republican National Committee, suggested that tax reform

Will go a long way toward making the Republican party the majority party. What we're reaching out for is the last bulwark of the Democratic party: working people, families – especially large families – and not only ethnics but blacks, Hispanics, Catholics. This is a reach by the conservative movement to bring these people into the Republican party.[18]

The passage of tax reform in 1986, despite the long odds against such legislation – 'The Making of a Miracle', as one source described it – provides a revealing case study of the American legislative process in action. It is often assumed that, in modern times, the executive branch has become virtually the sole initiator of major legislation. It is the president, we are often told, who is the prime mover behind public policy change with the legislature reduced to a relatively unimportant role. Such an analysis would be highly inappropriate in this case for the 1986 reform of the tax code can, by no means, be routinely listed as one of the achievements of the Reagan presidency and left at that. In its origins and its crafting the bill was a joint effort by the executive and legislative branches. The bill could not pass without the president's support, but it might not have emerged in the first place and would certainly have failed to pass without the contributions of key members of congress.

The starting place for the Tax Reform Act of 1986 was the 'Fair Tax' plan introduced simultaneously in the Senate and the House in 1982 by two Democrats, Senator Bradley of New Jersey and Representative Gephardt of Missouri. This called for a much simplified tax code with three income tax brackets and few deductions. Without support from the White House the Bradley–Gephardt initiative had no chance of becoming law. By the end of 1983, members of Reagan's senior staff, notably Donald Regan, began to take an interest in tax reform and this was reflected in the president's 1984 State of the Union address. In reference to tax policy he said, 'Let us go forward with an historic reform for fairness, simplicity, and incentives for growth. I am asking Secretary of the Treasury, Don Regan, for a plan for action to simplify the entire tax code so all taxpayers, big and small, are treated more fairly.'

For the moment, however, Reagan's support for tax reform remained tepid. His advisers were aware that the issue lacked appeal for the electorate and they deliberately soft pedalled the president's commitment in his campaign for re-election. Unlike the budget and tax cut proposals of 1981, there was no possiblity of the president claiming that he had a popular mandate for tax reform. Nevertheless, on 28 May 1985 Reagan sent a tax reform package to congress which

135

reduced the number of individual tax rate brackets from fourteen to three, lowered the top rate of tax for individuals from 50 per cent to 35 per cent and for corporations from 46 per cent to 33 per cent and eliminated a wide range of deductions and loopholes. Most importantly, the legislation was to be 'revenue neutral' – reform was to occur without raising taxes or reducing revenues. This was essential to meaningful reform. It required those seeking to amend the bill by restoring tax concessions eliminated at an earlier stage in the legislative process, to produce compensatory sources of revenue.

As the Constitution required, the bill was considered first in the House of Representatives, and during the summer of 1985 it was before the Ways and Means Committee chaired by Danny Rostenkowski, a Democrat from Illinois. Rostenkowski and Speaker O'Neill indicated their general approval of the president's plan while making it clear that they, 'would not rubber stamp the Reagan proposal but strive to make it fairer.'[19] After several months wrangling in Ways and Means and some deft manoeuvring from Rostenkowski that pulled the bill back on several occasions from seemingly certain defeat, a bill was reported out by the committee at the beginning of December. As it now stood, the bill retained the main thrust of the president's plan, but a Democratic imprint had been added. Instead of three tax brackets and a top rate of 35 per cent the Ways and Means measure included four brackets and a top rate of 38 per cent; the committee bill also toughened many of the provisions that applied to business and restored the deduction for state and local income taxes that the president wanted to eliminate.

These Democratic modifications were of great concern to Republican representatives, many of whom, from the beginning, had been unhappy with the anti-business cast of tax reform and were troubled by the informal alliance between Rostenkowski and Reagan. Consequently, when the House voted on the rule required to allow debate on the Ways and Means bill, it was defeated with only 14 out of 182 Republicans voting for the rule.[20] This was a crisis situation for the White House; Reagan was himself unhappy with the Ways and Means modifications to his plan, but could not afford to have his top priority in domestic policy defeated. He had crusaded for tax reform across the country in 1985 and his credibility would be badly damaged if the bill died at this point. His second term would certainly have gone into the terminal decline that media pundits were constantly predicting.

The Speaker informed the White House that he was not prepared to bring the bill up for debate again unless the president could guarantee that an additional fifty Republicans would vote for a rule.[21] This led to some frantic executive branch lobbying. James Baker, now Secretary of the Treasury, his deputy Richard Darman, B. Ogelsby the head of legislative liaison and Donald Regan began appearing on Capitol Hill in a concerted effort to bring sufficient Republicans into line. In their negotiations the president's men had few bargaining counters available; however, some Republican congressmen proved receptive to the argument that a humiliating defeat for Reagan would be harmful, not only to their party, but also to themselves when they faced re-election in 1986.

The president was also very active in this crucial lobbying – speaking with waverers on the telephone, conferring with small groups and making a personal appearance on the Hill to meet with 160 Republican representatives. Reagan's performance at this meeting was suitably low key. He made no opening statement, members were given the opportunity to air their grievances and the president, speaking only briefly, indicated his own dissatisfaction with the Ways and Means bill before telling his audience, 'if tax reform is killed, if it doesn't pass the House in any form, then there will be no tax reform. I just can't accept we would let this historic initiative slip through our fingers.'[22] The votes that the president so desperately needed appear to have been clinched, however, by a letter from him to Republican congressmen concocted by Jack Kemp, Baker and Darman. In this communication Reagan pledged to veto the tax bill if, after it had been to the Senate, it included a top rate of individual tax of more than 35 per cent, or if it did not provide for more incentives for industry than the Ways and Means version offered.

On 17 December 1985, the House adopted the rule required to make possible debate on the floor by a vote of 258–168 with 70 Republicans voting with 188 Democrats. The substantive bill passed later by voice vote. At the White House bipartisan celebration ceremony that followed, the president said, 'What's that I heard about lame duckery?', but as one source put it he 'had come perilously close to a major defeat and at the hands of his own followers. His salvage operation rescued him from a legislative wipe out.'[23] Furthermore the tax reform bill still had a long way to go and could expect, in Rostenkowski's words, 'a bumpy ride in the Senate.'[24]

In the Senate the key player in the struggle for tax reform was Senator Robert Packwood of Oregon, a moderate Republican and chairman of the Finance Committee. When reform had been mooted by the administration in 1984, Packwood had been quoted as saying, 'I sort of like the tax code the way it is.'[25] Nevertheless, when the bill, passed by the House, arrived in the Senate in early 1986, it fell to the

chairman of the Finance Committee to lead the efforts to fashion a Senate response. For the purposes of discussion in his committee, Packwood produced a draft bill that retained Reagan's revenue neutral principle and also provided for the 35 per cent top rate of individual tax that he had called for. Initially Packwood's attempts to marshal a majority behind a satisfactory bill were unsuccessful; he seemed unable to prevent his colleagues from reinstating tax concessions that had been eliminated in the House and thereby undermining the essential principle of revenue neutrality. By mid-April the White House concluded that Packwood had lost control of his committee and that tax reform was effectively dead.[26]

Packwood now advanced a strategy that brought tax reform back from the brink of extinction. His new plan called for cuts in individual tax far heavier than those contemplated by Reagan and Rostenkowski. The top rate of tax would be cut to 25 per cent (compared to the existing 50 per cent and the administration's proposed 35 per cent) and this would be financed primarily by the abolition of most tax shelters and the elimination of the special rate of capital gains tax. Packwood's bold change of tack fired the imagination of Congress and the country and revived the movement towards tax reform: 'The basic concept was so stunning that it attracted right wing conservatives as well as liberals and moderates. The liberals had long wanted tax loopholes closed and conservatives liked driving the tax rates way down to 25 per cent.'[27] Working with a bipartisan coalition of senators, Packwood now re-established control over his committee, obtaining unanimous approval for his bill which then, after some further modifications, swept through the Senate as a whole with only three votes against. After some tricky negotiations at the conference stage and the movement of the top rate of tax back up to 28 per cent, the Packwood bill eventually provided, in large part, the substance of the bill passed by congress.

The foregoing survey of the process whereby tax reform became law makes it clear that in any check list of Reagan's accomplishments the Tax Reform of 1986 has to be placed in a different category from the big economic policy victories of 1981. The latter were largely Reagan achievements. He had campaigned for them in 1980, they were initiated from within his administration and the strategic and negotiating skills provided by Reagan and his staff were crucial to the passage of the necessary legislation. Even in 1981 Reagan's spectacular success could not have occurred without weighty assistance from within congress – most notably in the person of Senator Howard Baker; nevertheless, the budget-cutting Omnibus Reconciliation Act of 1981 and the tax-reducing Economic Recovery Act of 1981 were both Reagan laws in a sense not true of the Tax Reform Act.

For a start, Reagan could hardly claim paternity of the tax reform idea. It had been launched in 1982 by Bradley and Gephardt; Jack Kemp helped to keep it alive and it was Donald Regan who prevailed upon the president to give the matter priority in his second term. Initially Reagan was only lukewarm; he declined to campaign on the issue in 1984 and not until well into his second term did tax reform assume great importance.

Reagan placed tax reform on the legislative agenda and generated support for the proposal around the country, but once he had set the ball rolling the passage of a bill became heavily dependent on the efforts and skills of such members of Congress as Rostenkowski and Packwood. For all that, once Reagan was committed, he threw his full weight behind the cause and, according to Hedrick Smith, his 'tenacity' was an essential ingredient in the bill's success. 'Reagan stubbornly clings to pet goals long after other politicians give up – a personal quality often underestimated by his critics, but essential to presidential success in the agenda game.'[28] Reagan and his staff worked closely with Rostenkowski and Packwood behind the scenes and lobbied vigorously for the bill when Republican defections threatened to destroy it in late 1985.

Subject to these qualifications tax reform must surely be counted as an important Reagan achievement and further testimony of his effectiveness in office. Tax reform was, of course, less earth shattering than the economic policy coups of 1981, but unlike the latter, it was accomplished without a groundswell of public opinion and in the face of considerable disunity among Republican members of the House of Representatives.

The passage of tax reform also showed that occasionally the American political system can produce, outside of crisis situations, policy change that aims at furthering the public interest; legislation that seeks more than the lowest common denominator and is not simply the result of bargaining between vested interests. In addition, these events demonstrate that important legislative initiatives in the United States are not the sole preserve of the executive branch. Legislators furthermore, in some circumstances, may play a substantial part in the crafting of legislative proposals.

Once again we are made aware of the contrast in such matters between the United States and other Western democracies. As this example confirms, congress remains an institution of great power and influence. Public policy-making is not monopolized, as in Britain, by an all-powerful executive branch fortified by the machinery of party and enveloped in a blanket of secrecy. In the UK, taxation policy is considered in conditions of maximum confidentiality by an inner circle within the executive branch; changes are unveiled by the Chancellor of the Exchequer on Budget Day and then, in practice, become effective immediately.[29]

At the beginning of his first term, Reagan was conspicuously successful in getting his economic policy accepted by Congress. His second term began much less auspiciously, but he could claim to have played a large part in passing a landmark measure of tax reform. Overall, during the first six years of his presidency, Reagan was, relatively speaking, a notably effective chief executive. Needless to say, he had suffered many reverses. His budgets had been mauled by congress, he had been obliged to swallow tax increases and there had been plenty of other setbacks. Nevertheless, when compared to other presidents and taking account of the many limits on presidential power, Reagan's record in mastering the American political system up to the end of 1986 was rather impressive. This perception changed dramatically when the Iran–Contra affair burst upon the scene in November 1986.

THE BORK NOMINATION AND REAGAN'S JUDICIAL STRATEGY

Reagan's credibility as an effective president was badly damaged by the Iran–Contra crisis and was further undermined, in the autumn of 1987, by the defeat of Robert Bork, his first choice for the US Supreme Court vacancy created by the resignation of Justice Lewis Powell. To a large extent Iran–Contra was a self-inflicted injury arising from the inadequacies of Reagan's style of management and the ineptitude of his staff. No doubt the Bork nomination could have been handled more deftly and with less complacency, but on this occasion it was circumstance rather than the behaviour of individuals that primarily accounts for the failure. The battle over Bork is yet another episode in the unending contest between the executive and legislative branches – a struggle that a president, well into his second term, nominating an intensely controversial candidate and lacking a majority in the Senate, was almost bound to lose.

If a president is to be effective, and if he is to translate his policy purposes into government action, he must master congress and the bureaucracy, but that alone will hardly be sufficient. As Franklin Roosevelt discovered in the 1930s, the federal judiciary is, in some circumstances, also able to thwart or to advance the president's agenda. To a degree unheard of in other countries, the courts in the United States often become involved in policy-making. They take decisions that elsewhere would be the prerogative of the legislative or executive branches. Judges in the American system are not restricted to the interpretation of laws made by the legislature; they frequently *make* law. Consequently. the man in the White House, if he is to be genuinely 'on top in fact as well as name', requires a judicial strategy to place alongside his strategies for dealing with the legislature and the administration.[30]

The president's power of appointing federal judges which he exercises subject to the advice and consent of the senate provides him with opportunities for bringing the judiciary into line with his ideological preferences. From time to time, replacements are required for nine US Supreme Court judges, 168 US Appeal Court judges and nearly six hundred federal district court judges. A president these days may expect to make approximately fifty nominations to the federal judiciary in any one year.

Appointments to the Supreme Court, the apex of the judicial system, obviously provide the greatest scope for presidential influence, and the resignation of Lewis Powell in June 1987 offered Reagan an especially inviting opportunity. Powell was widely seen as the swing vote on a court broadly divided between conservatives and liberals, and the appointment of an avowed conservative could be expected to have profound consequences for years to come. If the right sort of appointment was made, Reagan could hope also for progress towards the fulfilment of his 'social agenda' – the reversal or, at least, the modification of Supreme Court decisions (in other words national policy) in areas such as abortion, school prayer, pornography, school bussing, affirmative action and the rights of those suspected of criminal offences.

Article II, Section 2, Paragraph 2 of the United States Constitution gives a president the right to appoint federal judges subject to Senate agreement. This provision is one of the key compromises devised by the Constitution makers in 1787 and is designed to strike a balance between executive and legislative power.[31] From the president's perspective it is yet another constraint on his freedom of action that must be overcome if he is to meet his responsibility to lead – if he is to make any difference rather than merely to mark time while in office.

141

The nomination of the conservative Robert Bork, if approved, could be expected to make a difference. Similarly, it was to be anticipated that liberals would find the nomination deeply provocative. Bork was a most experienced jurist; a former law professor at Yale, Solicitor General in the Nixon administration and appointed by Reagan to the important Washington DC federal appeal court. In the course of this distinguished career Bork had displayed a judicial philosophy totally unacceptable to liberals in the senate and elsewhere. He shared Reagan's abhorrence of judicial activism, believing that judges should be 'strict constructionists' restricting their interpretations, as far as possible, to the 'original intention' of the Founding Fathers. Over a number of years, furthermore, Bork had directed a drum fire of often caustic criticism against some of the landmark decisions of the Warren and Burger Courts. He had inveighed against decisions on abortion, obscenity, pornography, free speech, the right of privacy, affirmative action, segregation in public accommodation, legislative reapportionment, bussing and school prayer. Represented in this list are some of the key articles of faith for American liberals in the late twentieth century. Edward Kennedy spoke for many others when, in immediate response to Bork's nomination, he said

> Robert Bork's America is a land in which women would be forced into back-alley abortions, blacks would sit at segregated lunch counters, rogue police could break down citizens' doors in midnight raids . . . and the doors of the Federal courts would be shut on the fingers of millions of citizens for who the judiciary is often the only protector of the individual rights that are the heart of our democracy.[32]

This rather lurid statement was one of the opening shots in a bitter and expensive war of words during the summer of 1987. Lobby groups like the NAACP, the ACLU, NOW, the Leadership Conference on Civil Rights and many others launched 'one of the biggest, most aggressive congressional lobbying drives in recent memory'.[33] According to one source, the anti-Bork forces spent around $12–$15 million on their lobbying effort; the pro-Bork camp also spent heavily, although significantly less than their opponents.[34]

In the run up to the Senate Judiciary Committee confirmation hearings, the administration strove to play down Bork's conservatism and to present him as a distinguished, mainstream jurist who was the victim of a smear campaign. In line with this essentially defensive strategy, executive branch spokesmen argued, as they are always likely to do, that ideological concerns were, in any case, irrelevant to the Senate's role in the appointment process. The president, so it was claimed, was entitled to pick a nominee who shared his views and the

Senate should restrict itself to considering the nominee's professional qualifications. Needless to say, this was not an interpretation of their role that liberal senators were willing to accept. The Reagan administration was also hopeful that when Bork appeared on televsion for the hearings his intellect and bearing would impress viewers; they were optimistic that he would prove to be, 'Ollie North without the medals'.

Bork's five days of appearances before the Judiciary Committee, widely carried on television, turned into an extended seminar on constitutional law, incidentally giving the US congress the opportunity to impressively fulfil its educational function once again. The Vietnam hearings in the late 1960s and the Watergate hearings in the 1970s had been exercises in public education and now the Bork confirmation hearings aired some of the great issues of jurisprudence in the 1980s. The pros and cons of judicial activism were discussed in detail; the arguments regarding the legalization of abortion were explored at length and the meaning of the equal protection provision of the 14th Amendment was probed.

In response to the vigorous assaults of liberal senators, Bork, following the strategy of the administration, endeavoured to present himself as a reasonable, flexible, mainstream jurist in contrast to the liberal image of him as a right-wing ideologue. He backed away from some of the more extreme views he had expressed in the past and indicated that he would not necessarily attempt to overturn decisions he continued to oppose like Roe v Wade, the 1973 decision legalizing abortion. The Judiciary Committee, after its lengthy quizzing of Bork, the longest that any Supreme Court nominee has had to endure, listened to 120 witnesses before eventually voting 5–9 against recommending the nomination. The nomination was then sent to the Senate floor where, after a bitter debate, it was rejected by a vote of 42–58, the largest such margin of defeat in history for a Supreme Court nominee.

How is this defeat to be explained and what were the implications for the Reagan presidency? It should be noted first of all that the defeat of a Supreme Court nomination is not, in fact, all that unusual: one in three nominees were not confirmed in the nineteenth century and even in the twentieth century, after a considerable shift in the balance of powers favouring the president at the expense of congress, one in five nominations have failed to gain Senate approval.[35]

It is often the case that Supreme Court nominees emerge from relative obscurity; however, Bork was anything but an obscure figure. He achieved notoriety in 1973 when he became acting

143

Attorney General and, on president Nixon's orders, fired Archibald Cox, the Watergate special prosecutor, after Attorney General Elliot Richardson and his deputy William Ruckelshaus had resigned rather than comply with the President's wishes. The taint of Watergate was itself enough to make Bork a controversial figure, and, in addition, as an academic he had written extensively on a wide range of contentious issues. In his writings Bork had done a lot of playing with ideas, working out his legal philosophy in public and often withdrawing from earlier stated positions. 'More than almost any other serious academic, in any field, Bork has dared. Hardly a notion has crossed his mind that has gone unexpressed in print. With flourish, he has regularly performed without a net.'[36] When Bork became the nominee, therefore, his opponents, both within the Senate and outside, had a lengthy public record available for scrutiny, one that was riddled with contradictions and provided many avenues of attack.

At the confirmation hearings, the administration's strategy of playing down Bork's conservatism was less than wholly successful. While the nominee came across as a gruff, amiable intellectual willing to adjust his views, that very flexibility led to charges of 'confirmation conversion'. Bork was accused, in other words, of changing his positions in order to secure the nomination. Nor did he prove to be an Oliver North in front of the television cameras, the public opinion polls revealing that his negative ratings increased after his appearances on the small screen.

The nomination could only gain approval in the Senate if the Republicans remained united and if sufficient defectors could be found from among the southern Democrats. At the beginning of his first term among Democratic members of Congress from the South, Reagan had been a man to be feared, but by 1987 the situation was different. The 1986 mid-term elections had shown the president unable to use his personal popularity in the region to prevent the defeat of his party's candidates for the Senate and the Democrats had regained control by a margin of 55–45. In the new politics of the South, moreover, Democratic senators were heavily dependent on black voters who were bound to find repugnant Bork's views on civil rights issues. The NAACP had announced, 'we will fight Bork all the way until hell freezes over and then we'll skate across the ice.'[37]

Southern Democratic luminaries such as Senators Lloyd Bentsen and Terry Sanford and former President Carter had also expressed serious concern about Bork and civil rights. Barbara Jordan, the distinguished, black former member of congress from Texas who saw

the Court as an essential defender of the interests of the underprivileged and minorities, said, 'I think that is the proper function of the
court, and the reason why so many people affected are opposed to the
nomination of Judge Bork is that they do not want to see – we do not
want to see – an articulate and persuasive voice on the Supreme Court
saying, "That is not your function".'[38] Southern Democrats in the
Senate were very conscious of the reservations in the region regarding
Bork's position on civil rights, and when the final roll call was taken
only Senator Ernest Hollings of South Carolina was willing to vote
for confirmation.

The Bork nomination defeat was a major setback for the Reagan
administration, but it should not be interpreted, as some have done,
simply as the result of weak and ineffectual leadership from the White
House.[39] This is not a good example of Reagan's 'hands off' style of
management. He took a keen interest in the matter, lobbied hard on
Bork's behalf, albeit rather late in the day, and stuck by his nominee
even after his defeat was assured. Reagan and his lieutenant Meese, the
Attorney General, can be faulted for overestimating their strength and
for not anticipating the problems that a candidate like Bork was bound
to encounter. However, it is difficult to see how the defeat could have
been avoided once the decision to nominate Bork had been taken.

The nominee was encumbered with a highly contentious and public
record that provided a rallying point for the mobilization of a
formidable coalition of lobby groups. There was no evidence of a
consensus either in Congress or in the country at large in support of
Bork's (or Reagan's) judicial philosophy. The senate was controlled
by the Democrats; the southern Democrats upon whom every
Republican president must rely were not disposed to cooperate with
the White House, whereas the liberals in the senate were only too glad
of the opportunity to strike back at an unusually successful conservative chief executive.

Any president at an advanced stage in his second term is bound to
have difficulties with the legislature. At this point congress is
inevitably more assertive and more mindful of its constitutional
prerogatives. The president is almost certain to be a spent force
electorally; he has little patronage to dispense and already attention
will have begun to shift from him to his potential successors. Lame
duck status, in other words, would be imminent, if not already
present, however gifted a leader the particular incumbent might be. If
the timing had been different – if Bork had been nominated in 1981 or
1985 – he might have been confirmed, but in 1987 such a controversial
candidate was doomed from the start.

The Bork nomination defeat can be seen as yet another episode in the constant struggle between the executive and legislative branches. It brings home the importance of not underestimating the significance of the separation of powers, particularly towards the end of a presidency. It also illustrates again the limits within which a president must operate as he strives to convert his policy ambitions into government action. In that regard, however, the defeat of the Bork nomination should not be considered in isolation.

The Reagan administration had taken elaborate steps to ensure that those appointed to key administrative positions were ideologically sound. Similarly, candidates for the federal judiciary at all levels were subjected to elaborate and unprecedented screening procedures. To be appointed to the federal judiciary during the Reagan years it was not enough to be a Republican, it was also necessary to be a 'strict constructionist' and to be otherwise in sympathy with the president's judicial philosophy. Other Republican presidents had been less alert to the possibilities inherent in the judicial appointment process. The conservative Eisenhower had even appointed to the Supreme Court William Brennan and Earl Warren, the latter as Chief Justice, both of whom were liberals.

By contrast, none but solid conservatives were placed on the Supreme Court by Reagan. Furthermore, he not only had the opportunity to appoint three associate justices and a chief justice during his two terms, he also selected 168 appeal court judges and 211 federal district court judges, all of whom had been subjected to 'the most thorough and comprehensive system for recruiting and screening federal judicial candidates of any administration ever'.[40] Only on very rare occasions did an unapproved candidate succeed, and this assiduous 'Reaganization' of the judiciary will inevitably have long-term policy consequences.

Reagan's critics have pointed with some satisfaction to his failure to win congressional approval for his social agenda – in other words, his preferred positions in regard to issues such as abortion, school prayer, bussing, pornography and affirmative action. But, if the president's legislative strategy failed him in those areas, his judicial strategy may ultimately prove far more successful. As he observed in 1986:

> In many areas – abortion, crime, pornography, and others – progress will take place when the federal judiciary is made up of judges who believe in law and order and a strict interpretation of the Constitution. I am pleased to be able to tell you that I've already appointed 284 federal judges, men and women who share the fundamental values that you and

I so cherish, and that by the time we leave office, our administration will have appointed some 45 per cent of all federal judges.[41]

In fact Reagan was able to appoint over 50 per cent of the federal judiciary himself. The Supreme Court now has a solidly conservative majority and eight out of thirteen federal appeal courts have Reagan appointed majorities. The election of Bush, furthermore (a result that may reasonably be attributed largely to Reagan's popularity), ensures that approximately three-quarters of all federal judges will be Reagan or Bush appointees by 1992. Many such appointees, if recent research is any guide, are likely to hand down decisions broadly in line with Ronald Reagan's social agenda.[42] In other words, what President Reagan failed to gain in congress he may, in the long term, win via the judiciary.[43]

The chances of Reagan's judicial strategy ultimately succeeding may not have been significantly damaged by the defeat of Robert Bork, and ironically, it may even have been enhanced. After a second abortive nomination, that of Douglas Ginsberg, the administration put forward the name of Judge Anthony Kennedy from the Ninth Circuit Court of Appeals. Kennedy's nomination was widely viewed as non-controversial; he was known to be a conservative, but was perceived to be a non-doctrinaire moderate rather than a hard liner like Bork. Bipartisan support for the nomination was forthcoming in the Senate. There was no serious opposition from lobby groups, apart from the National Organization for Women, and confirmation was swift. The Senate Judiciary Committee voted 14–0 in favour of confirmation, a recommendation approved by the whole Senate 97–0.[44]

Not for the first time, however, has a justice of the Supreme Court failed to live up to pundits' expectations. Since his appointment, Kennedy has helped to tilt the Court further to the right; his opinions have not been those of a moderate conservative in the mould of Sandra Day O'Connor, or of his predecessor Lewis Powell. Instead Kennedy has consistently aligned himself with the more hard-line conservatives, Chief Justice William Rehnquist and Antonin Scalia. Admittedly, as this is written, Kennedy has been a member of the Court for only little more than a year, but in that time he has voted with Rehnquist and Scalia 92 per cent of the time.[45]

As some conservative commentators have gleefully pointed out, Kennedy is not only ten years younger than Robert Bork he has also proved to be more of a traditional conservative in contrast to the latter's maverick tendencies. All this may change but, for the moment at least, the Kennedy appointment adds further weight to the claim that Reagan's judicial strategy was exceptionally successful and may, in the end, prove to be 'his most enduring legacy.'[46] Any assessment of President Reagan's effectiveness in translating his policy intentions into policy action must take account of the judicial dimension.

NOTES AND REFERENCES

1. See Table 1, p. 94, Chapter Five above.
2. *Public Opinion* (Sept./Oct. 1987), p. 40.
3. *Congressional Quarterly Weekly Report* (27 Oct. 1984), p. 2782.
4. Ibid.
5. See Hedrick Smith, *The Power Game; How Washington Works*. Random House, New York 1988, p. 488.
6. Ibid., p. 364.
7. Donald T. Regan, *For the Record: From Wall Street to Washington*. Harcourt Brace Jovanovich, New York 1988, p. 234.
8. Bernard Weinraub, 'How Regan Runs the White House', *New York Times Magazine* (5 Jan 1986), p. 14 and 27.
9. Regan, op. cit., p. 137.
10. Jane Mayer and Doyle McManus, *Landslide: The Unmaking of the President 1984–1988*. Houghton Mifflin, Boston 1988, p. 41.
11. Smith, op. cit., p. 363.
12. Regan, op. cit., p. 202.
13. Ibid., p. 195.
14. 'Congress Enacts Sweeping Overhaul of Tax Law'. *Congressional Quarterly Almanac 1986*. Congressional Quarterly, Washington DC 1987, p. 491.
15. Ibid., p. 499.
16. Ibid., p. 494.
17. Ibid., p. 506.
18. Smith, op. cit., p. 552.
19. Regan, op. cit., p. 284.
20. *Congressional Quarterly Almanac 1986*, op. cit., p. 506.
21. *Time* (30 Dec. 1985), p. 15.
22. *Congressional Quarterly Almanac 1986*, op. cit., p. 506.
23. *Time* (30 Dec. 1985), op. cit., p. 15.
24. *Congressional Quarterly Almanac 1986*, op. cit., p. 507.
25. Regan, op. cit., p. 214.
26. Smith, op. cit., p. 506.
27. Ibid.
28. Ibid., p. 383.
29. See *Economist* (23 Aug. 1986), p. 14.
30. See the discussion in Chapter Five above.
31. Henry J. Abraham, *Justices and Presidents*. Oxford University Press, New York 1985, p. 25.
32. *Congressional Quarterly Almanac 1987*, p. 271.
33. *Time* (21 Sept. 1987), p. 17.

34. Richard Hodder-Williams, 'The Strange Story of Judge Robert Bork and a Vacancy on the United States Supreme Court', *Political Studies* **XXXVI**, No 4 (Dec. 1988), pp. 613–37.
35. Abraham, op. cit., p. 39.
36. Michael Kramer, 'The Brief on Judge Bork', *US News and World Report* (14 Sept. 1987), pp. 18–24.
37. Ibid.
38. *Congressional Quarterly Almanac 1987*, p. 273.
39. Mayer and McManus, op. cit., p. 387.
40. Stephen Markman quoted in David O'Brien, 'The Reagan Judges: His Most Enduring Legacy?' in Charles O. Jones (ed.), *The Reagan Legacy*. Chatham House Publishers, Chatham, New Jersey 1988, pp. 60–101.
41. Message to the National Convention of the Knights of Columbus (5 Aug. 1986).
42. Al Kamen and Ruth Marcus, 'Liberal Judges:The Next Species for the Endangered List' *The Washington Post*, National Weekly Edition (6–12 Feb. 1989), p. 31.
43. One factor threatening that success, however, is the low pay for federal judges. Unless they are given substantial increases in the near future many Reagan appointees may be unwilling to make the considerable financial sacrifice involved in their staying on the bench. See David Broder, 'Judges Still Need a Raise', *The Washington Post*, National Weekly Edition (27 Mar.–2 Apr. 1989), p. 4.
44. *Congressional Quarterly Almanac 1987*, p. 276.
45. Al Kamen, 'The Bork Battle Revisited: A Pyrrhic Victory for Liberals?' *The Washington Post*, National Weekly Edition (17–23 Apr. 1989), p. 12.
46. O'Brien, op. cit.

CHAPTER SEVEN

Failure and Achievement in Foreign Policy

November 1986 was surely the worst month of the entire Reagan presidency. Shortly after mid-term election results disappointing to the Republicans, reports began circulating in the media regarding alleged covert shipments of arms to Iran by the US government in its attempt to obtain the release of hostages held by the pro-Iranian Hezoballah group in Lebanon. On 13 November, the president, speaking at a televised news conference, informed the nation that the United States had indeed been engaged in secret negotiations with Iran, denied that arms had been traded for hostages, but confirmed that he had 'authorized the transfer of small amounts of defensive weapons and spare parts for defensive systems to Iran'.[1]

These were astounding revelations. For some years a state of apparently unremitting hostility had existed between the United States and Iran. The seizure of the US Embassy in Teheran in 1979 and the taking of its staff hostage had outraged the American public and there had been no improvement in relations between the two countries since. Following the outbreak of the Iran–Iraqi War the Carter administration had imposed an embargo on arms being supplied to either side and the Reagan administration had taken the lead in denouncing Iran as a supporter of international terrorism. The Americans had also gone out of their way to pressure their allies into not selling arms to the Khomeini regime. As if all this was not embarrassing enough, twelve days after admitting the sale of arms Reagan was obliged to reveal that Edwin Meese, the Attorney General, had discovered evidence that profits from the arms sales had been diverted to Contra rebels in Nicaragua – an apparently flagrant attempt to evade congressional restrictions on such aid.

THE IRAN–CONTRA AFFAIR

The political backlash from what now came to be known as the Iran-Contra affair was devastating: congress was in an uproar; the media launched into a frenzy of investigative journalism reminiscent of Watergate; most seriously of all, Reagan's standing with the American public was substantially damaged, with his opinion poll ratings instantly plummeting. Until November, the president's job approval ratings in 1986 had, according to Gallup, averaged 64 per cent, making him by far 'the most popular sixth-year president since the advent of polling'.[2] In the wake of the Iran–Contra revelations, however, Reagan's Gallup job approval rating fell by 16 per cent and, according to some other polls it collapsed as much as 20 per cent. This was a major crisis for Reagan which might have led to his impeachment and seemed certain to ensure an ignominious end to his presidency.

Various investigations into the Iran–Contra affair by the press, congressional intelligence committees and the Tower Commission proceeded to outline a damning indictment of Reagan's foreign policy stewardship. In substance, the president's policy in the Middle East appeared to be riddled with inconsistency and uncertainty. As the Tower Commission noted, by selling arms to Iran, and thereby violating its own embargo, the United States

> could only remove inhibitions on other nations from selling arms to Iran. This threatened to upset the military balance between Iran and Iraq, with consequent jeopardy to the Gulf States and to the interests of the West in that region. The arms-for-hostages trades rewarded a regime that clearly supported terrorism and hostage taking. They increased the risk that the United States would be perceived, especially in the Arab world, as a creature of Israel. They suggested to other US allies and friends in the region that the United States had shifted its policy in favor of Iran. They raised questions as to whether US policy statements could be relied upon.[3]

According to Tower and his colleagues, this state of affairs had arisen as a result of the president's disengaged style of management which made it possible for policy-making and implementation to be hijacked by amateurs and adventurers. Sober-minded, experienced pro-fessionals in the Department of State and the Department of Defense were effectively short-circuited in the policy process. Instead, crucial decisions and the management of operations were in the hands of staff appointed as national security advisers to the president, first Robert

McFarlane and subsequently John Poindexter, assisted by Oliver North and others on the staff of the National Security Council.

The policy, when it became public, was, not surprisingly, universally denounced as misconceived, misguided and illegal. It shortly became apparent that the administration had been engaged for more than a year in covert action without informing the intelligence committees in congress, as required by law. Congress was also supposed to be informed of covert arms shipments and of any major weapons sales to foreign countries. In addition, the diversion of funds for Contra aid appeared to contravene the Boland Amendments, specifically designed by congress to limit US involvement in Central America.

How are we to account for the Reagan administration embarking on initiatives that flew in the face of the declared foreign policy of the United States; were of doubtful legality; were bound to generate a powerful political backlash when they inevitably became public; and were doomed to failure from their inception? The first thing to be said is that the policy of selling arms to the Iranians was not as irrational as it might seem. Ayatollah Khomeini was believed to be close to death and a succession struggle appeared imminent. As always, the US was nervous about losing ground to the Soviet Union in the Persian Gulf and overtures to possible moderates made sense. President Carter, after all, had been much criticized for the failure of his administration to develop adequate relationships with moderates before the Shah fell. Even the highly critical Tower Commission conceded afterwards that a 'strategic opening to Iran may have been in the national interest'.[4]

Something of a case can also be made for President Reagan's use of national security advisers and NSC staff as policy operators rather than restricting them to more obviously appropriate research and advice roles. The Assistant to the President for National Security Affairs (the National Security Adviser's official designation) is a member of the White House staff and his appointment is not subject to confirmation by the Senate. His relationship with the president, in other words , is quite unlike that of a cabinet member; he is, to a far greater extent, the president's man , answerable only to him. The nature of the National Security Adviser's role has varied from one president to another, but it has usually been assumed that his proper function is that of an 'honest broker'.[5] It is his responsibility to advise the president on national security matters and to make sure that he is aware of all the options available to him and the risks that they involve. He is also expected to monitor the actions of executive departments to ensure that they are in accordance with the president's national security objectives. The latter requirement touches upon a major theme of this book.

Chief executives face many difficulties in making sure that the actions of the government are in accord with their preferences. In particular, their wishes may be obstructed or diluted within the executive branch itself. Career civil servants may not share the president's predilections and strong-willed cabinet members may disagree with his position. Thus George Shultz, the Secretary of State, and Caspar Weinberger, the Secretary of Defense, were firmly opposed to the president's policy of selling arms to the Iranians, a judgement that, in the long term, was to be overwhelmingly vindicated. Nevertheless, irrespective of the morality, the legality or the practicality of his policy, Reagan was the president and as such was ultimately responsible for the national security of the United States. He was, therefore, entitled to take whatever steps that he believed necessary to meet that responsibility as he saw it.

As Carnes Lord has put it, 'It should not be necessary to make the elementary point that the president, as the nation's highest elected official, has not only the right but the duty to ensure that the policies with which he has identified himself publicly are fully reflected in the operations of the executive branch of the government. In our constitutional scheme, there is no basis for federal agencies to act autonomously in derogation of the power of the president.'[6]
Unlike cabinet members, the president's authority rests on an electoral mandate, a rather large one in Reagan's case, and he could be said to be obliged to use whatever means are available to overcome resistance to his policies in congress and within the executive branch itself. Reagan was often accused of being a weak president, irresponsibly delegating his authority to his staff, but that hardly fits the facts in this case.

The record shows that Reagan clung tenaciously to his arms sales policy over many months even though it failed to produce the desired results and was vigorously opposed by senior cabinet members.[7] Initially that policy involved approving the shipment of US made arms from Israel to Iran on the understanding that the Israelis would be allowed to buy replacements. Several months later, in January 1986, the president went further and took the fateful step of authorizing direct sales of weaponry from the United States to Iran. This evolving policy, kept alive by the president's commitment, was opposed at every opportunity by the Secretaries of State and Defense. Arguably the integrity of the policy making process required either the resignations of Shultz and Weinberger or the president acceding to their advice and changing course. In the event neither happened, and the president attempted to resolve the situation by working through NSC staff who were not intended to be involved in policy operations, lacked the appropriate expertise and were not properly accountable for their actions. Reagan can be reasonably accused of irresponsibly delegating the implementation of policy, but as he decided on the framework of that policy, the ultimate decisions were his.

Reagan, like many presidents before him in similar situations, did not keep the bureaucracy and congress informed about what was being done in the name of the United States. As always, when the facts came to light there was much pontificating in both the media and the legislature about improper secret actions by the executive, but Reagan's position, like that of his predecessors, was not without justification. The Department of State and the Department of Defense had made their opposition to the president's policy clear. Congress was controlled largely by the opposition and was, in any case, the president's deadly rival in a never-ending struggle for 'the privilege of directing American foreign policy'.[8] And then, of course, there was the extravagantly uninhibited American media, ever eager to embark on investigative binges. In such circumstances a president seeking to maintain his hold on the decision making process was well advised to maintain confidentiality as far as that was possible in an extraordinarily open political system. To put it another way, secrecy was required in the interest of presidential effectiveness – as he, *according to his lights*, tried to meet his responsibility to preserve the national security of the United States.

The Iran–Contra affair incorporated two separate strands of Reagan's foreign policy that eventually intersected with the diversion of funds derived from arms sales for Contra aid. When the latter scandal was investigated it became apparent that National Security Council staff, led by Lieutenant Colonel North, had, for some time, been channelling funds and covert military assistance to Contra rebels in apparently flagrant violation of the Boland Amendments. This was a clear case of law-breaking by the president's agents, if not the president himself. However, like the trading of arms for hostages, the matter of Contra aid needs to be considered in a wider context.

A number of clauses in the Constitution place the ultimate responsibility for the conduct of foreign policy firmly on the president. This interpretation was confirmed in 1936 in a famous decision of the US Supreme Court when reference was made to the 'exclusive power of the president as the sole organ of the Federal Government in the field of international relations – a power which does not require as a basis for its exercise an act of Congress, but which, of course, like every other governmental power, must be exercised in subordination to the applicable provisions of the Constitution.'[9] The president it seems is in charge of foreign policy, and congress has no more than secondary role.

Irrespective of the merits of the case, Reagan had developed a policy that called for a hard line in Central America. He had campaigned in 1980 on the theme of President Carter's alleged neglect of growing Soviet influence in the 'backyard' of the United States. In office, the Reaganites soon came to regard Nicaragua as another Cuba, a hot-bed of subversion, a Soviet surrogate and a threat to the security of the United States. Accordingly, the Reagan administration sought to destabilize, or perhaps overthrow, the Sandinista regime in Nicaragua by providing support to the Contra rebels. The public opinion polls showed that this policy did not meet with the approval of most Americans and congress, as a whole, did not support the president's policy. In 1982 the first Boland Amendment was passed stipulating that US aid should not be used to overthrow the government of Nicaragua and the following year 'Boland II' decreed that none of 'the funds available to the Central Intelligence Agency or the Department of Defense or any other agency or entity of the United States involved in intelligence activities may be obligated or expended for the purpose of . . . supporting, directly or indirectly, military or paramilitary operations in Nicaragua. . . .'[10]

One rather unconvincing argument used in defence of the Reagan administration continuing to aid the Contras despite the Boland amendments was that their wording did not apply to a White House agency like the NSC. A more plausible objection was advanced by those who argued that the amendments were constitutionally dubious. In effect they could be seen as 'an effort on the part of Congress to "micromanage"' foreign policy and, as such, a usurpation of the role of the executive.[11] The Reaganites could also argue, as presidential spokesmen are always inclined to do in such circumstances, that members of congress were ill qualified to manage the detail of foreign policy, or to pass judgement on immediate questions of national security. They had no access to military intelligence or State Department cables; they were chronically exposed to the ephemeral ambiguities of public opinion; and they represented the sum of the parts of the US while the president could claim to speak for the nation as a whole. The public opinion polls were, in this instance, not in the president's favour, but against that could be set his landslide victories in 1980 and 1984. In general terms, at least, his foreign policy rested on two large electoral mandates.

There were also some precedents that could be cited. Many other presidents had sought to break out of restraints imposed upon them by congress and had pursued foreign policies at odds with American public opinion. Franklin Roosevelt provides one of the best examples. In the early years of World War II he was convinced that Britain and France were in desperate straits and feared for the long-term security of the United States if they were defeated. His freedom to act, however, was constrained by public opinion and neutrality legislation that conservative isolationists in congress had sponsored. The effect of this was 'to remove a crucial area of foreign relations from executive control and to place American foreign policy in a straitjacket during the critical years before the Second World War. . . . The Roosevelt administration struggled to the very eve of Pearl Harbor to untie the knots in which Congress had bound it'.[12]

Like the Boland amendments, the neutrality legislation passed in the 1930s was intended to rein in the executive in foreign affairs. Roosevelt was an exceptionally astute politician and, unlike Reagan in 1985 and 1986, was careful to consult with congress as far as was practicable as he manoeuvred to get the United States into World War II. Nevertheless, like Reagan, Roosevelt was implicated in a variety of activities that ran counter to the express wishes of congress and similarly led to allegations of illegality. It has even been suggested that Roosevelt had foreknowledge of the attack on Pearl Harbor, but allowed it to happen as a means of swinging American public opinion behind his wish to enter the war. As has been pointed out, 'We in Britain, of all people, should remember our reason to be grateful for "crimes" committed by an American president.'[13] We may not agree with Reagan's Central America policy, but arguably he, no less than Roosevelt, had a duty to do whatever he deemed necessary in defence of the national security of the United States, an obligation rooted in the Constitution and supported by precedent.

There is much to be critical about in this episode of Reagan's presidency, but the behaviour of the president and his staff was not completely without justification. The sale of arms to Iran had its own logic, but even if it had not Reagan was within his rights in attempting to ensure that *his* policy rather that that of his opponents was reflected in the actions of the US government. In order to achieve this he had to overcome resistance not only in Congress, but also within the executive branch. If Reagan was to meet this acid test of presidential competence or effectiveness, he was bound to rely on secrecy, the assistance of personal staff loyal to his purposes and was obliged to resort to technically illegal tactics. It is, no doubt, the case that in some national security situations strict adherence to the letter of the law would be destructive of a president's efforts to meet his responsibilities.

The above argument puts the best possible gloss on an affair which, when looked at overall, has to be counted as a major disaster in the history of American foreign policy. By my yardstick of presidential success – the effectiveness of a chief executive in getting his intentions translated into governmental action – Reagan, at this juncture at least, was abysmally unsuccessful. If 1981 and economic policy had provided some object lessons in presidential effectiveness, 1985–86 and Iran–Contra dramatically illustrated some of the things that a president and his staff must avoid if their effectiveness is to remain unimpaired.

In situations such as this it becomes difficult to separate the substance of policy from matters of process. Reagan's attempt get his way collapsed in a welter of bitter recrimination, but beyond that the initiatives that he had embarked on failed to accomplish the goals that he sought. Hardly any hostages were freed; no bridges were built to moderates in Iran and the efforts of the US to unseat the Sandinistas were hopelessly counter-productive. Those who had opposed Reagan's policies were apparently vindicated. On the other hand, if the policies had succeeded, disquiet at the methods deployed would have been relatively subdued. As it was, the spillover effect from these spectacular failures of both policy process and policy substance seemed likely, at the time, to reduce Ronald Reagan to the role of a pathetic, ineffectual bystander for the remainder of his term. Conceivably he was saved from this ignominious fate only by an economy that continued to thrive and fortuitous triumphs in other areas of foreign policy.

Reagan's style of management – a style that seemed to serve him well at the beginning, but now failed him catastrophically – has received a lot of attention from students of the Iran–Contra affair. Unlike every other modern president, Reagan was never a man for detail. David Stockman, Donald Regan and Martin Anderson noted that in economic policy-making Reagan was content to give the most general guidance and to leave the details of implementation to his staff. This method of operation, according to the Tower Commission, proved to be grossly inadequate when applied to the trading of arms with Iran. 'Setting priorities is not enough when it comes to sensitive and risky initiatives that directly affect US national security. He must ensure that the content and tactics of an initiative match his priorities and objectives. He must insist upon accountability.'[14] The main burden of this criticism cannot be denied for it is clear that Reagan's loose management style permitted National Security Council operatives an extraordinary degree of latitude.

Such arguments cannot be taken too far. There is reason to question interpretations of events that suggest that President Reagan was totally out of touch with what was being done in his name. The 'No Hands presidency' thesis carried to extremes is not only *not* supported by the evidence – some of which emerged after the Tower Commission had published its report – it also plays into the hands of Reagan apologists anxious to shield the president from responsibility.[15]

President Reagan's grasp of the detail of policy implementation may have been remarkably hazy, but the policy directions selected were very much his own. It was the president who decided that everything must be done that could be done, including the incredibly risky ploy of trading arms, in order to secure the release of the hostages. Furthermore when the commitment of others in the White House to the policy of selling arms to the Iranians faltered, it was the president who kept the initiative going.[16]

The Tower Commission, in line with its strictures on the president's management methods, concluded that Reagan probably did not have prior knowledge of the diversion of funds for Contra aid. Tower and his colleagues may have thereby saved Reagan from impeachment. Subsequently, however, it became all too apparent that for several years the president himself had taken a close interest in the matter of aid to the Contras. Robert McFarlane gave evidence to congress that the president had approved a plan in 1983 for the mining of Nicaraguan harbours. After congress in 1984 voted to terminate aid to the Contras the president, according to McFarlane, impressed upon his staff the need to help the Contras 'hold body and soul together' and to work towards the reversal of the legislature's decision. The president's former National Security Advisor also reported that Reagan had been briefed 'dozens' of times on the progress of the Contras in the field. Reagan was also intimately involved in the efforts to obtain aid for the Contras from third countries; in particular, meeting with King Fahd in 1985 and persuading him that Saudi Arabia should double its contributions.[17]

At the trial of Colonel Oliver North in early 1989 defence lawyers produced a number of documents in support of their contention that North 'in arming and raising money for the Nicaraguan contras from a wide variety of sources – including arms sales to the Iranian government – was merely implementing the wishes' of President

Reagan.[18] It now seems implausible that Reagan had no knowledge of the diversion of funds from arms sales; it is most likely that he knew of and approved the diversion, but was protected by his staff from the consequences of disclosure. In July 1987 McFarlane's successor, Vice-Admiral John Poindexter, told a Congressional investigation that he had approved Oliver North's plan for a diversion without informing the president. 'I made a very deliberate decision not to ask the president, so that I could insulate him from the decision and provide some future deniability for the president if it ever leaked out. . . . I made the decision. I felt that I had the authority to do it; I thought it was a good idea; I was convinced that the president would, in the end, think it was a good idea.' Poindexter also said, 'On this whole issue, you know, the buck stops here with me.'[19]

The latter statement was very much at odds with any proper interpretation of the structure of responsibility in the political system; as Harry Truman made clear the 'buck' does not stop until it reaches the president's desk. Poindexter was, in any case, widely disbelieved, one congressman going so far as to describe him as 'a lying son of a bitch.'[20] Nevertheless, Poindexter was doing his duty as he saw it, acting as a lightning rod for the president, protecting his commander-in-chief from the political odium that would otherwise befall him.

In other respects, however, Iran–Contra revealed a president badly served by the people around him. If his style of management was hardly 'hands off' to the degree suggested by some observers, it did, for all that, depend heavily on delegation. As Reagan told interviewers for *Fortune*, 'I believe that you surround yourself with the best people you can find, delegate authority and don't interfere.'[21] In Reagan's first term this strategy worked well, but it proved disastrous during the first two years of his second term largely because of a sharp deterioration in the quality of his senior staff.

Reagan's dependence on his personal advisers has been stressed by Martin Anderson who served in that role himself

> Because he does not actively and constantly search out and demand things, he must rely on what is or is not brought to him. When his staff is very, very good, talented, wise and loyal, and almost selfless, it works brilliantly. But when his staff is ordinary – talented, smart but not wise, and loyal more to themselves than to Reagan policy or to the man himself – then mediocrity rules.[22]

This quotation, without naming names, neatly summarizes the crucial differences in Reagan's staff in 1981 and 1985–86. The troika was not without disadvantages, but Baker, Meese and Deaver provided Reagan in the earlier period with the loyalty, the self-effacement, the political nouse and the protection that his approach to government required. At the beginning of the second term the troika was effectively replaced by one man, Donald Regan.

Regan was personally close to Reagan, had no discernible policy agenda of his own and was dedicated to helping the president secure his objectives. On the other hand, Regan was also a man of considerable personal ambition not content with a low profile, behind-the-scenes position. 'He gloried in national television opportunities, insisted on being photographed standing by the president's side, looking over his shoulder or whispering in his ear, and boasted frequently about his power.'[23] Regan crudely exploited the vacuum created by the president's propensity to delegate, shouldered aside rivals and made sure that few people saw Reagan without going through him first. The chief of staff, however, while assuming a position of great importance badly failed to fulfil his responsibilities to the president in the Iran–Contra affair. According to the Tower Commission, he did not ensure that the proper procedures were followed in developing policy so that all the options were carefully weighed and the the risks adequately considered.[24] Furthermore, Regan was by temperament and background ill-suited to the rigours of pluralist politics. He had little understanding of the limits within which the president must operate and disdained to cultivate the media or to defer to congress, all of which helped to leave Reagan cruelly exposed.

The president was also ill-served by other senior advisers at the time of Iran–Contra. Robert McFarlane and John Poindexter as National Security Advisors shared a heavy responsibility for involving the president of the United States in ill-thought-out, risk-laden initiatives almost bound to end in disaster. Similarly, William Casey, the director of the CIA, had encouraged the activities of the NSC staff adventurer Oliver North and done nothing to warn the president of the hazards in the policies being pursued. The two senior cabinet members concerned, Shultz and Weinberger, meanwhile voiced their opposition to selling arms from time to time, but when the programme proceeded anyway they merely 'distanced themselves from the march of events. . . . They protected the record as to their own positions on this issue, (but) they were not energetic in attempting to protect the president from the consequences of his personal commitment.'[25]

President Reagan has been widely and correctly denounced for incompetence in the Iran–Contra affair – he spectacularly failed in his attempt to gain his policy objectives. In other words, he struggled unsuccessfully to exert his authority in the American political system; in this instance he was not 'on top in fact as well as name'. Some have interpreted these events in terms of presidential hubris, suggesting that Reagan and his staff, made arrogant and overconfident by public opinion poll findings and a second landslide, were determined to ram through their policies without regard for proper procedures or legal niceties. The sale of arms to Iran and aid to the Contras 'were parallel elements of the same foreign policy game undertaken by a president blocked by congress, frustrated by divisions in his inner circle, and determined to override all objections in pursuit of his goals.'[26] Such interpretations do not, of course, square with 'no-hands' theories of the Reagan presidency for they suggest an opinionated, wilful and resolute chief executive bent on having his own way at all costs.[27]

Reagan's efforts to circumvent opposition in his administration and to defeat his foes in congress has been the subject of much adverse comment, but the conclusion can be drawn that the nature of a president's position is such that he is virtually obliged to engage in such machinations. The Constitution places on him, the one nationally elected public official (apart from his vice president), onerous responsibilities for national security. However, the restraints on a president's freedom of action are such that he can sometimes meet those responsibilities only by cutting corners, even to the extent *in extremis* of technically breaking the law.

THE INF TREATY

At the end of May 1988 the media gave extensive coverage to President Reagan's trip to Moscow for an historic meeting with Mikhail Gorbachev. At this summit the two leaders formally ratified the INF Treaty banning the production and testing of intermediate range, ground launched, nuclear missiles, i.e. those with ranges of between 300 and 3,400 miles. The treaty also called for the destruction of all existing intermediate range missiles – 1,752 on the Soviet side and 859 held by the United States.[28] This was widely regarded as a breakthrough of great consequence; it was the first nuclear arms reduction treaty to be signed and the first to ban an entire class of nuclear weapons. The ratification of this agreement, moreover, symbolized the emergence of a profoundly altered relationship between the United States and the Soviet Union.

The INF Treaty and the inauguration of a new era of US–Soviet relations were the crowning achievements of Reagan's foreign policy stewardship, offsetting his failures in the Middle East and Central America and contributing much to his high standing in the public opinion polls as he left office. However, it is questionable whether these accomplishments can be legitimately credited to Ronald Reagan in the same sense as his economic policy coups of 1981. The latter could be seen as evidence of effective presidential leadership as defined earlier in this book; in those instances the president had successfully imposed his will, his preferences and his values on the American political system.[29] The INF treaty, by contrast, depended only partly on the president's capacity for leadership within the United States. To a very large extent, making a reality of this treaty turned on fortuitous developments in the USSR. It was merely Reagan's good fortune in his second term to be confronted by a new Soviet leader willing to take initiatives and to negotiate – a leader motivated by concerns and ambitions radically different from those of his predecessors. The INF accord was therefore the fruit of interdependence between the White House and the Kremlin rather than an accomplishment of the former alone.[30] Nevertheless, Reagan played a major part in making this important agreement possible and, contrary to the views of some, his success cannot simply be explained as a result of dumb luck.

'Dumb luck' interpretations of these events have gained added weight from the arguments of those who contend that for most of the period 1981–89 US foreign policy lacked order and direction. Until close to the end of his presidency, so it is suggested, Reagan and his senior officials engaged in much strident, anti-Soviet rhetoric and bellicose posturing while pursuing in practice 'an actual foreign policy that was often vacillating, ill planned and poorly executed'.[31] Experts expressed concern at the evidence of organizational chaos, disharmony and plain incompetence in the foreign policy apparatus during the Reagan years. The National Security Council was believed to be weakly led and derelict in meeting its responsibility to aid the president in making and implementing foreign and national security policy in an orderly and properly considered manner.[32] Alexander Haig, the first Secretary of State, proved to be headstrong and temperamental; he was never close to Reagan, was politically inept and was soon forced into resignation. Haig's successor, the more sober-minded George Shultz, was a better politician, but often seemed disinclined to provide leadership; on some important occasions, moreover, the Secretary of State was overridden or ignored.

Foreign policy during the Reagan years was also bedevilled by long-standing divisions and disagreements between the State Department and the Department of Defense. With Shultz at State and Caspar Weinberger as Secretary of Defense, interdepartmental conflict was increased by the intense personal rivalry between these two senior cabinet members. In policy terms, they differed on East–West issues; Weinberger favoured a hard line in dealing with the Russians while Shultz adopted a more conciliatory approach. In the actual use of American military power, on the other hand, Weinberger was intinctively more cautious than his cabinet colleague. Shultz, for example, in 1986, urged Reagan to attack Libya in response to terrorist outrages while Weinberger counselled caution.[33]

Incoherence and division in the foreign and national security policy apparatus would have been less troubling to the experts if the president had been more of a detail man and less inclined to an apparently passive style of leadership. It would have been better, in other words, if he had been more like Lyndon Johnson, Richard Nixon or Jimmy Carter. Unlike these predecessors, Reagan had little interest in, or understanding of, matters of detail. The complexities of the situation in the Middle East were beyond him and he had no grasp of the arcana of nuclear arms negotiations. Furthermore, like Stockman with regard to budgetary matters, foreign policy advisers were baffled by the president's apparent reluctance to lead. At NSC meetings to discuss arms control policy in the early months of the administration, one participant reported that the president 'seldom said anything that wasn't written on the card. He never weighed in. He was very passive. He wanted a consensus, and when it wasn't forged he didn't lay down the law. Everyone went off in a different direction. We'd leave a meeting and have no idea of what, if anything, had been decided.'[34]

There is nothing new about confusion and uncertainty in the making of American foreign policy, especially at the start of a new presidency. Internecine warfare between the State Department and the Pentagon compounded by the clashing of strong personalities, has afflicted most post-war administrations. Furthermore, the nature of the policy-making process is such that a degree of incoherence is inevitable and leadership is exceedingly difficult. Responsibility for the security of the United States and its relations with other powers is divided among a variety of official bodies. These include, among many others, the departments of State and Defense, the Central Intelligence Agency, the National Security Council, the Joint Chiefs of Staff, the Arms Control and Disarmament Agency and the Agency for International Development. In this mishmash of competing groups each has its own interests to defend and advance. 'The jurisdictions are so overlapping, the lines of responsibility so ambiguous, and the temptations to barge into each other's policy terrains so strong that only the most clear-headed, strong-willed president can impose order.'[35]

Undoubtedly there was a lack of order in the foreign policy-making apparatus during the Reagan years, but it is questionable whether the situation was any worse than usual and, in some respects, it may have been better. According to some eminent scholars at least, Reagan's foreign policy was far less incoherent than has been suggested.[36] It is true that he did not arrive in the White House in possession of a grand strategy into which could be slotted all foreign and national security policy eventualities, but that would not have been appropriate anyway. 'It would have been difficult, even in the luxury of one's analytical imagination, to invent a single strategic concept to embrace the full complexity of the international conditions of 1981.'[37] Nevertheless, unlike some of his predecessors, Reagan did, from the beginning, have broad foreign policy ends that he was determined to pursue. As in domestic policy, Reagan had a broad sense of where he wanted to go and was not content merely to tinker with the status quo; he entered office committed to foreign and national security policy objectives that were not only unusually ambitious, but also provided a logical thread linking the strident rhetoric of the earlier years with the peace mongering that came later.

Few fully recognized the connection, however, and Ronald Reagan's arrival in Moscow in May 1988 for his fourth summit with Gorbachev precipitated a rash of newspaper comment about how far the president had travelled ideologically in the past seven years. The *New York Times* subtitled one such story 'Reagan's Evolution: A Change of Heart As Well as Tactics'; the *Washington Post* referred to 'The Reagan Odyssey: From "Evil Empire" Speech to Four Summits'.[38] Articles such as these added to the impression of incoherence in US foreign policy in the 1980s; they suggested that there had been little consistency, central purpose or direction and inferred that the Reagan administration merely reacted to initiatives taken elsewhere. Such interpretations give insufficient credence to the evidence that Reagan remained throughout remarkably consistent in his attachment to a handful of basic assumptions. The fact, for instance, that in 1988 he was willing to negotiate with Gorbachev and to praise his efforts at reform within the Soviet Union did not mean that Reagan had abandoned the rabidly chauvinistic and primitive anti-communist views that had marked his thinking since the late 1940s.

As if to demonstrate this, Reagan, while in Moscow, brandished his ideological credentials by insisting on meeting with dissidents and by harping on the human rights issue. Similarly, at a meeting with students at Moscow University the president regaled his audience with his thoughts on the virtues of capitalism and the advantages of Western democracy while pointedly referring to the horrors of governments that intrude too far into the lives of their citizens.[39] When asked at a press conference to reconcile his present cordiality towards the Soviets with earlier speeches bitterly denigrating the leaders of the USSR Reagan, not unreasonably, said that was, 'another time, another era'.

Seven years previously, at his first press conference, the president had denounced detente as a 'one way street that the Soviet Union has used to pursue its own aims . . . their goal [is] the promotion of world revolution and a one world socialist or communist state . . . [Soviet leaders] reserve unto themselves the right to commit any crime, to lie, to cheat in order to attain that . . .'. Two years later Reagan depicted the Soviet Union as an 'evil empire' and the 'focus of evil'. In 1988 Reagan's approach was very different, not because his powerful aversion to communism had in any way weakened, but because the Soviet Union and its leadership had undergone fundamental change. In the place of the reactionary and unscrupulous Breshnev there now stood Gorbachev, a man whom, in Mrs Thatcher's celebrated phrase, it was possible 'to do business'. Gorbachev was no hard-line communist ideologue openly committed to world domination, but a moderate reformer intent on *glasnost* and *perestroika*, apparently anxious to concentrate on internal problems and to move the Soviet Union closer to values and ideals that Reagan held dear.

When Reagan entered the White House, the situation had been very different. At home the United States was still recovering from the trauma of Vietnam – an experience which, in conjunction with other humiliations in the 1970s, had contributed to a crisis of confidence and self doubt. Americans, it seemed, had lost faith in their leaders and their institutions. Meanwhile, the United States' principal rival in the outside world had become increasingly menacing. From a conservative perspective the Breshnev regime was no more than a marginal improvement on that of Stalin. Moreover, detente and the arms agreements of the previous decade had allowed the United States' principal adversary to gain a significant advantage in armaments, a development paralleled by the Soviet Union's strategy, at that time, of extending and consolidating its influence in the third world.

Reagan and his senior advisers in 1981 took the view that before turning in any detail to foreign policy they should first attend to problems at home. National morale had to be restored, the economy revived and resources diverted towards strengthening the nation's defences. Once this essential groundwork had been laid the administration would be able to address more specifically the problems associated with the national security of the United States and its place in the international arena.

For much of Reagan's first term, it seemed that the foreign policy objectives of his administration did not extend beyond vigorous reassertions of American power and a facing down of the Soviet Union. However, a number of sources have suggested that Reagan's objectives were, in fact, far more ambitious than they at first appeared. Robert Tucker, for example, believes that the president's ultimate goal was

> nothing less than the alteration of the essential conditions that had come to define American security in the postwar world. One such condition had resulted from the acquisition by the Soviet Union of strategic nuclear missile force capable of striking the United States. The other condition had followed from the development by the Soviet Union of the capability for global intervention.[40]

The American response to the first condition had been mutual deterrence and the Truman doctrine had arisen from the second. To take this second strategy first, President Truman in 1947 said, 'It must be the policy of the United States to support free peoples who are resisting attempted subjugation by armed minorities or by outside pressures.' This was a major statement of American foreign policy inaugurating the era of containment where, in the words of George Kennan, 'The main element of any United States policy toward the Soviet Union must be that of a long-term, patient but firm and vigilant containment of Russian expansive tendencies.'[41] Conservatives, like Reagan, had always been sceptical about the policy of containment, regarding it as too negative and inherently defeatist – reservations that they believed had been amply upheld by the expansion of Soviet influence throughout the third world in the 1970s.

The Reagan doctrine, which superseded the Truman doctrine, was considerably more ambitious, going beyond containment to the provision of tangible assistance to rebel groups attempting to overthrow third world governments aligned to the Soviet Union. The Reagan doctrine was an offensive as well as a defensive strategy; accordingly, the administration aided the resistance forces in Afghanistan and gave support to anti-communist forces in such places as Kampuchea, Angola and Nicaragua. The doctrine as a policy has had no more than mixed success; it was notoriously unproductive in its application to Nicaragua, whereas the Soviets have withdrawn from Afghanistan and the Vietnamese are about to leave Kampuchea. What is relevant for the argument of this book, however, is that an important alteration in policy direction was brought about. Reagan changed the terms of foreign policy debate and demonstrated once more his capacity for effective presidential leadership.

The Reagan doctrine was consistent with conservative Republican doubts about the adequacy of containment, but many of the same conservatives did not share the president's remarkably radical attitude towards nuclear weapons. It eventually became clear that Reagan was horrifed by the implications of the policy of mutual deterrence on which the West (and the Soviet Union) had relied since the end of World War II. The Cold War rhetoric on the campaign trail and the sabre rattling in the early years of his presidency notwithstanding, Reagan, we are assured by a variety of sources, was from the beginning a closet nuclear disarmer. John Newhouse, for example, in his article 'The Abolitionist', is heavily critical of Reagan's management of foreign policy, but writes: 'What the Soviets didn't understand (any more than the national security bureaucracy in Washington did) was that Ronald Reagan wasn't an adventurer who saw nuclear arms as usable weapons: instead he was an abolitionist – a far more convinced disarmer than Carter.'[42] Similarly, Donald Regan, an embittered ex-Reaganite, notes in his memoirs that 'Reagan's every action in foreign policy . . . had been carried out with the idea of one day sitting down at the negotiating table with the leader of the USSR and banning weapons of mass destruction from the planet'.[43] Robert Tucker goes further:

> Mr Reagan's antinuclear disposition . . . has been one of the great surprises of his long tenure. Having come to office condemning the arms control efforts of his predecessors and committed to a military build-up; having taken, once in office, what appeared to be a casual attitude toward nuclear weapons; and having appointed to office men who had never been known to utter a word about the moral enormity of ever using nuclear weapons, the sudden discovery that the president was not only deeply offended by the arrangement (mutual deterrence) that forms the limiting condition of all our lives, but intent on taking measures to alleviate this condition, if not to escape entirely from it, was clearly startling – so much so that many refused to credit what they viewed as too sudden, and suspect, a conversion. And yet Reagan's antinuclear outlook was genuine.[44]

The genuine and long-standing nature of Reagan's antipathy to nuclear weapons is confirmed by Martin Anderson, who was close to him for a number of years. According to Anderson's analysis, Reagan had held such views since at least 1976. For some time he had been convinced that nuclear war between the superpowers would lead to the destruction of civilization; the strategy of Mutual Assured Destruction (MAD) was 'morally unacceptable'; arms limitations treaties and nuclear freezes did not go far enough, and it was essential that arms *reductions* took place. The Soviet Union, Reagan had no doubt, was an implacable foe that understood only the language of military power, but lacked the economic strength to compete in an arms race with the United States, provided the latter showed sufficient commitment.[45]

It is necessary to make a distinction in these matters between Reagan and some of the Reaganites. Many of the latter were irreconcilably distrustful of the Soviets, had no faith whatsoever in arms control negotiations and used them only for tactical purposes.[46] Reagan, too, was deeply sceptical of the motives of Soviet leaders and was most unimpressed by the arms limitation agreements of the 1970s. However, unlike some of his fellow conservative Republicans, President Reagan did not see the build up of American arms as an end in itself, but as a means of driving the Russians into the serious negotiations over nuclear weapons that the future of mankind demanded.

The possiblity of such negotiations taking place seemed remote in the early years of the Reagan presidency. In 1981 the United States had proposed the so-called 'zero option' whereby all intermediate range nuclear weapons in Europe would be eliminated – both those that the Soviet Union already had in place and those that were about to be installed in NATO countries. The following year at Strategic Arms Reduction Talks (START), the Americans had also proposed big cuts in long-range strategic weapons in combination with stringent verification procedures. However, given the belligerent anti-Soviet rhetoric and the ritual denunciation of earlier arms limitation agreements by Reagan and his spokesmen, it was widely believed that the 'zero option'and the START proposals were tactical ploys rather than indications of a willingness to engage in serious negotiation. Although this was the position of administration hawks like Richard Perle, the Assistant Secretary of Defense and no doubt others with little interest in meaningful negotiation, it was not true of the president himself, who 'took his negotiating position seriously and at face value'.[47]

Nevertheless, the prospects for reaching agreements appeared to recede even further when President Reagan, on 23 March 1983, launched his Strategic Defense Initiative which the media quickly dubbed Star Wars. In effect, SDI called for a defensive umbrella or astrodome to be erected above the United States as a protection against the penetration of nuclear missiles. Such missiles would be destroyed in mid-flight and nuclear weapons would thereby be rendered 'impotent and obsolete'.

The president's unveiling of the Star Wars initiative created uproar at home and abroad. Within the United States it was ridiculed as a crackpot Reagan fantasy, illegitimately conceived and sprung upon the nation without proper consideration. Heavyweight members of the defence establishment denounced the proposal as impracticable and deplored what they saw as the reckless abandonment of the strategy of mutual deterrence which had kept the peace between the super powers for nearly forty years.[48] NATO allies were outraged by the absence of consulation and apalled by the implication that the Americans might withdraw behind a shield of insularity. The Soviets, for their part, were deeply shocked and troubled by the disruption of the status quo of deterrence. Andropov, the Soviet leader of the moment, in a *Pravda* interview, said 'Engaging in this is not just irresponsible, it is insane. . . . Washington's actions are putting the entire world in jeopardy.'

Five years later, at the Moscow summit, Reagan proudly claimed paternity of SDI: 'the whole thing was my idea', and this is broadly confirmed by the faithful Anderson. The latter also provides chapter and verse in support of the view that SDI was not a harebrained scheme dreamed up overnight, but a carefully researched proposal that had been gestating for some time. In the summer of 1979 it had been borne in on Reagan how devastatingly vulnerable the United States was to a nuclear attack. He learned that if a Soviet missile was launched against an American city the North American Aerospace Defense Command would pick it up immediately on its radar screens, but there was nothing that could be done to stop such a missile and within ten to fifteen minutes it would hit its target. In pondering the dilemma of the President of the United States in these fleeting moments, Reagan noted that 'The only options he would have would be to press the button or do nothing. They're both bad. We should have some way of defending ourselves against nuclear missiles.'[49]

With the above statement as their starting point, a small group of advisers from within and outside the White House began secretly investigating whether a system of nuclear missile defence was feasible. Within the administation the group included Anderson, Edwin Meese then Counsellor to the president, Richard Allen, Reagan's first National Security adviser and George Keyworth the president's science adviser. From outside came Edward Teller the distinguished nuclear physicist, General Daniel Graham, a former chief of the Defense Intelligence Agency, Karl Bendetson, an undersecretary for the army under Truman; and three Reagan friends from the world of business – Jaquelin Hume, William Wilson and Joseph Coors. In early 1982 these advisers informed the president of their view that a missile defence system was possible and a year later the Joint Chiefs of Staff recommended that research and development should go ahead.

The SDI proposal was developed in secret by a small coterie around the president and launched without consultation with the State Department, the Department of Defense, congress or NATO allies. Not surprisingly, this surreptitious way of proceeding led to adverse comment, but some sort of justification is to be found in the notorious difficulties that attend policy-making in the American system. Reagan and his senior aides were attempting to bring about a radical policy change – one which might ultimately lead to the abandonment of deterrence. Such an ambitious initiative, if pursued in a more conventional manner, would almost certainly have been defeated for it faced much weighty opposition. The majority of scientists with relevant expertise did not believe that the technology was available to convert the president's pipedream into a reality. Defence establishment luminaries were against, Congress in general was most unenthusiastic and the media tended to be scornful. The Defense Department bureaucracy moreover, was most unlikely to be cooperative.

> To begin with, missile defence would be seen as a new idea, and nothing threatens an entrenched bureaucracy like a new idea, especially an idea they have not thought of themselves. Second, the military budget was, as usual, very tight, and you could smell the fear that missile defense money would have to come out of other defense programs.[50]

There are interesting parallels here with the Iran–Contra affair. In that situation too, Reagan was bent on a policy that did not command the support of bureaucrats within his own administration, not to mention the fervent opposition to his plans in congress and the country at large. Both Iran–Contra and Star Wars are examples not of a weak 'no hands' chief executive, but of a strong-willed president determined to impose his policy choices on an unruly, if not chaotic, political system and prepared to use constitutionally suspect and otherwise dubious methods to achieve his objective.

SDI may have lacked credibility at home, but the Soviets took it very seriously indeed. They were much alarmed at the possibility of being forced into a debilitating arms race in outer space and terrified by the prospect of the Americans acquiring a defensive shield that would make possible a first strike against the Soviet Union without fear of retaliation. Even vigorous critics of Reagan's foreign policy management have conceded that SDI was a key factor in getting the Soviet Union back to the arms control negotiating table, willing to make a whole series of concessions.[51]

The Russians had withdrawn from INF and START talks when the Americans went ahead with the installation of intermediate range nuclear weapons in Europe and said they would not return until those missiles were removed. However,

> when that approach failed, the Soviets said they would return to the bargaining table, but only to talk about banning space weapons: when that failed, they agreed to resume START and INF talks, but only if they were linked to a ban on SDI; when that failed, they agreed to 'delink' the negotiations and reach a separate INF accord, but only covering Europe; when that failed, they agreed to ban medium range missiles worldwide.[52]

Eventually the Russians also agreed in principle to cut the number of strategic nuclear weapons by half, made concessions regarding chemical weapons and accepted the need for cuts in conventional arms. Reagan's strategy for dealing with the Soviet Union could be said, in other words, to have been dramatically successful. The build up of American arms in the early years of his presidency and, above all, the Strategic Defense Initiative 'seemed to have frightened the Soviets and convinced them to bargain in earnest. . . . Reagan had somehow managed to use the threat of this nothing of an SDI program to obtain Soviet concessions that were something very tangible indeed.'[53]

The INF treaty and the onset of a new improved relationship between the US and the Soviet Union were, to be sure, heavily dependent on factors over which Reagan had no control. Without Gorbachev and his reformist aspirations, we may assume that little of this progress would have been made; Reagan's legendary luck held until the very end of his political career. Nevertheless, the president's personal contribution is not to be underestimated; in his first term his foreign policy appeared to lack direction, and certainly there were problems of disharmony and disorder among the competing entities and individuals that share responsibility for the United States' relationships with the outside world. Yet there was nothing especially new about this phenomenon and despite the appearance of confusion, Reagan did have a rudimentary sense of where he stood and where he wanted to go.[54] The assumptions upon which he based his foreign policy may have been oversimplistic, but his intentions were far more ambitious that those of most presidents.[55]

Ronald Reagan was not content to be a passive president merely responding to events, he sought a change in the terms of foreign policy debate in the US no less fundamental than the one he had attempted in the realm of economic policy. The fact that he succeeded, at least partially, in this endeavour is a mark of his effectiveness in the White House. Much has been made of Reagan's lack of taste for, or understanding of the detail of policy, 'yet this same detached president dominated policy . . . (he) may not have grasped, or cared about, the details; he may not have faced the contradictions; but *his* priorities, *his* values were being pursued.'[56] This crucial and, in the context of the American political system, most unusual ability to gain acceptance of his policy preferences owed much to Reagan's sense of vision and the tenacity or 'awesome stubbornness' with which he clung to the objectives he had decided upon.

NOTES AND REFERENCES

1. Address to the nation (13 Nov. 1986).
2. Shannon, op. cit., p. 34.
3. *The Tower Commission Report*. Bantam Books, New York 1987, p. 65.
4. Ibid.
5. Ibid., pp. 90–3.
6. 'Executive Power and Our Security', *National Interest* (Spring 1987), pp. 3–13.
7. 'Special Report: The Iran Contra Affair', *Congressional Quarterly Almanac 1986*, pp. 415–47.
8. Edward S. Corwin, *The President: Office and Powers*. New York University Press, New York 1957, p. 171.
9. U.S v Curtiss-Wright Export Company, 299 US 304 (1936).
10. *Congresssional Quarterly Almanac 1985*, p. 77.
11. Hadley Arkes, 'On the Moral Standing of the President as an Interpreter of the Constitution: some Reflections on Our Current "Crises"', *PS* (Summer 1987), pp. 637–42.
12. Arthur Schlesinger Jr, *The Imperial Presidency*. Popular Library, New York 1973, p. 104.
13. London *Times* Editorial (19 Nov. 1987).
14. Op. cit., p. 80.
15. See Jane Mayer and Doyle McManus, *Landslide: The Unmaking of the President 1984–1988*. Houghton Mifflin, Boston 1988, Ch. II.

16. Smith, op. cit., p. 622.
17. *Time* (25 May 1987), p. 33.
18. *Sunday Times* (26 Mar. 1989), p. A17.
19. Mayer and McManus, op. cit., p. 192.
20. Ibid., p. 194.
21. Ann Reilly Dowd, 'What Managers Can Learn from Manager Reagan' (15 Sept. 1986), pp. 21–29.
22. *Revolution*, op. cit., pp. 291–2.
23. Norman Ornstein, 'What Sununu Should Do', *Washington Post National Weekly* (9–15 Jan. 1989), p. 29.
24. *Iower*, op, cit., p. 81.
25. Ibid., p. 82.
26. Smith, op. cit., p. 620.
27. See Mayer and McManus, op. cit., Ch. II.
28. *Congressional Quarterly Weekly Report* (28 May 1988), pp. 1431–5.
29. See Chapter One.
30. Richard Rose, *The Postmodern President: The White House Meets the World.* Chatham House Publishers, Chatham, New Jersey 1988, pp. 243–4.
31. David Ignatius, 'Reagan's Foreign Policy and the Rejection of Diplomacy' in Sidney Blumethal and Thomas Byrne Edsall (eds), *The Reagan Legacy.* Pantheon Books, New York 1988, p. 174.
32. See, among others, *Iower*, op. cit., *passim*.
33. Smith, op. cit., p. 582.
34. John Newhouse, 'Annals of Diplomacy: The Abolitionist – I', *New Yorker* (2 Jan. 1989).
35. Smith, op. cit., p. 571.
36. See, for example, Robert Tucker, 'Reagan's Foreign Policy', *Foreign Affairs* **68**, No. 1 (1988–89), 1–27; Robert E. Osgood, 'The Revitalisation of Containment' in William G. Hyland (ed.), *The Reagan Foreign Policy.* New American Library, New York 1987, pp. 19–56.
37. Osgood, op. cit., p. 25.
38. Section 4, p. 1 (29 May 1988), and p. A1 (29 May 1988).
39. *New York Times*, p. A12 (1 June 1988).
40. Tucker, op. cit., p. 10.
41. Both the Truman and Kennan quotes are from *The Economist*, 'The Truman Doctrine' (14 Mar. 1987), pp. 21–4.
42. Op. cit.
43. *For the Record.* Harcourt Brace and Jovanovich, New York 1988, p. 294.
44. Op. cit., p. 22.
45. *Revolution* Harcourt Brace and Jovanovich, New York 1988, Ch. VIII.
46. Tucker, op. cit., p. 22.
47. Ibid., p. 23.
48. See McGeorge Bundy, George F. Kennan, Robert S. McNamara and Gerard Smith, 'The President's Choice: Star Wars or Arms Control' in Hyland, op. cit., pp. 165–79.
49. Anderson, *Revolution*, op. cit., p. 83.
50. Ibid., p. 93.
51. Ignatius, op. cit.
52. Ibid., p. 194.
53. Ibid., p. 195.

54. Jan Lodal, 'An Arms Control Agenda', *Foreign Policy*, No. 72 (Fall 1988), pp. 152–72.
55. Tucker, op. cit., p. 11 says Reagan's objectives were 'far more ambitious than any administration's since that of Kennedy'.
56. I. M. Destler, 'Reagan and the World: An Awesome Stubborness' in Charles O. Jones (ed.), *The Reagan Legacy*. Chatham House Publishers, Chatham, New Jersey 1988, pp. 241–61.

CHAPTER EIGHT
Presidential Leadership

The questions to be asked of every new president are: Will he be able to master the political system? Does he have what it takes to turn his campaign commitments into government action? Will his presidency make a significant difference in terms of public policy outcomes or will he be forced to settle for achieving no more than a modest degree of incremental change? In short, will this particular chief executive be capable of effective presidential leadership?

In 1981 it seemed to many commentators that Ronald Reagan was unlikely to meet these tests, but eight years later they had reason to reconsider. Reagan's record in office was uneven and he suffered more than a few defeats and disasters, but his overall performance was still more impressive than that of most modern presidents. Quite apart from his triumphs in the field of foreign policy, which owed much to fortuitous developments in the outside world, Reagan presided over a sea change in the terms of domestic policy debate. In other words, he proved to be one of the most effective presidents since World War II.

Not everyone takes easily to the idea of Reagan as an unusually effective president. The perceptions of some are coloured by their dislike of Reagan's policies and, looked at from abroad, there often seems to be more than a little truth in the media caricatures of him as an aging, empty headed, grade B movie actor who somehow stumbled into the White House. Any reservations we may have regarding Reagan's policies are irrelevant to assessments of effectiveness as defined in this book. Personal concerns about the treatment of poor people in the United States during the Reagan years, or the bullying of small countries in Central America, have no place in such assessments. It is also necessary to take media caricatures for what they are and to be careful not to lose sight of the uniquely American nature of the office of president.

The latter point is of particular importance. All of us are products of a particular political culture, and there is a natural inclination to see the politics of other countries in terms that are necessarily alien. It is, however, grossly inappropriate to evaluate an American president in accordance with criteria applicable to a British prime minister. The two roles are fundamentally different. The president must be not only prime minister but chief of state. He is not fortified by a disciplined party machine and does not operate in a system where the separation of powers between the legislative and the executive is virtually without meaning. As one observer has noted, it is not a president's job

> to defend a detailed program of legislation in give and take with the
> political opposition from the commanding heights of a clear
> parliamentary majority. It is rather to muster ad hoc coalitions on behalf
> of a few major issues in a political system where power is
> constitutionally divided and has been further fragmented by the decline
> in the importance of the two major political parties. The American
> President must arouse popular enthusiasm for his program in order to
> get his way. This requires not mastery of legislative detail but the
> capacity to make broad themes compelling to a mass audience.[1]

Ronald Reagan would have made a very poor prime minister indeed, but, by the same token, Mrs Thatcher possesses neither the temperament nor the skills required of a president. It is inconceivable that someone like Mrs Thatcher could be elected president in the first place, but if we take that leap of imagination and place her in the Oval Office it is impossible to see her as anything but a disastrous president.

ROOSEVELT IN THE WHITE HOUSE

The two former presidents with whom Reagan is most often compared are Roosevelt and Eisenhower, and a brief discussion of the leadership styles of these two presidents will make a useful preliminary to our examination of the Reagan approach. Reagan had hero worshipped FDR as a young man and long after he became disenchanted with liberalism he remained an enthusiastic admirer of Roosevelt's style and endeavoured to model his own on it. According to Cannon, 'Though Reagan's politics ultimately would evolve into opposition to some of the most enduring legacies of the New Deal, his style has remained frankly and fervently Rooseveltian throughout his

to the White House; he was never at ease with the inefficiency and the irrationality of decision-making in a pluralist system – problems that Roosevelt had taken in his stride. For twenty years after Roosevelt's death, president watchers were to remain obsessed by the example of his presidency and even now no incumbent can escape the comparison.

EISENHOWER REVISIONISM

The Roosevelt model is not, in fact, appropriate for all seasons and all presidents, a conclusion supported by the revisionist literature on Eisenhower that began appearing in the 1970s. This suggested that to picture Eisenhower as an amiable, naive and rather idle chief executive, bemused and baffled by the problems of presidential power, was to deal in caricature. Eisenhower was, we were then told, a highly skilled and subtle leader; his techniques and strategies were undoubtedly different from those suggested by the Roosevelt/ Neustadt model, but for all that his methods were highly effective and his achievements sufficient to place him in the front rank of modern presidents.

The most notable of the revisionists, Fred Greenstein, points out that, in retrospect, Eisenhower stands out among the presidents from Harry Truman to Jimmy Carter if only because, unlike the others, he at least succeeded in winning and completing a second term. Eisenhower, furthermore, enjoyed an extraordinary average of 64 per cent popular approval in Gallup findings throughout his administration, whereas every other president in the period, excepting John Kennedy who was only briefly in office, suffered a spectacular collapse of public opinion poll support.[9]

Eisenhower also compiled a record of achievement in foreign and domestic policy which, although unimpressive to observers at the time, has come to look much better in later years. In contrast to the agony of Vietnam which engulfed the United States in the 1960s, Eisenhower quickly brought the Korean War to a conclusion and no American lives were lost in combat for the next seven and a half years. On the domestic front, Eisenhower's cautiously conservative economic policy is more impressive from the perspective of the 1980s than it appeared to liberal pundits in the 1960s. Despite appearances, Eisenhower, is now perceived as a hard-headed workaholic, with a keen understanding of the problems of man-management.[10] In addition, far from disdaining politics, he had an acute sense of the political, making him more than a match for contemporary arch-politicoes like Sam Rayburn, Lyndon Johnson and Everett Dirksen.

Eisenhower's performances at press conferences, according to Richard Neustadt, had been harmful to his 'professional reputation'; that is to say, they weakened his standing in the all-important Washington community. It is now suggested that Eisenhower's evasive, ambivalent and sometimes seemingly uninformed remarks were actually carefully contrived answers designed to confuse his questioners and preserve his freedom of manoeuvre while protecting him from the odium that would follow from more straightforward responses.

> Overall both the calculated and unintentional aspects of Eisenhower's press conference style had the same effect as his approach to delegation of authority: they damaged his reputation among the political cogniscenti, but protected his options as a decision maker and insulated him from blame by the wider public for controversial, or potentially controversial utterances and actions. [11]

In contrast to the confused, uncertain and somewhat incompetent figure that Eisenhower sometimes cut in public, the revisionists insist that, in fact, he had a clear and sharply analytical mind. And in organizing the White House, he demonstrated a sophisticated understanding of the value of team work, carefully ensuring that his colleagues felt that they were all part of a great collective enterprise. Again, contrary to popular illusion, it is maintained that Eisenhower kept the reins of decision-making firmly in his own hands, monitoring closely the actions of principal aides such as John Foster Dulles and Sherman Adams, while not hesitating to use them as lightning rods in the interest of protecting himself from controversy and criticism.

Eisenhower demonstrated that it was possible to make a success of the presidency without becoming a Roosevelt clone. He did not seek sweeping changes in public policy and had no taste for high profile leadership of the sort glorified by Roosevelt admirers and exponents of the 'text book' presidency like Richard Neustadt, Arthur Schlesinger Jr *et al.* [12] Nevertheless, according to Greenstein, Eisenhower was a masterly practitioner of a different but, for all that, effective brand of leadership. Rather than aggressively leading from the front, engaging in rhetorical bombast, vilifying opponents, trampling on congressional sensitivities and allowing himself to be seen as being deeply immersed in the detail of policy making, Eisenhower specialized in quiet and subtle leadership, in large part, exercised from behind the scenes.[13]

It will become apparent from the discussion that follows that Ronald Reagan has provided another style of presidential leadership, one that includes elements found in both Roosevelt and Eisenhower, but has also distinctive characteristics of its own.

PRESIDENTIAL LIKEABILITY

One intangible but important quality that Roosevelt, Eisenhower and Reagan shared was likeability, a major political resource in an anti-authority political culture where leadership is so dependent on persuasion. Like the other two, Reagan was a physically attractive man with an agreeable upbeat personality; he moved easily and comfortably on the public stage, radiating warmth and charm and generating affection among others. The absence of such personal characteristics was a considerable handicap to some otherwise highly successful American politicians. Richard Nixon was sufficiently respected to win re-election by a landslide, but likeability was not one of his strengths even before the Watergate revelations. When Lyndon Johnson queried why he was not well liked, he had to endure Dean Acheson bluntly telling him 'Well, Mr President, you are not a very likeable man.' If people had liked Johnson more, he would almost certainly have been re-elected. Similarly, if Nixon had been more likeable, Watergate might never have occurred, or the president might have survived the crisis.

Throughout his life others have found Reagan to be an especially pleasant man. As president, both in face-to-face situations and from a distance, he came across as an unpretentious person relatively free of the pomposity and sense of self importance that afflicts most of those prominent in public life. As Garry Wills noted, 'He is endlessly likable, without the edgy temperament, the touchy pride, that drives some who become superstars.'[14] Many critics have accused Reagan of vacuity and sloth, but few would deny him the 'nice guy' label.

Erwin Duggan in an article with the title, 'Presidential Likeability: Is Niceness Enough?'[15] not surprisingly concluded that niceness, by itself, was not enough, but that it was an asset to Reagan in the exercise of his ceremonial duties as head of state. Reagan was, undoubtedly, especially good in the ceremonial role, but the political significance of his likeability surely extends further than that. For instance, it provides part of the explanation for his hold on American public opinion. This can be exaggerated; in fact, Reagan was not especially popular for much of his first term and his standing in the polls depended on matters other than likeability, such as the state of the economy. Nevertheless, the fact that so many Americans liked Reagan personally, in many cases notwithstanding their dislike of his policies, was, in itself, one of his great political strengths.[16]

This also helps to account for his unusually good relationship with the media – another advantage of great political consequence which Roosevelt and Eisenhower also enjoyed. Liberal commentators often expressed concern at the 'easy ride' that President Reagan was given by the print and broadcast media and alluded darkly to the machinations of image makers like Michael Deaver.[17] No doubt these activities helped, but it was also the case that journalists, cameramen and others in the media warmed to Reagan in a way that was not the case for some other presidents. He went out of his way to be obliging and civil to those who worked in the news industry. Reagan had been a reporter himself and knew it made good political sense, but, beyond that, such behaviour came naturally to him. One source illustrates this point by reference to Reagan's habit of freely responding to questions thrown at him by reporters. The latter soon found out, 'that if they shouted a question to Reagan, loudly enough for him to hear, he was incapable of not stopping, turning and answering. . . . It seems to be an instinctive part of Reagan's personality to respond to anyone who addresses him.'[18] Such politeness, unusual among politicians, was greatly alarming to the president's advisers, but furthered his popularity with journalists and, no doubt, influenced their presentations. Hedrick Smith, a senior figure in the White House press corps, notes:

> Sheer likability . . . has been a great asset to Ronald Reagan . . . news coverage of a public figure can be affected by the personal feelings of the press corps. Popular, likable presidents such as Eisenhower and Reagan have fared better with the press than others, such as Johnson, whom White House reporters saw as too raw and manipulative; Nixon, whom many reporters distrusted and disliked; or Carter, who was ultimately regarded as meanspirited and holier-than-thou.[19]

Reagan's likeability was also of incalculable value in his dealings with legislators. Reagan shared with Roosevelt and Eisenhower the ability to strike up friendly and productive relations with members of Congress. If a president is to govern, he needs an effective legislative strategy and a professional legislative liaison operation is essential, but in addition there must be frequent use of the most precious presidential resource – the president himself. Telephone calls to wavering members, meetings with important congressional groups, intimate give-and-take sessions with important legislators and close working arrangements with congressional leaders are all necessary to maintain the broad net of relationships a president needs in Congress if he is to get anything done. A president who wishes to be successful with Congress will be willing to commit precious personal time to persuading members and will carry out the task of persuasion eagerly and cheerfully.[20]

There is ample evidence that Reagan was especially adept in this role. His relaxed, wisecracking, self-effacing manner put legislators at their ease and inclined them towards cooperation. 'One Roosevelt-like quality that [helped] Reagan with the modern presidential role [was] his impressive capacity to be ingratiating' a talent that few other modern presidents have possessed.[21] Reagan did not bully and overpower representatives and senators in the manner of a Lyndon Johnson; he did not share Nixon and Carter's thinly veiled contempt for congress, its personnel and its methods. There was no danger of Reagan humiliating or intellectually upstaging Congressmen who met him in the Oval Office. 'His demeanour was one of cordiality and respect.'[22] He came across as an unassuming and agreeable man anxious to like and be liked by his visitors. Thus the president's main adversary in Congress, Tip O'Neill, found Reagan to be 'an exceptionally congenial and charming man. He's a terrific story teller, he's witty, and he's got an excellent sense of humor.'[23]

AN 'AMIABLE DUNCE'?

Although congressmen personally enjoyed visiting the White House during Reagan's incumbency more than a few legislators, even in his own party, were troubled by his relentlessly anecdotal style and his apparent lack of command of the detail of policy. Senator Robert Packwood, chairman of the Senate Finance Committee, complained in 1982 that, when senators expressed concern about the mounting budget deficit, the president responded with a fatuous anecdote.[24] Similarly, Robert Michel, leader of the House Republicans, said: 'Sometimes I think, my gosh, he ought to be better posted. Where are his briefing papers?'[25]

Reagan's preference for anecdotes over analysis, his tendency to distance himself from the detail of policy-making and his heavy reliance on staff have all fed the suspicion that he was really not very bright. Many have concluded that he lacked the mind needed to deal with abstractions and other complexities and have shared Clark Clifford's view that Reagan was no more than an 'amiable dunce'. The *Spitting Image* caricature, some would have us believe, was not too far removed from the truth.

There is not much doubt that Reagan is not a man of exceptional intelligence in the conventional sense, but far too much has been made of his limitations in this regard. Many of those who knew Reagan in his youth and middle age clearly did not regard him as a 'dunce'. They found him a reasonably intelligent, impressively articulate and well-informed man. When he entered the White House, however, Reagan was on the verge of his seventieth birthday and doubts about his intelligence were widespread. These concerns received added weight in 1985 with the publication of David Stockman's memoirs. The portrait he painted of the president was most unflattering. Of his first encounter with Reagan during the 1980 campaign, when he was enlisted to help in the preparations for the televised presidential debates, Stockman says,

> Reagan's performance was, well, miserable. I was shocked. He couldn't fill up the time. His answers just weren't long enough. And what time he could fill, he filled with woolly platitudes. There was one question about the upcoming MBFR (Mutual and Balanced Force Reductions) conference. After a few lines he broke off, smiled, and said, 'You guys will have to forgive me now. . . . I've just lost that one completely.' You felt kind of sorry for the guy, but his lack of agility was disquieting.[26]

Stockman decided that the president was a 'kind, gentle and sentimental' man whose 'body of knowledge is primarily impressionistic: he registers anecdotes rather than concepts'.[27] He was an economic illiterate who could be diverted from the path of true revolution by hard luck stories and who derived his enthusiasm for supply-side theory from his personal experience of paying 90 per cent tax at the end of World War II.[28] During the battle to secure a massive tax cut in 1981, Stockman was appalled to discover that 'the President did not have great depth of understanding about the tax code. The complexities, intricacies, and mysteries involved in the tax breaks that the Congress wanted were simply beyond him. In essence, he didn't understand the link between the federal tax structure and the budget.'[29] In early 1984 when Stockman urged upon the president the immediate need for a major tax increase, Reagan responded with a rambling twenty-minute lecture on economic history and theory, leading Stockman to gloomily observe, 'What do you do when your

President ignores all the palpable relevant facts and wanders in circles. I could not bear to watch this good and decent man go on in this embarrassing way.'[30] Stockman's patronizing, view of Reagan's intellectual limitations has been very influential, but it needs to be set alongside the perceptions of other witnesses, some of whom knew the president far better.

Donald Regan is a case in point. He was a hard-headed former businessman and as a disaffected Reaganite he is often severely critical of the president in his memoirs. Nevertheless, his overall view is far more balanced than Stockman's. Regan describes the president as 'a formidable reader and a talented conversationalist with a gift for listening'; moreover, 'his grasp of basic economic theory as it had been taught in his time was excellent, and he had kept abreast of later theory. He had no trouble understanding the leading ideas of the day, or in making reasonable judgments about the effects produced by policies based on Keynesian theory, of which he was deeply suspicious.'[31] Regan noted further that the president had a 'formidable gift for debate' and observed that he had seen him 'defend his ideas and critique the proposals of other heads of state with the best of them at six international economic summits.'[32] Regan had his own doubts about the president's style of leadership, but he clearly dissents from Stockman's low view of President Reagan's intellect.

Another, even better qualified, witness who also contradicts Stockman's opinion in these matters was Martin Anderson. Over a period of seven years Anderson spent much time in Reagan's company, eventually becoming head of the Office of Policy Development and chief domestic and economic policy adviser to the president. Anderson's assessments of Reagan's intelligence must surely be taken seriously for he is no political hack; he is a conservative Republican activist, but he is also an economist and an academic of some distinction. Anderson says that Reagan, 'is highly intelligent with a photographic memory. He has a gift for absorbing great amounts of diverse information, and is capable of combining parts of that information into new, coherent packages, and then conveying his thoughts and ideas clearly and concisely in a way that is understandable to almost anyone.'[33]

Reagan, Anderson leads us to believe, was the true architect of Reaganomics. He drew on the advice of a large number of professional economists, but, Anderson insists, 'over the years [Reagan] made all the key decisions on the economic strategies he finally embraced. He always felt comfortable with his knowledge of the field and he was in command all the way.'[34] According to

Anderson, 'Reagan did not know the latest nuances of economic theory, but he had the basics down as well as any of his economic advisers.'[35] For more than twenty years, moreover, Reagan 'observed the American economy, read and studied the writings of some of the best economists in the world, including the giants of the free market economy – Ludwig von Mises, Friedrich Hayek and Milton Friedman – and he spoke and wrote on the economy, going through the rigorous mental discipline of explaining his thoughts to others.'[36] Those who persist in regarding Reagan as some sort of genial moron are obliged to find answers to the quite different perceptions of these highly qualified observers.[37]

Ronald Reagan was much more intelligent than he sometimes appeared on the television screen or to visitors to the Oval Office. He lacked intellectual curiosity, displayed remarkably little interest in the detail of policy and had a style of leadership that was, in some respects, oddly passive. However, a high IQ, although much valued by journalists and academics, is no guarantee of success in the White House. Some extremely intelligent presidents have been failures in office, whereas Franklin Roosevelt, the most successful of modern presidents, was said to possess 'a second rate intellect, but a first class temperament'.[38] Reagan certainly did not share Roosevelt's obsessive interest in the minutiae of policy-making, but he too had advantages of temperament. His sense of politics equalled that of Roosevelt, in marked contrast to the stridently critical and very intelligent David Stockman whose grasp of politics appears to be negligible, especially for a man who had been a member of congress. In his book Stockman reveals his revolutionary purpose; he treated budget making as an intellectual exercise and was appalled that professional politicians did not share his grandiose ambitions. Reagan, by contrast, was a political realist rather than a utopian. The president also had a healthy belief in the division of political labour; he had himself established the broad framework of economic policy whereas it was the duty of Stockman and others to work out the details. After that had been done the chief executive was primarily responsible for selling the resultant product to Congress and the public.

CHIEF DELEGATER

Reagan's well-known inclination to delegate the details of policy-making to his staff has been constantly referred to by his many critics.

They have assumed that he lacked the mind and the willingness to work that is necessary to come to grips with detail. Unlike Eisenhower who delegated extensively, but who, the revisionists argue, kept the reins in his own hands, Reagan's was supposedly the 'no hands' presidency where no one was really in charge and 'policy-making was literally up for grabs'[39] Such critics have delighted in the colourful metaphor used by Alexander Haig to convey his view of leaderless confusion in the Reagan White House – 'To me the White House was as mysterious as a ghost ship; you heard the creak of the rigging and the groan of the timbers, and sometimes even glimpsed the crew on deck. But which of the crew had the helm? . . . It was impossible to tell.'[40] This is all very entertaining, but not all witnesses would accept it as a fair representation of the White House under Reagan.

David Stockman, while agreeing with Haig on little else, shared his concerns about the president's methods and declared Reagan to be 'as far above the detail work of supply side as a ceremonial monarch is above politics'.[41] At informal meetings before the new administration got underway, the president-elect 'simply, listened, nodded and smiled. 'We have a great task ahead of us.' he would presently say, but he never finished the sentence. He gave no orders, no commands; asked for no information; expressed no urgency. . . . He conveyed the impression that since we all knew what needed to be done, we should simply get on with the job.'[42] Stockman initially found the lack of direction disconcerting, but consoled himself with the thought that he, unlike most other people in the administration – including, as he saw it, the president – did know what had to be done.

Donald Regan as Secretary of the Treasury was also troubled at first by the lack of direction from the president, but like Stockman he too was too confident of his own abilities to remain nonplussed for long. Apart from military service, Regan's prior experience had been exclusively in the world of business; he was 'accustomed to management by objective, where people have *in writing* what is expected and explicit standards are set'. While at the Treasury, however, the secretary never had the opportunity to sit down alone with the president to discuss economic policy, 'From first day to last at Treasury, I was flying by the seat of my pants. The president never told me what he believed or what he wanted to accomplish in the field of economics. I had to figure these things out like any other American, by studying his speeches and reading the newspapers.'[43]

Martin Anderson offers a different perspective on these matters. He concedes that Reagan's management style was, in some respects, curiously passive, but denies any suggestion that he was indecisive.

'Rarely did he ask searching questions and demand to know why someone had or had not done something. He just sat back in a supremely calm and relaxed manner and waited until important things were brought to him. And then he would act, quickly, decisively, and usually, very wisely.' Anderson also directly refutes the Stockman/ Regan allegations regarding the lack of direction in the Reagan administration. 'He knew what he wanted to do and we knew what he wanted done. For five years before he was elected president he staked out clear positions on hundreds of policy issues, and on major issues he spelled out his proposals in some detail.'[44] There was, apparently, less mystery than some of Reagan's cabinet members supposed about the president's policy intentions, in his first term at least. By suggesting otherwise, men like Stockman and Regan maximize their own places in history; they become the real architects of policy and the president's contribution is diminished.

When asked to describe his management style, Reagan himself said:

> I believe that you surround yourself with the best people you can find, delegate authority, and don't interfere as long as the overall policy that you've decided upon is being carried out. . . . I use a system where I want to hear what everybody wants to say honestly. I want the decisions made on what is right or wrong, what is good or bad for the country. I encourage all the input I can get. . . . And when I've heard all that I need to make a decision. I don't take a vote. I make the decision.[45]

This idealized interpretation presents a picture of a chief executive fully in charge. He has decided on the overall policy, but depends on his staff to lay before him the nature of the problem being dealt with, the various choices of action available and the costs and benefits of those alternatives. Once that process has been completed the president himself makes the decision. If this is the theory, how far did it work like that in practice? Was Reagan in control: Were the decisions really his, or was policy-making 'up for grabs'?

A number of sources suggest that Reagan was more in control than sometimes seemed to be the case, and that he did make the key decisions in his administration. In January 1982, for example, the president was under intense pressure from senior White House staff and cabinet members to move closer to a balanced budget by cutting defence expenditures and raising taxes, advice which he rejected. According to one of the president's aides, 'He made the decision. He makes the decisions here, all the major ones. In foreign policy, he makes all the decisions that come to him, and quite a few do. . . . He is not as involved as Jimmy Carter in the day-to-day operations of the presidency, but I don't think he has to be. . . . The suggestion that he's only going through just the ceremonial motions is just not true.'[46]

According to Anderson, 'In the White House all major decisions were made by Reagan' and in the making of economic policy he was 'in command all the way'.[47] Even during the Iran–Contra affair, when the weaknesses of Reagan's management style were most severely exposed, it was the president himself who took and held to the decision to trade arms with Iran against the advice of senior advisers George Shultz and Caspar Weinberger.[48] It has also become increasingly apparent that in the matter of Contra aid the president was far more heavily involved in the decision making than some sources suggested earlier.[49] Robert McFarlane, John Poindexter and Oliver North were, it is now clear, not acting off their own bat, but were following presidential direction.[50]

The crucial question of how far Reagan, notwithstanding his tendency to delegate, retained control over decision making is directly addressed by another insider Terrel Bell, Reagan's first Secretary of Education. The feisty, outspoken Bell is a useful witness. He was no Reagan acolyte; he had never met the president before appointment and was a moderate rather than a conservative Republican. There were many issues on which Bell disagreed with Reagan, yet he recognized the advantages in his style of management. He directly contradicts Stockman's suggestions that in economic policy matters the president gave inadequate direction. 'I never saw evidence of this. He often made decisions on budget and other matters that I did not like, some of which made me angry. But I never felt that his policies were aimless or wandering or lacked clear focus. . . . Reagan was a decisive leader and it is inaccurate to portray him otherwise.'[51]

Bell outlines the role of cabinet councils in the first term. He attended many meetings of these sub-units of the cabinet where reports and data from lower level agencies were considered in detail and the various policy alternatives were evaluated. Subsequently the group would meet with the president and he would be apprised of the essentials of their deliberations before making his decision.

> In this way [President Reagan] could be thoroughly informed without subjecting himself to the impossible burden of countless hours of study late into the night. In other words he delegated effectively. He did not get bogged down in details. He had time to evaluate perspectives to see the picture as a whole. He had the time to relax occasionally, riding horses at Camp David, time to be on the telephone and to keep

appointments in his office and for the endless process of working with Congress. He worked us hard so he could do his job and still be relaxed. That is the mark of the skillful executive. He knew how to delegate and when to monitor. He had a laid back style, but this did not mean he was not effective. Indeed,it enabled him to be effective.[52]

This is a particularly useful assessment of Reagan's style. Bell was right there in the cabinet, but was more of a disinterested observer than men like Stockman and Regan. He displays a better understanding of politics and his recollections are not distorted by intellectual arrogance, nor tainted by bitterness and thwarted ambition.

As Bell recognizes, delegation is an entirely legitimate and desirable management technique that any president is well advised to use. It makes possible a sensible division of labour within the executive branch. The president's primary responsibility is to lead, to provide overall policy direction and, arguably, he is better able to do that if he is not distracted by peripheral detail. Policy-making requires much more than hammering out the details behind the scenes; policies must also be sold to the public and congress and the president is best able to do that. Indeed, in the case of Reagan, he rightly believed himself to be uniquely qualified for this role, although, not for a moment, did he accept that he was therefore reduced to the role of a mere salesman. 'He viewed himself as the creator of the message as well as the chief messenger.'[53]

In the right conditions there are many advantages to delegation. The infinite complexity of the problems of modern government guarantee that no president can come to grips with all the detail and it is foolhardy for him to even try to do so. What may have been possible for Roosevelt in the 1930s was an impossiblity half a century later. Presidents who attempt to emulate Roosevelt today place at risk their physical health, their sanity and their sense of perspective. In the present era, they are better advised to concentrate their attention on setting the general directions of policy and acting as salesmen for the policies agreed while leaving the details to their staff. Such a strategy has the additional advantage of making possible the 'Teflon' effect; that is to say, when policies go wrong, the president is less likely to incur the public odium that may follow if he is closely involved with the planning and execution of policy. As Eisenhower understood, staff can act as lightning rods and so help the president to preserve his personal popularity – an essential requirement if he is to remain effective.[54]

There are dangers in delegation, however. It is obviously important that a president who delegates should not lose ultimate control of the decision-making process. The electorate have placed him, and not his staff, in charge of the government and if accountability is to have any meaning the key decisions must remain in his hands. The implied distinction between the 'big' questions of policy and the detail may not work in some situations – an understanding of the 'nitty gritty' by the president himself may be indispensable to good policy-making. To put it another way, delegation is appropriate in some policy areas, but much less so in others. For example, it served Reagan well with regard to tax reform and provided an instructive contrast with the relentlessly 'hands on' style of his immediate predecessor, Jimmy Carter, who

> read reams of Treasury documents on tax reform and plunged into the drafting of a final proposal, which got nowhere. Reagan relies on staff analysis plus his own principles and instincts. In his tax reform drive he established his objectives – among them lower rates, fairness, simplicity, revenue neutrality, and stimuli for growth. Then he delegated the details to Treasury and weighed in at key moments with appeals to Congress and the voters, plus strategic advice to [James] Baker on pushing the program.[55]

Delegation worked for tax reform, but the strategy is much less suitable in sensitive and complicated foreign policy matters. Although Reagan played a larger part in decision making during the Iran–Contra affair than is commonly believed, his style of management gave too much scope to adventurers and egotists on the White House staff. As John Tower and his colleagues noted, the issues at stake were too complicated and too potentially explosive politically for Reagan's permissive style of management. 'Setting priorities is not enough when it comes to sensitive and risky initiatives that directly affect US national security'.[56] It is reasonable to assume that a more 'hands on' president would have reined in irresponsible aides and avoided some of the more disastrous mistakes.

The Iran–Contra affair brought out very clearly how dependent on his staff is a president who delegates extensively. In his first term, Reagan's management style had worked well because he was surrounded by a good staff. The troika of senior White House aides of Edwin Meese, James Baker and Michael Deaver, in conjunction with the system of cabinet councils, ensured that issues were thoroughly researched and policy options carefully weighed before Reagan was required to make a decision. With capable responsible staff surrounding him, Reagan was protected from the danger of half baked and politically catastrophic decisions. When the troika was replaced by Donald Regan as chief of staff and the system of cabinet councils became largely defunct, the potential for disaster in Reagan's style of management was devastatingly revealed. As Anderson puts it, in Reagan's second term 'the high rolling, high risk methods that served him so well earlier now betrayed him. His unique management style had enormous power and efficacy when implemented properly, but it was a flawed style, with high risk and potential for disaster. Its Achilles' heel was exposed by the Iran–Contra affair.'[57]

Delegation is an essential strategy for all presidents, but it can be carried to excess, and this undoubtedly occurred during the Reagan years. Eisenhower, the revisionists argue, struck a better balance; he delegated extensively, but at the same time was sufficiently familiar with the detail of policy-making. He kept his senior staff under close control and exercised a subtle form of 'hidden hand' leadership from behind the scenes.

PRESIDENTIAL MODESTY

One of the more interesting explanations of the logic behind Reagan's tendency to delegate his authority has been provided by John Sears, his former campaign manager. According to Sears, Reagan's capacity to delegate derives from his experience as a film actor. 'A lot of people in political and corporate life feel that delegating is an admission that there's something they can't do. But actors are surrounded by people with real authority – directors, producers, scriptwriters, cameramen, lighting engineers, and so on. Yet their authority doesn't detract from the actor's role. The star is the star. And if the show's a hit he gets the credit.'[58]

Arguably, Reagan's fondness for delegation reflected a modesty, or a sense of his own limitations, that was not only a managerial strength but also carried with it other important advantages. This is not, of course, to suggest that he was lacking in self-confidence; he had few doubts about his ability to perform the tasks required of a president as he saw it, but he recognized that he could not do it all and that he needed the help of experts. In 1980, in a revealing comment to a group of economic advisers, Reagan said, 'I'd like you to tell me what has to be done to restore the health of the economy. Don't worry about the politics of what has to be done. That's my job. I'll take care of that.'[59] Other activist presidents have been less restrained and less diffident; they have sought not only to lead but also to micromanage.

Reagan's different and, apparently, more modest approach to his job also served him well in a political culture where leaders of all description are regarded with suspicion. For historical and other reasons Americans remain ambivalent about leadership; presidents are expected to lead, but at the same time they are hedged about with restraints that prevent them from meeting that responsibility. Presidents must be careful to avoid arousing age-old suspicions and resentments; their standing will be weakened if the perception gains ground that they are 'power mad' and not properly respectful of the constitutional and other limits placed on presidential power. As Woodrow Wilson, FDR, Lyndon Johnson and Richard Nixon discovered, such allegations can have devastating negative reper-cussions.

By contrast, Ronald Reagan was largely immune to the charge of megalomania. His readiness to delegate his authority and his 'relaxed nine-to-five style . . . made him seem less "Washington", less power hungry and less menacing'.[60] Furthermore, unlike many of his predecessors, Reagan's head was not turned by the trappings and myths attached to the presidency; he remained remarkably free of the egomania that afflicts most men who sit in the White House. He did not take himself too seriously, was not 'puffed up' by his high office and did not 'treat himself like a statue of himself'.[61]

George Reedy has written convincingly about the corrupting, court like atmosphere of the White House where a president is treated like a quasi monarch and is surrounded by sycophants only too willing to flatter their master's ego.[62] Reagan, unlike say Lyndon Johnson or Richard Nixon, remained unaffected by this fawning attention and deference. He put on no airs and graces and left people with the impression that despite his high office he remained essentially one of them. This non-threatening style of leadership was attuned to the American democratic tradition and helped him to retain both his popular support and his credibility among other political leaders.

TOUGHNESS AND VISION

The picture of Reagan conveyed so far, leaves out of account (and, indeed, tends to obscure) two of the great strengths of Reagan's leadership: his toughness and his vision. Despite his legendary affability Reagan was, beneath it all, an exceptionally tough-minded and fiercely ideological president; one who had a clear sense of direction and stuck stubbornly to the paths he had chosen. Martin Anderson, describes Reagan simply as 'one of the toughest men I have ever known; far tougher, for example, than his predecessors, Carter , Ford and Nixon. Once Reagan has determined what he thinks is right, and what is important to do, then he will pursue that goal relentlessly.'[63]

Donald Regan was also clearly impressed by the president's resolution: 'it was not uncommon for him to render courageous decisions on domestic economic questions in the face of nearly unanimous advice and pressure to do the opposite.' Regan noted also, 'When he has made a decision, he lives with it. He doesn't fret over it. And most of all he doesn't change his mind. Therefore he doesn't confuse Congress or the public as to what he stands for.'[64] The hypercritical David Stockman recognized that, on occasion, Reagan could be very tough. He observed his coming down 'like a ton of bricks', on Governor Hugh Carey of New York who presumed to criticize his economic policy. The big tax cut passed in 1981 was, according to Stockman, an impressive display of strength by the president. Later in the first term when Stockman had decided that the case for a 'major tax increase was unassailable, inescapable and self evident' he found Reagan stubbornly refusing to budge, 'No, we have to keep faith with the people. Everywhere I go they say, "Keep it up! Stick to your guns!" Well, isn't that what we came here to do?'[65]

In early 1982 many of Reagan's senior staff were concerned about the mounting deficit and pressed the president to consider raising taxes and cutting defence expenditures. When James Baker, at a White House meeting, spoke along these lines Reagan responded sharply, 'If that's what you believe, then what in the hell are you doing here?'[66] This was an exchange between a pragmatist and an ideologue. No doubt with an eye to the 1984 election, Baker was deeply troubled by the political implications of the deficit and other signs of weakness in the US economy. The president, however, believed passionately in the virtues of cutting taxes and a strong defence and stubbornly resisted the pressure on him to make short-term adjustments.

The tax reform bill that passed in Reagan's second term was the result of the efforts of many others besides the president. Nevertheless, it would not have become law without his tenacious insistence on staying with the proposal once he had decided to support it. 'The tax bill's survival', according to Hedrick Smith, 'was testimony not only to the support of Democratic leaders but also to Reagan's tenacity. Reagan stubbornly clings to pet goals long after other politicians give up – a personal quality often underestimated by his critics, but essential to his success in the agenda game.'[67] It was also the case that that same tenacity came close to wrecking Reagan's presidency when he stubbornly insisted on trading arms for hostages, against the advice of his secretaries of State and Defense. Similarly, he recklessly pressed ahead with aiding the Contras despite the Boland Amendments and the absence of public support.

Reagan's tough mindedness was paralleled and reinforced by his sense of vision; few presidents have gone to the White House with a clearer sense of what they intended to do when they got there. Eisenhower, for example, had no preconceived plan and Roosevelt's intentions, in 1932, were very unclear. As Theodore Lowi has observed, 'no one knew Roosevelt's specific positions and plans until after he became president in 1933. If there was a referendum on the Roosevelt program, that was in 1936, not in the campaign of 1932. In contrast, Ronald Reagan's program was clear for all to see before the 1980 election.'[68].

Reagan possessed a political gyroscope; he had a sense of direction and was not contantly adjusting his position take account of what he thought the voters wanted to hear. His vision may have been banal, oversimplistic or just plain wrong, but its very existence was an important strength that his contemporaries have lacked. Jimmy Carter, for instance, was racked by doubt. Similarly, Michael Dukakis was an earnest, hard-working, highly intelligent political manager, but the American people were hardly any better informed about what he really stood for at the end of the 1988 campaign than they had been at the beginning.[69]

George Bush, in the same campaign, was irritated by reporters asking what his 'vision' might be, and according to his staff

> the reason the questions nettled him . . . was that [he] never accepted the need for an overarching vision. Rather, he believes he possesses the right training and the intuitive sense to make correct decisions as problems come his way. He is the embodiment of pragmatism: self confident about his ability to find solutions without holding to a master blueprint.[70]

This outright disavowal of any sense of vision will conceivably detract from Bush's effectiveness in the White House, dooming him to the role of mere presider rather than a genuine leader. Articles about the Bush administration have already begun to appear in the American press with titles such as, 'A Ship Without a Rudder: The White House Appears to Lack Direction or Purpose'.[71] One senior official in the administration has argued that Bush has been handicapped by his lack of an, 'ambitious agenda comparable to Reagan's. "This administration is like a canoe standing still in a pond. Every little ripple can knock you over. Reagan was a boat moving forward so the little ripples caused little troubles, but you had this momentum and kept moving.""[72]

Invidious comparisons have also been made between Bush and his predecessor in regard to the latter's greater resolution in adhering to his principles. During his visit to China early in his presidency, Bush ignominiously backed down, apparently for diplomatic reasons, when the Chinese authorities refused to allow a leading dissident to attend a barbecue hosted by the president. Lou Cannon has interestingly contrasted Bush's behaviour with that of Reagan in similar circumstances:

> He raised human rights issues in every one of his five meetings with Mikhail Gorbachev and insisted on inviting Soviet dissidents to the U.S. Embassy in Moscow. On his trip to China in 1984, Reagan reacted angrily and promptly when the Chinese censored part of a nationally televised speech in which he sharply criticized the Soviets and made favorable references to religion and capitalism. . . . While Reagan could at times be rigid beyond reason, he also conveyed a sense of constancy that even his adversaries respected.[73]

Bush, lacking in vision and clear-cut resolve, is unlikely to command similar respect.

Tough-mindedness and a clear sense of direction are characteristics that Reagan shared with his great personal friend and ideological ally Margaret Thatcher, and they are qualities which go a long way towards explaining the success of two otherwise very different politicians operating in very different political systems. Zbigniew Brzezinski draws the parallels as follows. 'They are . . . not particularly intellectual in their approach. They are what political leaders ought to be, individuals with a relatively simple but clear grasp of what their priorities are, and they happen to have the willpower to try to implement what they believe in. And those are the essentials of effective leadership. . . .'[74]

To write off Ronald Reagan, as so many in Europe have done, as a bone-headed, idle and incompetent president is to underestimate the man grossly and to misunderstand seriously the needs of the presidency in the late twentieth century. Reagan may be no intellectual, and his management style may have had some major drawbacks, but he had a number of strengths and proved to be an astute politician who mastered the problems of presidential power rather better than anyone else possibly since Roosevelt. His approach to the problems of presidential leadership on occasion brought him to the brink of disaster, but, at its best, it made it possible for him to be effective in office to an unusual degree.

Liberal critics, in particular, have scorned and derided Reagan without appearing to recognize that this allegedly incompetent chief executive mastered the political system sufficiently to bring about fundamental policy change, an accomplishment that few presidents can claim. One prominent American liberal, however, has been prepared to give Reagan his due even if the compliment is somewhat back-handed. Arthur Schlesinger Jr, otherwise a trenchant critic of the substance of Reagan's policies, has recognized the former president's exceptional ability to get the system to work.

> If the President can point the country and persuade the voters that it is the right direction in which to go, and if he can find reasonably competent subordinates to figure out the details, it does not matter so much politically that he himself hardly knows what is going on. Reagan's success proved that the presidency, if you know how to work it, is not all that tough a job. He spent fewer hours at his desk and more on holiday than readers of this book are accustomed to doing. Yet in short order he brilliantly dispelled the learned doubts of the late 1970s about the capacity of Presidents to govern and brilliantly restored national confidence in the workability of the office and the system.[75]

Schlesinger, it should be noted, is a Roosevelt biographer and admirer, yet he seems to be saying that it is not necessary after all to be a carbon copy of FDR in order to be an effective president. It appears that the man in the White House does not have to be a Superman – a hyperactive, omniscient being, harbouring his authority and working all hours of the day on behalf of a wide-ranging legislative programme.

Judged by such standards, Reagan must be counted a failure, but not all the criteria implicit in the Roosevelt model of presidential power are relevant in the former's case. Unlike Roosevelt and others in the same mould – Truman, Kennedy and Johnson – Reagan wished to shorten rather than to extend the reach of government, a posture reflected in his approach to his job as president. 'As opposed to the hyperactivity of Democratic presidents and the mushrooming expectations placed upon them, President Reagan [worked] at his dominant priority (limiting domestic government) by not becoming involved, by not thinking up new things to do, by not claiming to solve other people's problems.'[76]

Ideologically Reagan had much more in common with Eisenhower. Comparisons between Eisenhower and Reagan, however, tend to be unflattering to the latter. According to the latest interpretations, Eisenhower, while publicly engaging in delegation was, in private, a detail man, carefully controlling his subordinates and skilfully exercising leadership from behind the scenes. By contrast, Reagan is so often presented to us as a vacuous, slothful figure incapable of the leadership subtleties now associated with Eisenhower.[77] It should be recognized that Reagan was far more ambitious and in that regard more of a leader than was his Republican predecessor. Eisenhower was not bent on fundamental change. He did not seek to dismantle the New Deal only to resist its extension; his overall purpose was the maintenance of the status quo. For all his apparent indolence, Ronald Reagan was not content to be a mere machine minder. He was a radical innovator determined to use the machinery of government to reverse the thrust of past policies. In that sense, Reagan was closer to Franklin Roosevelt than to Dwight Eisenhower.[78]

NOTES AND REFERENCES

1. Michael Mandelbaum, 'The Luck of the President' in William Hyland (ed.), *The Reagan Foreign Policy*, op. cit., p. 141.
2. Cannon, op. cit., p. 18.
3. Op. cit.
4. See especially William Leuchtenberg, *In the Shadow of FDR*. Cornell University Press, Ithaca 1983.
5. Some of the material that follows on Roosevelt and Eisenhower has previously appeared in a slightly different form in David Mervin, 'Presidential Power: Roosevelt, Eisenhower and Reagan', *Teaching Politics* 17, No. 2, pp. 230–43.
6. Neustadt, op. cit., p. 229.
7. Ibid., p. 231.
8. Fred Greenstein, *The Hidden Hand Presidency: Eisenhower as Leader*. Basic Books, New York 1982, p. 5.
9. Ibid., p. 4.
10. Ibid., p. 38.
11. Fred Greenstein, 'Eisenhower as an Activist President', *Political Science Quarterly* (Winter 1979–80).
12. On the 'text book' presidency, see Thomas Cronin, *The State of the Presidency*. Little Brown, Boston 1980.
13. Greenstein, *The Hidden Hand Presidency*, op. cit., pp. 58–65.
14. Gary Wills, *Reagan's America: Innocents at Home*. Doubleday, New York 1987, p. 33.
15. *Public Opinion* 8, No. 2 (Apr./May 1985).
16. From April 1982 to May 1984, for instance, close to 30 per cent of those polled liked Reagan personally even though they disapproved of his policies. See William Adams, 'Recent Fables about Ronald Reagan', *Public Opinion* 7, No. 5 (Oct./Nov. 1984).
17. For example, Anthony Lewis, 'Why the Kid Gloves for Reagan's Presidency', *New York Times* (Feb. 1982).
18. Anderson, op. cit., p. 291.

19. *The Power Game*. Random House, New York 1988, p. 426.
20. Norman J. Ornstein, 'The Open Congress Meets the President' in Anthony King (ed.), *Both Ends of the Avenue*. American Enterprise Institute, Washington DC 1983, p. 205.
21. Fred Greenstein, 'Reagan's Presidential Leadership' in E. Sandoz and C. Crabb (eds), *Election 84: Landslide Without a Mandate*. New American Library, New York 1985, pp. 66–85.
22. C. O. Jones, 'A New President, a Different Congress, a Maturing Agenda' in Lester Salamon and Michael Lund (eds), *The Reagan Presidency and the Governing of America*. The Urban Institute Press, Washington DC 1984, p. 276.
23. *Man of the House*. Random House, New York 1987, p. 335.
24. Morton Kondracke, 'Reagan's IQ', *New Republic* (24 Mar. 1982), p. 10.
25. Stephen Wayne, 'Congressional Liaison in the Reagan White House' in Norman J. Ornstein, *President and Congress: Assessing Reagan's First Year*. American Enterprise Institute, Washington DC 1982, p. 59.
26. *The Triumph of Politics*. Hodder and Stoughton, London 1986, p. 48.
27. Ibid., pp. 12 and 95.
28. Ibid., pp. 10–11.
29. Ibid., p. 251.
30. Ibid., p. 400.
31. *For the Record*. Harcourt Brace and Jovanovich, New York 1988, pp. 249 and 191.
32. Ibid., p. 250.
33. Op. cit., p. 279.
34. Ibid., p. 164.
35. Ibid., p. 171.
36. Ibid., p. 164.
37. See also Larry Speakes, *Speaking Out*. Avon Books, New York 1989, p. 373.
38. Oliver Wendell Holmes quoted in James MacGregor Burns, *Roosevelt: The Lion and the Fox*. Harper and Row, New York 1956, p. 157.
39. Jane Mayer and Doyle McManus, *Landslide: The Unmaking of the President 1984–1988*. Houghton Mifflin, Boston 1988, p. 21.
40. *Caveat: Realism and Foreign Policy*. Macmillan, New York 1984, p. 5.
41. Op. cit., p. 93.
42. Ibid., p. 81.
43. Op. cit., p. 142.
44. Op. cit., pp. 290 and 210.
45. Ann Reilly Dowd, 'What Managers Can Learn From Manager Reagan' *Fortune* (15 Sept. 1986), pp. 21–29.
46. Kondracke, op. cit.
47. Op. cit., p. 220.
48. See, for example, 'Special Report: The Iran Contra Affair', *Congressional Quarterly Almanac 1987*, pp. 415–47.
49. For example, *The Tower Commission Report*. Bantam Books, New York 1987; and Mayer and McManus, op. cit.
50. See *Time* (25 May 1987), p. 33 and John Cassidy, 'North the Fall Guy all set to Point the Finger', *Sunday Times* (26 Mar. 1989), p. A17.
51. *The Thirteenth Man: A Reagan Cabinet Memoir*. The Free Press, New York 1988, p. 31.

52. Ibid., p. 32.
53. Laurence Barrett, *Gambling with History: Reagan in the White House*. Penguin Books, London 1984, p. 22.
54. See Greenstein, *The Hidden Hand Presidency*, op. cit., pp. 238–9.
55. Dowd, op. cit.
56. *Tower*, op. cit., p. 80.
57. Op. cit., p. 295.
58. As quoted in Dowd, op. cit.
59. Anderson, op. cit., p. 165.
60. Smith, op. cit., p. 426.
61. Cannon, op. cit., pp. 305–6.
62. *The Twilight of the Presidency*. New American Library, New York 1970, p. 18.
63. Anderson, op. cit., p. 288.
64. Regan, op. cit., p. 250. The second quotation is from Dowd, op. cit.
65. Stockman, op. cit., pp. 159, 246 and 399.
66. 'How Reagan Decides', *Time* (13 December 1982).
67. Smith, op. cit., p. 383.
68 'Ronald Reagan – Revolutionary?' in Salamon and Lund, op. cit., pp. 29–56.
69. See David Osborne, 'On a Clear Day He Can See Massachusetts', *The Washington Post*, National Weekly Edition (25 Apr.–1 May 1988), p. 24.
70. David Hoffman, 'Patrician With The Common Touch' *The Washington Post*, National Weekly Edition (14–20 Nov. 1988), p. 6.
71. David Hoffman and Ann Devroy, *The Washington Post*, National Weekly Edition (13–19 Mar. 1989), p. 6.
72. Ibid.
73. 'Danger Signals For the President', Ibid., p. 28.
74. Quoted in Hugo Young and Anne Sloman, *The Thatcher Phenomenon*. BBC Publications, London 1986, p. 108.
75. *The Cycles of American History*. Andre Deutsch, London 1987, pp. 293–4.
76. Hugh Heclo, 'Reaganism and the Search for a Public Philosophy' in Palmer, op. cit., pp. 31–63.
77. See Wills, op. cit., p. 320.
78. Greenstein, *The Reagan Presidency*, op. cit., p. 239.

CHAPTER NINE

The Reagan Legacy

President Reagan had many shortcomings; his administration had its share of crises and disasters and the final record of achievement was, at best, mixed. Nevertheless, there is no doubt that Ronald Reagan was one of the most successful presidents of modern times. He met the challenges of presidential power better, and was therefore more effective in office than, perhaps, any president since Roosevelt.

As the analysis in previous chapters has shown, there are innumerable obstacles to the exercise of presidential power and it sometimes seems little short of miraculous that any chief executive ever succeeds in achieving major objectives outside of crisis situations. Furthermore, no modern president has established complete and consistent mastery over the political system. Some have enjoyed fleeting periods of dominance, but sustained presidential success has been a remarkably rare commodity.

EFFECTIVENESS IN THE WHITE HOUSE

President Truman's stature rests largely on his position as an architect of the policy of containment that became the foundation of American foreign policy after World War II but, on the home front, his relations with congress were notably unproductive and his domestic policy achievements negligible. There may have been more to Eisenhower than was once thought and, to be fair, he had no aspirations towards activism in the realm of domestic policy. However, whatever the reasons, conservative Republicans seeking to roll back the New Deal derived little solace from Eisenhower's tenure – a presidency devoted largely to preserving things as they were. John Kennedy was not president long enough to fulfil the promise that some believed he possessed, but, in office, his commitment to radical change in areas such as civil rights weakened and his positive achievements were few. For a while in the mid-1960s Lyndon Johnson was an impressively effective president. He dominated the policy-making apparatus and brought about some important changes. Johnson's policies were, however, built on New Deal foundations rather than breaking with the past. And, in any case, Johnson's dominance was brief and eventually he was driven from office leaving both the presidency and his party seriously weakened.

Neither Nixon nor Ford nor Carter could be described as effective presidents in the sense used here. Nixon enjoyed some triumphs in the international arena, but failed to bring about a significant change of direction in domestic policy. Nixon's successor, Gerald Ford, was crippled from the beginning by the absence of a popular mandate and achieved nothing of consequence in the way of public policy change. Jimmy Carter, unlike his Republican predecessors, had the benefit of healthy majorities in both houses of the legislature and yet he too failed to realize the high hopes he had entertained as his presidency began.

Given the obstacles to the exercise of presidential power and the historical precedents it seemed most unlikely that Ronald Reagan would be able to avoid the failure that had befallen so many others. In the long run, Reagan's policies may be deemed to have failed. If the dire prognostications of his many critics are fulfilled, the American economy will eventually founder as a result of the actions of his administration. The burden of massive budget and trade deficits, a gigantic national debt and the enormous sums owed to foreign investors may, ultimately, cause the economic system to collapse. Similarly, if the lynch pin of Mikhail Gorbachev is removed from the international scene and a return to the intense rivalry between the superpowers takes place, Reagan's foreign policy may, ultimately, be found badly wanting. Spectacularly disastrous consequences arising from Reagan's policies at home and abroad are still entirely possible and will remain so for some time to come – the final verdict on the wisdom of those policies, in other words, is not yet in. Even if those policies are ultimately shown to be, beyond all doubt, misconceived this will not detract from Reagan's record of effectiveness in obtaining acceptance of his policies – the principal measure of presidential success or failure in this book.

When he first entered the White House Reagan's principal objectives were to reduce the size and role of government, to reinvigorate the economy and to strengthen the nation's defences. In pursuit of those aims Reagan sought policy change aimed at increasing defence expenditure, cutting taxes and curtailing domestic programmes. Broadly speaking, Reagan achieved these ambitious ends.

> Even critics must admit that a determined president was able to accomplish many of his stated goals. Reagan gained the largest increase in peace time defense spending, a step he felt was necessary in order for the country to regain its position as the world's preeminent military power. Reagan cut tax rates sharply and dramatically altered the income tax system, policies to which his administration was also deeply committed. Reagan sheared back a great number of domestic programs, thus carrying out in good part his promises to reduce the scope of the domestic side of government.[1]

Inevitably Reagan enjoyed only partial success in translating his objectives into policy change. In particular, the reductions in domestic expenditure were far more modest than were necessary to prevent ballooning budget deficits, given the reductions in tax revenue and the increases in defence spending. Reagan failed spectacularly to deliver his 1980 campaign promise to balance the budget; large budget deficits and an enormous national debt are part of the legacy of Reaganomics. Budget deficits – in constant dollars (1982) – averaged $161 billion for the first six years of the Reagan administration as compared to an annual average of $28 billion since 1950.[2] The national debt, meanwhile, tripled during the Reagan years to more than $2.6 trillion.

Many commentators have expressed alarm at the deficits incurred during Reagan's presidency; however, responsibility for balancing the budget falls as much on congress as on the president. Reagan could plausibly argue that the legislature was responsible for the budget deficit; if members of Congress had been more cooperative and less determined to defend domestic programmes, expenditure cuts could have been made sufficient to bring the budget into balance. The majority in Congress, on the other hand, were bound to blame the president for his stubbornness in refusing to raise taxes or to decrease defence spending sufficiently to eradicate the deficit. This stalemate between the executive and the legislature merely reflected American public opinion in the 1980s. Polls regularly revealed majorities against reducing spending for social programmes paralleled by majorities opposed to tax increases and in favour of increased defence expenditure. There was widespread agreement on the undesirability of a big deficit, but no consensus in support of the measures necessary for its elimination.[3]

It cannot be denied that Reagan's inability to come even close to his avowed intention to balance the budget counts against his claim to be regarded as an especially effective president. He had failed after all, in this instance, to impose his preferences on the political system. In the president's defence it has been argued that although he was as anxious as anyone to see the budget balanced he was working to an order of priorities that placed cutting taxes and strengthening America's defences ahead of eliminating the deficit. Former Representative Jack Kemp has said, 'I remember very clearly Reagan being asked, "What about the deficit?" He said, "I would take a deficit if by a deficit I were able to implement my tax cut and my defense build-up." I am sure Reagan talked about a balanced budget as a theoretical point. But the defense build-up and the tax cuts were sacrosanct.'[4] Reaganites could claim that the achievement of two out of three principal goals was a level of accomplishment that few other presidents have enjoyed.

It has also been suggested that the deficit was part of Reagan's political strategy, 'game plan' or 'hidden agenda'. According to this argument Reagan and his staff shortly after taking office were required to address some of the realities of budgetary politics. In campaigning Reagan had railed against the 'welfare mess' and promised to eliminate 'waste, fraud and abuse'; but balancing the budget would require more than rhetoric, it needed some substantial cutting of federal programmes. In practice very little of the budget was amenable to cutting. Defence, 'untouchable' entitlement pro-grammes and the interest on the national debt taken together accounted for approximately three quarters of the federal budget.[5] In other words, the big savings in expenditure required to compensate for cutting taxes were, from the outset, not possible and large deficits were inevitable.

Perversely, however, deficits made a major contribution to Reagan's central purpose of limiting government. Everyone agreed that deficits were bad and should be reduced as soon as possible, but to do so by increasing taxes was unacceptable to the majority of Americans. In this context, liberal Democrats in congress were forced on to the defensive. The revenue was not available to support the programmes that they might otherwise have advanced to deal with various pressing social problems. 'The federal budget deficit makes it impossible for Democrats to talk about any major new domestic spending programs unless they also talk about raising taxes. Which is exactly what the Republicans want them to talk about.'[6] Budget deficits coupled with tax cuts helped Reagan to bring about a fundamental change of ethos in the United States, one where extensions of the role of the federal government were no longer acceptable.

In his final television address to the nation in January 1989 the president asserted, 'We weren't just marking time, we made a difference.' This undeniable claim summarizes the single most important accomplishment of the Reagan administration. United States domestic and foreign policies were significantly different under Reagan than they had been before. So many presidents come and go without bringing about such change. They may compile respectable legislative records; they may even have more impressive *Congressional Quarterly* presidential support scores than Reagan, but the overall effect of their having been in office has been slight – they were 'just marking time'.

Repeatedly, presidents have gone to Washington declaring their intention to move the country in this or that direction, insisting that they would bring about real change. Typically such promises have remained undelivered; in almost all cases the realities of office have forced presidents to lower their sights and to settle for keeping the machinery of government ticking over rather than trying to bring about major alterations in direction. As James MacGregor Burns noted, the pundits fully expected Reagan to follow a similar path:

> Had not Eisenhower departed from his 1952 rhetoric to embrace most of the New Deal program? Had not both Richard Nixon and Jerry Ford moved from the right or moderate right wing of the GOP to its center. Democrats had done the same . . . only in the opposite direction. Both John Kennedy and Jimmy Carter had entered office as 'rhetorical radicals' and soon turned into fiscal moderates.[7]

Within weeks of George Bush taking office, the press was to be found reporting evidence of the new president distancing himself from the conservative programme on which he was elected and moving towards the ideological centre.[8]

Irrespective of widespread popular impressions, Ronald Reagan proved to be far more resolute than most other presidents. He, too, fell a long way short of his original objectives. Many compromises were necessary and he suffered some considerable reverses in attempting to gain acceptance of his policies. It is also the case that almost all of Reagan's great legislative triumphs occurred at the beginning of his first term. Nevertheless despite the qualifications and the setbacks, taken as a whole, the effect of Reagan's tenure was to bring about policy change of a sort that had not been seen in the United States for half a century. 'He was a strong president and imposed his policies on the country,' James Sundquist commented.

'He turned the whole trend of American government around. We were headed in the direction of the welfare state and all Republicans could do before was to slow the trend. Reagan halted it.'[9] In the same vein Louis Harris has said,

> Eisenhower, Nixon and Ford had been conservative on many issues. But they all had one characteristic in common that Ronald Reagan did not share; none of them had the daring to assault the federal government as the last haven for help in solving social ills. All tacitly assumed that the basic thrust of the New Deal would remain intact. None dared to make the federal government an object of attack, as the root of most of the evil.[10]

Unlike other Republican presidents, Reagan was prepared to challenge directly the assumptions upon which the New Deal was based. He failed to bring about a revolution or an electoral realignment and he certainly was not able to dismantle the New Deal. What Reagan did was to provide the leadership necessary for a change in the terms of debate; he presided over the emergence of a new public philosophy.

A NEW PUBLIC PHILOSOPHY

A public philosophy has been briefly defined as 'the outlook on public affairs that seems to be taken for granted in a particular period'.[11] Thus, in the first decade or so of the twentieth century a consensus developed behind progressive notions of political and economic reform; progressivism permeated mass and élite thinking, was embraced by both political parties and thereby took on the form of a new public philosophy. Similarly, in the 1930s, a body of ideas evolved in support of the New Deal providing an intellectual underpinning for Roosevelt's policies and his theory of governance. Not everyone, but certainly a vast majority of Americans, came to accept that the presidency should, in peace or war, be the main focus and the principal initiator in the federal government. It was widely accepted that the problems and complexities of modern society could no longer be left to the vagaries of market forces and the ministrations of local and state governments; social and economic ills had to be addressed by the federal government in Washington.

For close to half a century before Reagan became president, the public philosophy of the New Deal dominated American politics. Journalists, voters and politicians of both parties had taken as given the assumptions upon which it was based. Its staying power was apparently demonstrated in 1964 when Barry Goldwater, the Republican candidate for the presidency and an openly declared foe of the New Deal, went down to crushing defeat. On the other hand, more prudent conservative Republicans such as Eisenhower and Nixon avoided head-on collisions with the New Deal, doing no more than seeking 'to slow the trend'.

Reagan was no less a radical conservative than Goldwater, but an infinitely more skilful political leader. While many Americans had found Goldwater to be a rather frightening figure who just might abolish social security and precipitate World War III, the smiling, non-threatening image projected by Reagan was far more reassuring. Yet beneath the mask of affability, there was a man of uncommon resolution intent on replacing the New Deal with Reaganism.

Reagan enjoyed only mixed success in translating his intentions into policy change. Federal programmes were cut and eliminated, but far fewer than had been hoped for. Devolution to the states did occur, but again the achievement fell short of the goal. Big cuts in taxation did take place, but the reductions in federal expenditure were insufficient to make balancing the budget possible. A limited degree of deregulation did take place and the Pentagon entered a new era of plenty. This is a limited, uneven and yet impressive record. It is not impressive, of course, if measured against some abstract model of executive leadership, or if judged in terms appropriate to Mrs Thatcher. But, if properly placed in context, it represents a level of achievement superior to that of most White House incumbents.

In gaining partial acceptance of his programme, Reagan was instrumental in the creation of a new public philosophy. The evidence for that is best seen in the extent to which Democratic candidates and elected officials came to accept Reaganite assumptions. This was apparent in the 1984 election when the president's

> steadfast support of across-the-board tax cuts in the face of intense pressure from established opinion led his Democratic party opponent, Walter Mondale, to make the achievement of a balanced budget into a positive moral virtue. Thus a Republican issue . . . became the mainstay of Democratic speeches and advertisements. . . . Virtually nothing was heard from the Democratic party about social welfare. Hardly a peep sounded in regard to a massive jobs program . . . [Reagan] shifted the entire debate in an economically conservative direction.[12]

In the 1980s liberal Democrats in the national legislature, the keepers of the New Deal grail, 'had to accommodate the widespread view that the government cannot afford major new domestic expenditures and that public support is flagging for the kind of government programs that were a key tool of Great Society liberalism'.[13] As Henry Waxman, a liberal Democratic congressman from California, ruefully explained, 'It's disappointing and frustrating. We're not doing what we ought to be doing. The liberal agenda is fighting to keep what we have.' The terms of the debate had clearly changed; liberals were reduced to damage limitation exercises and rearguard actions. They could do little more than fend off the worst excesses of programme cutting by the administration. As Waxman put it, 'I have to look at stopping the Reagan Administration from gutting the Clean Air Act as one of the great successes, and salvaging many of the health programs as an accomplishment.'[14]

In the 1988 national elections there was ample evidence of Democrats taking to the wearing of Reaganite clothes. Dukakis set his face against any reversal of Reagan's tax cuts either as a way of cutting the deficit or of financing new programmes and 'the extent to which the prevailing Democratic philosophy incorporates elements of Reaganomics' was widely commented upon.[15] As *Time* magazine noted after Bush's nomination:

> At the very least [the President] has defined the debate. Opinion polls show some vague unease about the economy's future, along with renewed interest in federal solutions for a variety of social ills. Still, Reagan's preachments about the evils of Big Government and high progressive tax rates continue to dominate the political landscape. Even his failures, the most monumental being the nation's mounting debt, have served to constrain the discussion.[16]

It was with more than a little justification that Martin Anderson boasted, 'What Reagan and his comrades have done is to shape America's policy agenda well into the twenty-first century. The prospects are nil for sharply progressive tax rates and big, new social welfare programs, some of the former mainstays of the Democrats domestic policy agenda. Everyone is for a strong national defense, differing only in the degree and quality of it.'[17]

A situation that was a source of great satisfaction to a conservative like Anderson was a cause for bitter regret to Democratic Senator Ernest Hollings. Although a trenchant critic of Reagan's domestic policy, Hollings, unlike some other liberals, was enough of a realist to recognize how successful the former president was in gaining his objectives:

> When Ronald Reagan came to Washington in 1981, he made no bones about his intention to slash government spending and trash the federal bureaucracy. He flaunted his contempt for government. Eight years

later liberal pundits crow that the Reagan Revolution has failed, that the federal fortress stands stronger than ever. They are dead wrong. The reality is that President Reagan dealt Uncle Sam a crippling blow. He left a federal treasury that is paralysed by debt; a federal work force that is demoralized and discredited; a public infrastructure that is literally crumbling. What's more by mobilizing the nation's voters as 'an overpowering bloc vote against necessary taxation' (David Stockman's words),Reagan sapped the government's capacity to put its house – and books – in order.[18]

Hollings goes on to identify a few of the areas of public policy where evidence of 'the demise of government' that Reagan sought can be found. The Reagan administration failed in its aim of abolishing the Department of Education, but reduced its staff by a quarter and cut its programmes savagely. Education block grants to the states were reduced by 63 per cent; grants for bilingual education were cut by 47 per cent; for vocational education by 29 per cent and for college work study by 26.5 per cent. Federal funding for subsidized housing was cut by 81 per cent during the Reagan years. The level of benefits and the range of coverage was reduced for 'safety net' programmes like Aid to Families with Dependent Children. In 1978, 3 per cent of the federal budget was devoted to natural resources, environmental protection and conservation programmes whereas by 1988 that percentage was halved.[19] In those few areas of public policy not immune to cutting, Reagan had 'made a difference' even if it was a difference that liberals like Hollins deplored.

Reagan's policies also had significant consequences for federalism in the United States. Like other Republican incumbents he was troubled by the seemingly incessant growth of the national government in Washington at the expense of the states since the 1930s. Eisenhower and Nixon had sought to redress the balance by devolving federal responsibilities to state and local governments. For them bringing government closer to the people was a desirable end in itself as well as a means of providing for a more efficient and effective delivery of services.[20] Reagan's approach was far more radical in its implications; he too was wedded to the federal ideal, but this was of secondary importance compared to his primary purpose of substantially reducing the role of government *per se*. As he said in his first inaugural address,

> Government is not the solution to our problem; government is the problem. . . . It is time to check and reverse the growth of government. . . . It is my intention to curb the size and influence of the federal establishment and to demand recognition of the distinction between the powers granted to the federal government and those reserved to the states or to the people.

In some respects Reagan's actions fell far short of this statement of intention. Total civilian employment in the federal government in fact rose by 3 per cent from 1980–1987. Much of this increase is explained by the shift of priorities towards defence, an area of government activity where civilian employment grew by 11.5 per cent in the same period, but even non defence federal civilian employment only declined by 1.4 per cent.[21]

It is also the case that total federal budget outlays (measured in constant 1982 dollars) increased from $699.1 billion in 1980 to $859.3 billion in 1987 and even non defence federal budget outlays increased from $535.1 billion to $609.5 billion in the same period. However the increases in federal domestic expenditures 1980–87 are partly accounted for by payments to individuals and the interest payments incurred by the large deficits of the Reagan years.[22]

A more favourable picture of Reagan's effectiveness in achieving his goal of limiting the scope of government can be derived from statistics concerned with federal aid to state and local government. During the 1970s such aid had risen steeply increasing annually by an average of 14.43 per cent. By contrast, Reagan succeeded in sharply reducing the rate of increase and actually brought about declines in 1982 and 1987.[23] It should also be noted that federal grants-in-aid as a percentage of total federal outlays declined from 15.5 per cent to 10.8 per cent between 1980 and 1987. Meanwhile federal grants as a percentage of state and local government outlays dropped from 25.8 per cent to 18.2 per cent; similarly, during the same period, federal aid as a percentage of GNP fell from 3.4 per cent to 2.5 per cent.[24] Once again Reagan's record was uneven, but there is no doubt that he had an impact on the relationship between the federal government and the states that few other presidents have been able to equal.

In foreign and national security policy Reagan could also claim to have succeeded in bringing about significant change. He entered office believing that previous administrations had neglected the nation's defences and been too passive in the face of relentless Soviet expansionism. The long-standing US policy of containment needed to be replaced with a more positive and aggressive stance; Marxist regimes in the third world were to be actively undermined by providing aid to rebel groups sympathetic to the West. In addition, as the Soviets only understood the language of strength, the United States needed to rearm, not as an end in itself, but as a means of bringing about serious arms reduction negotiations. Despite his bellicose rhetoric, Reagan was appalled by the implications of the policy of 'mutually assured destruction' and was convinced of the need to rid the world of the menace of nuclear weapons – a concern that eventually led him to make 'Star Wars' or SDI the centrepiece of his nuclear strategy. Many doubted the wisdom of these policy changes and not all of them were fully implemented, nevertheless, substantial movement in the directions chosen by Reagan did occur.

POLICY SUBSTANCE

Throughout this book I have endeavoured to focus on the policy process and to avoid considerations of policy substance.[25] However, a president's reputation, his place in history, his legacy will turn not simply on whether he has mastered the system, but also on whether his policies are perceived to have worked, and passing reference to these matters is necessary here. Conclusive judgements regarding the consequences of a president's policies are not possible until many years after he has left the White House, and even then the historians are likely to disagree. In addition, there is always the danger, especially relevant in the case of presidents only recently in office, that the political preferences of the analyst will distort his conclusions. Notwithstanding these important problems, it is clear that the evaluation of any modern president will be greatly influenced by overall perceptions of his performance in two principal policy arenas – management of the economy and foreign policy. Ultimately the historians will want to ask what was the state of the economy during and at the end of a particular president's term of office? Were his policies beneficial to the economic well-being of the nation? Similarly, in the realm of foreign policy general questions will, in the long run, be posed regarding a president's record in advancing and protecting the interests of the United States in the world. Was the position of the country in international affairs strengthened or weakened during the course of the administration under consideration?

In assessing Reagan's record as manager of the economy, his critics have naturally fastened onto indicators such as the large budget and trade deficits, the enormous additions to the national debt and the heavy dependence on foreign investors, all of which arose during his tenure. These negatives are not conclusive proof that Reagan's economic policy failed and there are other statistics that justify more favourable conclusions. When Reagan took office inflation was the issue of economic policy, the matter that concerned the American public most.[26] By 1989 the problem of inflation had largely disappeared;

during the last year of the Carter administration inflation rose to 13.5 per cent but was down to 4.7 per cent as Reagan's second term came to an end. Unemployment in 1980 was 7 per cent whereas it stood at 5.2 per cent at the end of 1988. Administration spokesmen repeatedly pointed out, as Reagan prepared to leave office, that after the recession early in his first term the United States had experienced its longest ever period of economic growth in peace time, making possible the creation of 17 million new jobs.[27]

Conceivably at some point in the future it will be possible to say definitively whether Reaganomics failed. In the end, those many commentators who expect the worst over the long term may prove to be right. Arthur Schlesinger, for instance, may be vindicated in his speculation that, 'Reagan's tax reduction act may be the most disastrous piece of legislation since the Second World War'.[28] For the moment, however, no conclusive assessments are possible, even if it is clear that, in 1988, Reagan's management of the economy was favourably perceived by the public at large, aiding rather than disadvantaging the Republican party in the presidential election.

A similar lapse of time will be required before much of a conclusive nature can be said about the merits of Reagan's foreign policy. At this stage, the signing of a major arms control agreement and the inauguration of a new era of reasonably amicable relations with the Soviet Union would seem to represent large achievements for Ronald Reagan, far outweighing the accomplishments of most presidents in the foreign policy arena.

It is the case that these breakthroughs in foreign policy were much dependent on factors outside the president's control. However, it is possible to argue that Reagan was primarily responsible for bringing about the substantial redirection of foreign policy that ultimately proved beneficial to the United States. Under his leadership a large increase in armaments occurred and the United States adopted, initially, an uncompromising stance towards the Soviet Union and its satellites around the world. This new aggressive posture, so it could be claimed, was a major factor in bringing the Soviet Union to the arms control negotiating table and in curbing its expansionist inclinations abroad.

There were, of course, various foreign policy disasters, including incidents such as the ignominious and costly withdrawal from Lebanon, defeats by congress over South Africa and the Philippines and, surpassing all else, the Iran–Contra débâcle. By any standard the latter was a massive set back for the president personally and for American foreign policy. Reagan appeared to be grossly incompetent with little respect for the law, while the United States was made to look foolish and unreliable in the eyes of the outside world. Furthermore, the Reagan administration failed miserably to accomplish one of its principal foreign policy purposes, the unseating of the Sandinista regime in Nicaragua. As Reagan left office his policy in Central America had lost credibility and United States influence in the region was at its lowest ebb for many years. Overall, however, it seems likely that the historians will eventually give Reagan's foreign policy fairly high marks.

REVITALIZING THE PRESIDENCY

By making a reality of his intentions, in successfully imposing his preferences, his choices, Reagan revitalized the presidency and restored confidence in the political system. In the previous decade many commentators had pondered the inadequacy of American political institutions and had queried whether the United States might be becoming ungovernable. The polls showed that public confidence in political leaders was at a low ebb; congress appeared to be more chaotic than ever; political parties had been chronically weakened and special interests loomed large. The presidency appeared to have lost its institutional integrity. Nixon had brought disgrace on the office and his successor proved to be pathetically ineffectual. Carter had gone to the White House with high hopes, but was eventually reduced to agonizing in public over his inability to surmount the obstacles to presidential leadership.

The situation was dramatically transformed during Reagan's first term. He and his staff demonstrated that all the pessimism of the late 1970s notwithstanding, the political system was workable. Congress could be brought to order and the disadvantages of weak parties overcome given the right type of leadership by the White House. Not surprisingly, public opinion polls later showed that confidence in the Reagan presidency was badly damaged by the Iran–Contra scandal, but it seems that this decline by no means completely offset the important gains made in the earlier years. Irrespective of later disasters, Reagan and his team demonstrated that the system could be made to work and that the presidency is even yet a viable institution. Very few incumbents pass on the presidency in strengthened and revitalized form to their successors, but Reagan, despite some setbacks, was able to join this select group.

This has been confirmed by some well-qualified witnesses from both parties. Thus Richard Cheney, chief of staff to President Ford, later Republican Whip in the House of Representatives and now Secretary of Defense, told David Broder,

> Discount if you wish for the fact that I'm a Republican and a Reagan supporter, but you have to believe the office is in better shape now than when he came to town. He had some rocky moments, but the country has the feeling that Ronald Reagan proved the presidency is not an impossible job, that a nice guy can take it on, and without being an intellectual giant, make it work. The job isn't bigger than any man. Maybe it was luck, but problems that Nixon, Ford and Carter encountered and could not survive, he has withstood.[29]

Similarly, on the Democratic side, Harry McPherson, a senior assistant to Lyndon Johnson, noted that 'Reagan restored a lot of the confidence and good disposition towards the president. He made it seem a more natural thing for the country to follow a president.' Another Democratic luminary, Stuart Eizenstat, who had first-hand experience of the frustrations of presidential power as Carter's domestic policy assistant, remarked, 'Reagan has strengthened the office simply by being a two term president. What had been written off eight years ago as an impossible job, destined to crush any mortal, has been turned around. It now appears that a mortal can handle the job and be successful.'[30]

Reagan was also unusual in that he remained, to the end, an electoral asset rather than a liability to his party, an accomplishment denied not only to undistinguished presidents, but also to some of the more outstanding like Wilson and Johnson. Presidents are party leaders and temporarily, at least, they represent what the party stands for. As is well known, American parties are very loosely structured and in the modern age presidential coat-tails are not what they were; nevertheless, the fates of presidents and parties remain inextricably entwined. The party of a president who leaves office a failure is bound to be diminished and damaged. Party candidates for lesser offices will find it that much more difficult to win election and the fallout for presidential candidates may well prove fatal. This was the case for Hubert Humphrey in 1968, Gerald Ford in 1976 and Walter Mondale in 1984. By the same token a phenomenally successful president like Franklin Roosevelt did wonders for the fortunes of his party at all levels of the political system.

Ronald Reagan was no Roosevelt in electoral terms, even if he did win two landslide victories for his party. In 1980 the Republicans also won a majority in the Senate for the first time since 1955 and held control for six years. These were large achievements and who can doubt that Reagan contributed massively to the revival of Republican party fortunes in the 1980s? On the other hand, it is not possible to speak of an electoral realignment. Realignments involve seismic shifts in the electoral terrain that extend right down through the political system. But, throughout the Reagan years, the Democrats remained firmly in control of the House of Representatives and reasserted their supremacy in the Senate in 1986; they also continued to hold a majority of state governorships and two-thirds of state legislative chambers. Reagan's electoral success, it would seem, was largely personal rather than party based. He failed to carry significant numbers of his party's candidates into office with him and even when he campaigned extensively for fellow partisans, as he did in the mid-term elections of 1986, the effects of his intervention were slight.

Various factors, most notably the new importance of constituency service for members of Congress, help to account for the fact that presidential popularity is no longer easily transferable and it may be that party realignments have become outdated historical phenomena. Reagan's legacy to his party was, for all that, a formidable one and George Bush's election to the White House was much dependent on the continued popularity of his predecessor. According to a Washington Post/ABC poll in October 1988, voters approving Reagan's presidency supported Bush rather than Dukakis by a margin of 4 to 1. Bush was strongest, furthermore, in those areas of the country – the Midwest and the South – where Reagan was most popular.[31] Unlike many other retiring chief executives, Reagan was no millstone around the neck of his party's candidate for the presidency – 1988 was not comparable to 1968, 1976 or 1984.

Reagan emerges from this analysis as a president who brought about a change in the terms of debate with regard to both foreign and domestic policy, revitalized the office of chief executive and made possible his replacement by a candidate of his party. No one but Roosevelt among modern presidents could claim a comparable record. And even the great Roosevelt had many advantages denied Reagan, including taking office at a moment of great crisis and being flanked throughout his presidency by large majorities in both houses of the legislature.

Nevertheless, Reagan himself enjoyed some good fortune. Public disillusionment with big government and the thrust of New Deal and Great Society programmes began to set in well before he took office. Keynesian economic policies fell out of favour in the 1970s and during the same period the public became increasingly nervous about the possibility that the Soviet Union was gaining a military advantage over the United States. The Reagan administration, therefore, was able to exploit currents of élite and popular thinking that had begun their course well before 1981. Developments within the Soviet Union also presented the Reagan administration with unusual opportunities. In the early 1980s an ageing and decrepit leadership and a weak Soviet economy provided a favourable context for the first stage of Reagan's foreign policy. Subsequently, the accession of Gorbachev and related consequences made possible arms agreements, the furthering of detente and other developments favourable to Reagan's standing.

Reagan's success is also to be explained in part by the professionalism of his staff. This was reflected in the carefully thought out administrative strategy adopted in 1981. By carefully vetting not only cabinet and sub-cabinet appointees, but also lower level political appointments, the Reaganites guarded against the real possibility of the president's intentions being subverted within the federal administration. The same high level of professionalism was apparent in the legislative strategy of the Reagan administration. They understood that the beginning of any president's first term provides him with a window of opportunity that will not be there later. Accordingly, they 'hit the ground running' and from the outset established a clear order of priorities, two precautions that Carter had noticeably failed to take. An impressive legislative liaison operation was established and astute use was made of the president's formidable skills as a communicator.

The high professionalism of Reagan's staff in tandem with the talents of the president himself allowed him to take advantage of a qualified movement to the right of American public opinion and to accomplish, in his first term, some major legislative breakthroughs in economic policy. According to one political journalist, writing for a newspaper generally critical of Reagan, these alone were achievements sufficient to place Reagan in the front rank of chief legislators in the last half century.

> Between January and August of 1981, he pushed through Congress sweeping reductions in tax rates, eliminated or reduced scores of domestic programs and launched a major increase in defense spending. That was the most dazzling political tour de force for any president since Roosevelt's New Deal and Lyndon Johnson's 1965 Great Society Congress. Like those earlier presidential achievements, it leaves a lasting legacy.[32]

Broadly speaking, the thrust of these changes was sustained during the remainder of Reagan's two terms thereby providing the president with his principal claim to effectiveness in the White House.

The legislative route proved to be inappropriate for Reagan's agenda of social issues. Administration-backed proposals regarding abortion, school prayer, bussing, pornography and affirmative action made little headway in congress. But the Reagan forces also mounted an impressive judicial strategy taking careful steps to ensure that the federal judiciary would be packed at all levels with judges who shared the president's preferences. What Reagan failed to gain in the legislature while in office he could reasonably hope to secure, in the long term, via the judiciary.

Another important part of the explanation for Reagan's success lies in his sense of vision and his tenacious hold on a few simple beliefs. For most of his life he has been convinced that the scope of govenment should be as restricted as possible; that taxation is inherently objectionable and that the evil of communism must be vigilantly resisted at every opportunity. These guiding beliefs can be criticized for being excessively simplistic, but they gave the Reagan administration a clear sense of direction, an important quality that other administrations have lacked. This Reagan strength is recognized by the more astute of his critics,

> Reagan is the triumph of a man who earnestly believed in something. And he believed in it in bad times as well as good. He went up and down the country expounding his gospel, and eventually the cycle turned from public purpose to private purpose, and it was his time. I don't think it was a triumph of packaging; I think it was a triumph of commitment. Substantive commitment. Reagan, whatever he did got where he is by *not* compromising on his convictions whatever the polls said. I think that Reagan is proof of the power of conviction politics.[33]

As this quotation suggests, Reagan was one of the most intensely ideological of presidents. On the other hand, he displayed a capacity to give way, to compromise when it became necessary to do so. As another commentator put it, Reagan

> demonstrated an unerring sense of just how far to go. This is an invaluable, indeed an essential, political skill. A leader in a democracy must present himself as a person of firm principles. He or she must, however, compromise those principles in order to govern. A leader without any guiding principles is spineless and aimless; one who will never bend them is a fanatic. The successful statesman is the one who can navigate between the two extremes, earning a reputation for being principled but not bull-headed. Mr Reagan has that reputation. His predecessor did not.[34]

Possibly one of the least appreciated of Reagan's qualities was his relaxed attitude towards political power. 'Antigovernmentalism' is embedded deep in the American political culture; at all costs, politicians must avoid any suspicion of being 'power hungry'. The atmosphere of the White House is terribly corrupting in this respect, however, and most presidents eventually fall under suspicion. It happened to Roosevelt and also to Johnson, Nixon and Carter, but Reagan was never accused of this particular crime. 'Reagan stays detached. He's got a Zen approach to power. He doesn't care about power for power's sake alone. Eisenhower is the only other person who had the same detached way of holding power.'[35]

THE BUSH COMPARISON

The early months of the Bush administration provided some revealing contrasts with the Reagan era. In the 1988 election Bush secured 53 per cent of the vote compared to the 51 per cent won by Reagan eight years previously; in addition, the early public opinion polls gave Bush much higher levels of public approval than Reagan at the comparable stage. However, Bush was denied the important bonus of party control of one house of the legislature and his own electoral success was not a personal victory in the sense of Reagan's in 1980. For other reasons Reagan's mandate at the beginning was not notably substantial; nevertheless, in 1981, many members of Congress, including the Democratic leadership, were convinced that the president had an especial rapport with the American people. This led them to believe that it would be imprudent to resist too vigorously Reagan's economic policy proposals.

Congressional perceptions of Reagan's hold on public opinion owed much to his undoubted skill before television cameras, whereas George Bush showed little sign of being similarly gifted. Robert Lichter, the director of The Center for Media and Public Affairs, said of President Bush, 'The guy knows he's no good on television. You get the impression he held his nose and did it during the campaign because he was convinced he had to. But now that's over and he's back mumbling and babbling and cutting off his words in mid sentence.'[36] The Bush staff, furthermore, quite unlike Reagan's, demonstrated in the first half of 1989 little awareness of the importance of television for government in the United States in the late twentieth century.

The Reaganites were criticized for their attempts to manipulate television news to their advantage, whereas the Bush administration has been condemned for seeming to go to the other extreme. According to Lesley Stahl of CBS News, 'This White House doesn't care if the president gets on the evening news or not.'[37] Assuming that Stahl is correct, and this continues to be the case, such an attitude is likely to make Bush a less effective president than his predecessor. 'In the television age, the battle between the president and the media has become a kind of proxy for governing. Ronald Reagan regularly won this combat and was able to set his own agenda; and, in part for that reason he was seen as a strong president.'[38]

The Reagan administration had seen the appointments process as an important means of helping to bring about policy change. They had applied ideological litmus tests to potential appointees – a procedure that was not used during the Bush transition. Incoming cabinet members were provided with lists of likely candidates, but there was little pressure on them to appoint accordingly. 'We say to them, here are our suggestions. In some cases, here are our strong suggestions . . . . But nobody is trying to cram guys down secretaries' throats'. Between seven and and eight hundred lower level political posts were reserved for Bush campaign aides and long-time supporters, but their ideological soundness was not at issue. According to one official concerned with appointments, 'Our people don't have agendas. They have mortgages. They want jobs.'[39] Edwin Meese, Pendleton James and others who dealt with appointments under Reagan took a much less relaxed view of their responsibilities.

In the early part of 1989 Bush's legislative strategy appeared less impressive than Reagan's eight years previously. One source rudely suggested that Bush 'hit the ground crawling' and months after his inauguration congress had no clear idea of his priorities in foreign and domestic policy. 'The conventional wisdom on both sides of the political divide is that Bush has made a terribly slow start and that his administration is floundering.'[40] In dealing with the legislature Bush began with an approach quite different from Reagan's. He was more conciliatory, less ideological and more ready to placate his Democratic opponents.

In his anxiety to develop a cooperative relationship with congress Bush freely abandoned, in most un Reagan-like fashion, positions he had adopted earlier. Just before the election he had scorned the idea of the federal government bailing out the savings and loan industry, but shortly after taking office sent to congress a $157 billion rescue plan for that purpose. Throughout the Reagan years Bush was a hard line supporter of military aid for the Contra rebels in Nicaragua, yet in the White House, at an early stage, he struck a deal with congress whereby military aid was abandoned with humanitarian aid being continued for a further year.[41]

The budget deficit had been a major issue of the 1988 campaign. Bush had repeatedly reaffirmed his pledge not to introduce new taxes and committed himself to a 'flexible freeze' as a way of curtailing domestic expenditure. This arrangement was intended to balance the budget within five years by preventing the overall total for domestic programmes, other than Social Security, from growing faster than inflation. By May 1989, however, the idea of a 'flexible freeze' appeared to have been jettisoned with the administration reaching a budget agreement with congressional leaders that provided for a 10 per cent increase in appropriations for domestic 'discretionary' programmes.[42]

President George Bush's style of leadership has proven to be markedly different from that of Ronald Reagan. He has been more willing to negotiate behind the scenes with the legislature and less inclined to resort to 'vivid oratory and direct appeals to the voters to advance his agenda'. Throughout his political career the present incumbent has been a pragmatist, adjusting his views to take account of changing circumstances rather than stubbornly adhering to fixed positions in the manner of Reagan. As Fred Greenstein remarked of Bush,

> You have to think of the broader pattern of his career, running on Goldwater themes in 1964 and then coming into the House a couple of years later as a pretty moderate Republican. He's not an ideologue in the traditional sense – he's not a conceptualizer in the way that Nixon was. With Bush I think it's like a baby waking up after a nap-every day is a new day.[43]

George Bush is certainly much less of a detached president than his predecessor; he is far more closely involved in the detail of policy-making. Nevertheless, in one sense, Bush's style is more passive than Reagan's; his presidency in unlikely to be characterized by the strength and effectiveness displayed by Reagan. Rather than following in Reagan's footsteps as an innovative, radical conservative president, ready to address problems and confront adversaries head on, Bush seems to be adopting an approach to presidential power more akin to that of Eisenhower.

Unlike these other two Republican presidents, Reagan possessed vision and an 'awesome stubbornness'; he had a sense of where he wished to go and a determination to achieve objectives. Irrespective of any doubts we may have regarding the substance of his policies, Reagan was an effective president, a strong president in that he successfully imposed his preferences on the political system; he moved the country in the directions that he had chosen. To that extent he was 'on top in fact as well as name'. Reagan's was not 'hidden hand' leadership, he led from the front rather than from behind. It was a style of leadership not without serious flaws and not suitable for all seasons, but it also had merits worth pondering.

NOTES AND REFERENCES

1. Paul Peterson and Mark Rom, 'Lower Taxes, More Spending and Budget Deficits' in Jones, *The Reagan Legacy*, op. cit., pp. 213–40.
2. Ibid., p. 215.
3. Smith, *The Power Game*, op. cit., p. 725.
4. Quoted by William Schneider in 'The Political Legacy of the Reagan Years' in Sidney Blumenthal and Thomas Byrne Edsall (eds), *The Reagan Legacy*. Pantheon Books, New York 1988, pp. 51–98.
5. Jack Meyer, 'Social Programs and Social Policy' in Palmer, *Perspectives on the Reagan Years*, op. cit., pp. 65–89.
6. Schneider, op. cit.
7. *Power to Lead*, op. cit., p. 45.
8. John Cassidy, 'Bush Erects a Tower of Hope for Democrats', *Sunday Times* (12 Feb. 1989), p. B7.
9. Quoted by Charlotte Saikowski, 'What US Scholars Think of the Reagan Presidency', *Christian Science Monitor*, World Edition, (12–18 Jan. 1989), p. 2.
10. *Inside America*. Vintage Books, New York 1987, p. 281.
11. Hugh Heclo, 'Reaganism and the Search for a Public Philosophy', in Palmer, *Perspectives on the Reagan Years*, op. cit., pp. 31–63.
12. Aaron Wildavsky, 'President Reagan as Political Strategist', *Society* (May/June), pp. 56–62.
13. Janet Hook, 'Liberal Democrats Adapt to a Hostile Climate', *Congressional Quarterly Weekly Report* (9 Aug. 1986), pp. 1797–801.
14. Ibid.
15. David Broder, 'The Democrats Together At Last', *The Washington Post*, National Weekly Edition (18–24 July 1988), p. 6.
16. 'The Torch is Passed' (22 Aug. 1988), p. 6.
17. *Revolution*, op. cit., p. 438.
18. 'Decaying America: The Underside of the Reagan Legacy', *The Washington Post*, National Weekly Edition (8–14 May 1989).
19. Ibid.
20. See Timothy Conlan, *New Federalism: Intergovernmental Reform from Nixon to Reagan*, The Brookings Institution, Washington D.C., 1988 p. 1.
21. *U.S. Statistical Abstracts, 1989*, Government Printing Office, Washington, 1989, Table 514.
22. Ibid., Table 491.
23. Ibid., Table 419.
24. Ibid., Table 450.

25. Parts of the discussion in this chapter have appeared in a different form in David Mervin, 'Ronald Reagan's Place in History', *Journal of American Studies* **23** (1989).
26. Schneider, op. cit., p. 74.
27. *Sunday Times* (18 Dec. 1988).
28. 'Reagan: Failed Revolutionary', *The Times* (17 Jan. 1989).
29. Quoted in David Broder, 'After Reagan, the Presidency No Longer Seems an Impossible Job', *The Washington Post*, National Weekly Edition (16–22 Jan. 1989), pp. 8–9.
30. Ibid.
31. *The Washington Post*, National Weekly Edition (17–23 Oct. 1988), p. 36.
32. Broder, 'After Reagan . . .', op. cit.
33. Arthur Schlesinger Jr in an interview 'Seeing Daylight', *Playboy Magazine* (March 1988).
34. Michael Mandelbaum, 'The Luck of the President' in William Hyland (ed.), *The Reagan Foreign Policy*. New American Library, New York 1987, pp. 127–46.
35. Lee Atwater, quoted in Smith, *The Power Game*, op. cit., p. 55.
36. Quoted in Ann Devroy, 'If a President Falls in the Forest and No One Hears', *The Washington Post*, National Weekly Edition (8–14 May 1989), p. 14.
37. Quoted in David Ignatius, 'After Reagan the Media Miss Being Manipulated', *The Washington Post*, National Weekly Edition (15–21 May 1989), p. 23.
38. Ibid.
39. Ann Devroy, 'Victors and Spoils', *The Washington Post*, National Weekly Edition (23–29 Jan. 1989).
40. John Cassidy and Mark Hosenball, 'Indecisive Bush in Danger of catching the Carter Disease', *Sunday Times* (12 Mar. 1989).
41. David Hoffman, 'One Hundred days of Solicitude', *The Washington Post*, National Weekly Edition (8–14 May 1989), p. 13.
42. David Hoffman and Paul Blustein, 'Remember Bush's "Flexible Freeze" Budget Proposal?' *The Washington Post*, National Weekly Edition (1–7 May 1989), p. 13.
43. Quoted in Hoffman, 'One Hundred days . . .', op. cit.

Bibliography

Aberbach, Joel and Rockman, Bert, 'Clashing Beliefs in the Executive Branch: The Nixon Administration Bureaucracy', *American Political Science Review* **LXX**, No. 2 (June 1976), pp. 456–68.

Abraham, Henry J., *Justices and Presidents*. Oxford University Press, New York 1985.

Adams, William, 'Recent Fables About Ronald Reagan', *Public Opinion* **7**, No. 5. Oct./Nov. 1984.

Almond, Gabriel and Verba, Sidney, *The Civic Culture*. Princeton University Press, Princeton 1963.

Almond, Gabriel and Verba, Sidney, *The Civic Culture Revisited*. Little Brown, Boston 1980.

Anderson, Martin, *Revolution*. Harcourt Brace and Jovanovich, New York 1988.

Arkes, Hadley, 'On the Moral Standing of the President as an Interpreter of the Constitution: Some Reflections on Our current Crises', *PS* (Summer 1987), pp. 637–42.

Ashford, Nigel, 'A New Public Philosophy' in John Lees and Michael Turner (eds), *Reagan's First Four Years*. Manchester University Press, Manchester 1988, pp. 7–20.

Barrett, Laurence, *Gambling with History: Reagan in the White House*. Penguin Books, London 1984.

Bell, Terrell, *The Thirteenth Man*. The Free Press, New York 1988.

Blumenthal, Sidney and Edsall, Thomas Byrne (eds), *The Reagan Legacy*. Pantheon Books, New York 1988.

Bowles, Nigel, *The White House and Capitol Hill*. Clarendon Press, Oxford 1987.

Broder, David, 'The Democrats Together At Last', *The Washington Post*, National Weekly Edition, (18–24 July 1988), p. 6.

223

Broder, David, 'After Reagan, the Presidency No Longer Seems an Impossible Job', ibid. (16–22 Jan. 1989), pp. 8–9.

Broder, David, 'Judges Still Need A Raise', ibid. (27 March–2 April 1989), p. 4.

Bundy, McGeorge, *et al.*, 'The President's Choice: Star Wars or Arms Control' in William Hyland (ed.), *The Reagan Foreign Policy*. New American Library, New York 1987, pp. 165–79.

Burns, James MacGregor, *Roosevelt: the Lion and the Fox*. Harcourt Brace and World, New York 1956.

Burns, James MacGregor, *Leadership*. Harper and Row, New York 1978.

Burns, James MacGregor, *The Power to Lead: The Crisis of the American Presidency*. Simon and Schuster, New York 1984.

Califano, Joseph, *A Presidential Nation*. W.W. Norton, New York 1975.

Cannon, Lou, *Reagan*. G.P. Putnam's Sons, New York 1982.

Carter, Jimmy, *Keeping Faith*. Collins, London 1982.

Cassidy, John 'Bush Erects a Tower of Hope For Democrats', *Sunday Times*, (12 Feb. 1989), p. B7.

Cassidy, John 'North the fall guy all set to point the finger', ibid. (26 Mar. 1989), p. A17.

Cassidy, John and Hosenball, Mark, 'Indecisive Bush in Danger of Catching the Carter Disease', ibid. (12 Mar. 1989).

Ceaser, James, *Presidential Selection: Theory and Development*. Princeton University Press, Princeton 1979.

Charlesworth, James (ed.), 'A Design For Political Science: Scope, Objectives and Methods', Monograph 6, *American Academy of Political and Social Science*, Philadelphia, 1966.

Chubb, John and Peterson, Paul, *The New Directions in American Politics*. The Urban Institute Press, Washington DC 1986.

Clark, Joseph, *The Senate Establishment*. Hill and Wang, New York 1963.

Cooper, Joseph and Mackenzie, G. Calvin (eds), *The House at Work*. University of Texas Press, Austin 1981.

Corwin, Edward S., *The President: Office and Powers*. New York University Press, New York 1957.

Crewe, Ivor, 'Britain evaluates Ronald Reagan', *Public Opinion* 7, No. 5 (Oct./Nov. 1984), pp. 46–9.

Cronin, Thomas, 'A Resurgent Congress and the Imperial Presidency', *Political Science Quarterly*, **95**, No. 2, (Summer 1980).

Cronin, Thomas, *The State of the Presidency*. Little Brown, Boston 1980.

Dahl, Robert, *Congress and Foreign Policy*. W.W. Norton, New York 1950.

Dahl, Robert and Lindblom, Charles, *Politics, Economics and Welfare*. Harper and Row, New York 1953.

Dallek, Robert, *Ronald Reagan: The Politics of Symbolism*. Harvard University Press, Cambridge, Mass. 1984.

Davis, Eric, 'Legislative Liaison in the Carter Administration', *Political Science Quarterly* **94**, No. 2, (Summer 1979), pp. 287–301.

Destler, I.M., 'Reagan and the World: An Awesome Stubborness' in Charles O. Jones (ed.), *The Reagan Legacy*. Chatham House Publishers, Chatham, New Jersey 1988, pp. 241–61.

Devroy, Ann, 'Victors and Spoils', ibid. (23–26 Jan. 1989).

Devroy, Ann, 'If a President Falls in the Forest and No One Hears', *The Washington Post*, National Weekly Edition, (8–14 May 1989), p. 14.

Dowd, Ann Reilly, 'What Managers Can Learn from Manager Reagan', *Fortune* (15 September 1986), pp. 21–9.

Drew, Elizabeth, *Portrait of an Election*. Simon and Schuster, New York 1981.

Duke, Paul (ed.), *Beyond Reagan: The Politics of Upheaval*. Warner Books, New York 1986.

Edwards, Anne, *Early Reagan: The Rise of an American Hero*. Hodder and Stoughton, London 1987.

Edwards, George, *Presidential Influence in Congress*. W.H. Freeman, San Francisco 1980.

Ehrlichman, John, *Witness to Power*. Pocket Books, New York 1982.

Ferguson, Thomas and Rogers, Joel, *Right Turn: The Decline of the Democrats and the Future of American Politics*. Hill and Wang, New York 1986.

Fiorina, Morris, *Congress: Keystone of the Washington Establishment*. Yale University Press, New Haven 1977.

Fulbright, J. William, 'The Fatal Arrogance of Power', *New York Times*, Sunday Magazine, (15 May 1966), p. 104.

Green, Mark, *Who Runs Congress?* Dell Books, New York 1984.

Greenstein, Fred, 'Eisenhower as an Activist President', *Political Science Quarterly* **94** (Winter 1979–80), pp. 575–99.

Greenstein, Fred, *The Hidden-Hand Presidency: Eisenhower as Leader*. Basic Books, New York 1982.

Greenstein, Fred (ed.), *The Reagan Presidency: An Early Assessment*. Johns Hopkins University Press, Baltimore 1983.

Haig, Alexander, *Caveat: Realism and Foreign Policy*. Macmillan, New York 1984.

Harris, Joseph, *California Politics*. Chandler Publishing, San Francisco 1967.

Harris, Louis, *Inside America*. Vintage Books, New York 1987.

Hart, John, *The Presidential Branch*. Pergamon Press, New York 1987.

Heclo, Hugh, 'Reaganism and the Search for a Public Philosophy' in John Palmer, *Perspectives on the Reagan Years*. The Urban Institute Press, Washington DC 1986, pp. 31–63.

Hinckley, Barbara, *The Seniority System in Congress*. Indiana University Press, Bloomington 1971.

Hodder-Williams, Richard, 'The Strange Story of Robert Bork and a Vacancy on the United States Supreme Court', *Political Studies* **36**, No. 4 (Dec. 1988), pp. 613–37.

Hodgson, Godfrey, *All Things to all Men*. Weidenfeld and Nicolson, London 1980.

Hoffman, David, 'Patrician with the Common Touch', *The Washington Post*, National Weekly Edition, (14–20 Nov. 1988), p. 6.

Hoffman, David, 'One Hundred Days of Solicitude', ibid. (8–14 May 1989), p. 13.

Hoffman, David and Devroy, Ann, 'A Ship Without a Rudder: The White House Appears to Lack Direction or Purpose', ibid. (13–19 Mar. 1989), p. 6.

Hoffman, David and Blustein, Paul, 'Remember Bush's "Flexible Freeze" Proposal?', ibid. (1–7 May 1989), p. 13.

Hogan, Joseph, 'Legislative Liaison in the Reagan Administration' in Lees and Turner, op. cit., pp. 69–94.

Hollings, Ernest, 'Decaying America: The Underside of the Reagan Legacy', *The Washington Post*, National Weekly Edition (8–14 May 1989), p. 23.

Hook, Janet, 'Liberal Democrats Adapt to a Hostile Climate', *Congressional Quarterly Weekly Report* (9 August 1986), pp. 1797–801.

Howard, Anthony (ed.), *The Crossman Diaries*. Hamish Hamilton and Jonathan Cape, London 1979.

Hunt, Albert, 'The Campaign and the Issues' in Austin Ranney (ed.), *The American Elections of 1980*. American Enterprise Institute, Washington DC 1981, pp 142–76.

Huntington, Samuel, *American Politics: The Promise of Disharmony*. Harvard University Press, Cambridge, Mass. 1981.

Huntington, Samuel, 'Congressional Responses to the Twentieth Century' in David Truman (ed.), *The Congress and America's Future*. Prentice Hall, Englewood Cliffs 1973.

Hyland, William G. (ed.), *The Reagan Foreign Policy*. New American Library, New York 1987.

Ignatius, David, 'Reagan's Foreign Policy and the Rejection of Diplomacy' in Blumenthal and Edsall, op. cit., pp. 172–212.

Ignatius, David, 'After Reagan the Media Miss Being Manipulated', *The Washington Post*, National Weekly Edition (15–21 May 1989), p. 23.

Jones, Charles O., 'Congress and the Presidency' in Thomas Mann and Norman Ornstein (eds), *The New Congress*. American Enterprise Institute, Washington DC 1981.

Jones, Charles O. (ed.), *The Reagan Legacy*. Chatham House Publishers, Chatham, New Jersey 1988.

Kamen, Al, 'The Bork Battle Revisited: A Pyrrhic Victory for Liberals?', *The Washington Post* (17–23 Apr. 1989), p. 12.

Kamen, Al and Marcus, Ruth, 'Liberal Judges: The Next Species for the Endangered List', ibid. (6–12 Feb. 1989), p. 31.

Kellerman, Barbara, *The Political Presidency: Practice of Leadership*. Oxford University Press, New York 1984.

Key, V.O., *The Responsible Electorate*. Vintage Books, New York 1966.

King, Anthony (ed.), *The New American Political System*. American Enterprise Institute, Washington DC 1978.

King, Anthony (ed.), *Both Ends of the Avenue*. American Enterprise Institute, Washington DC 1983.

King, Anthony, 'How Not to Select Presidential Candidates: A View From Europe' in Ranney, op. cit., *The American Elections of 1980*, pp. 303–28.

King, Anthony, 'Margaret Thatcher as a Political Leader' in Robert Skidelsky (ed.), *Thatcherism*. Chatto and Windus, London 1988, pp. 51–64.

Kondracke, Morton, 'Reagan's IQ', *New Republic* (24 Mar. 1982), p. 10.

Kramer, Michael, 'The Brief on Judge Bork', *US News and World Report* (14 Sept. 1987), pp. 18–24.

Ladd, Everett, 'The Brittle Mandate: Electoral Dealignment and the 1980 Election', *Political Science Quarterly* (Spring 1981), pp. 1–25.

Ladd, Everett, 'The Reagan Phenomenon and Public Attitudes Towards Government' in Lester Salamon and Michael Lund (eds), *The Reagan Presidency and the Governing of America*. The Urban Institute Press, Washington DC 1984.

Laski, Harold, *The American Presidency*. George Allen and Unwin, London 1940.

Lees, John and Turner, Michael (eds), *Reagan's First Four Years*. Manchester University Press, Manchester 1988.

Leuchtenberg, William, *In the Shadow of FDR*. Cornell University Press, Ithaca 1983.

Lewis, Anthony, 'Why the Kid Gloves for Reagan's Presidency?', *New York Times* (22 February 1982), p. 17.

Light, Paul, *The President's Agenda*. Johns Hopkins University Press, Baltimore 1982.

Lindsey, Robert, 'California Rehearsal' in Hedrick Smith *et al*, *Reagan the Man, the President*. Macmillan Publishing Co., New York 1980.

Lodal, Jan, 'An Arms Control Agenda', *Foreign Policy* No. 72 (Fall 1988), pp. 152–72.

Lord, Carnes, 'Executive Power and Our Security', *National Interest* (Spring 1987), pp. 3–13.

Lowi, Theodore, *The Personal President: Power Invested Promise Unfulfilled*. Cornell University Press, Ithaca 1985.

Lowi, Theodore, 'Ronald Reagan – Revolutionary?' in Salamon and Lund, op. cit., p. 48.

McClosky, Herbert and Zaller, John, *The American Ethos: Public Attitudes toward Capitalism and Democracy*. Harvard University Press, Cambridge, Mass. 1984.

McKay, David, *American Politics and Society*. Basil Blackwell, Oxford 1983.

Malbin, Michael, 'Delegation, Deliberation and the New Role of Congressional Staff' in Mann and Ornstein, op. cit., pp. 134–77.

Mandelbaum, Michael, 'The Luck of the President' in Hyland, op. cit., pp. 127–46.

Mann, Thomas and Ornstein, Norman (eds), *The New Congress*. American Enterprise Institute, Washington DC 1981.

Mansfield, Harvey Snr (ed.), *Congress Against the President*. Praeger, New York 1975.

Matthews, Donald R., *US Senators and Their World*. Vintage Books, New York 1960.

Mayer, Jane and McManus, Doyle, *Landslide: The Unmaking of the President 1984–1988*. Houghton Mifflin, Boston 1988.

Mervin, David, 'Individualism and the New Congress' in Lynton Robins (ed.), *The American Way*. Longmans, London 1985, pp. 90–101.

Mervin, David, 'The President and Congress' in Malcolm Shaw, *Roosevelt to Reagan: The Development of the Modern Presidency*. C. Hurst, London 1987.

Mervin, David, 'The Competence of Ronald Reagan', *Parliamentary Affairs* **40**, No. 2 (Apr. 1987), pp. 203–17.

Mervin, David, 'Has There been a "Reagan Revolution"?', *Social Studies Review* **3**, No. 2 (Nov. 1987), pp. 77–81.

Mervin, David, 'Presidential Power: Roosevelt, Eisenhower and Reagan', *Teaching Politics* **17**, No. 2 (May 1988), pp. 230–43.

Mervin, David, 'Ronald Reagan's Place in History', *Journal of American Studies* **23** (August 1989), pp. 269–86.

Meyer, Jack, 'Social Programs and Social Policy' in Palmer, op. cit., pp. 65–89.

Mitchell, William, *The American Polity*. Free Press, Glencoe 1962.

Nathan, Richard, *The Plot that Failed: Nixon and the Administrative Presidency*. John Wiley and Sons, New York 1975.

Nathan, Richard, *The Administrative Presidency*. Macmillan, New York 1986.

Nathan, Richard, 'Institutional Change Under Reagan' in Palmer, op. cit., pp. 121–45.

Nelson, Michael, 'The Case For the Current Nominating Process' in George Grassmuck (ed.), *Before Nomination*. American Enterprise Institute, Washington DC 1985.

Neustadt, Richard, *Presidential Power: The Politics of Leadership*. John Wiley and Sons, New York (1976 edition – first published 1960).

Newhouse, John, 'Annals of Diplomacy: The Abolitionist' *New Yorker* (2 Jan. and 9 January 1989).

Newland, Chester, 'Executive Office Policy Apparatus: Enforcing the Reagan Agenda' in Salamon and Lund, op. cit., pp. 135–68.

Nicholas, H.G., *The Nature of American Politics*. Clarendon Press, Oxford 1986.

Nixon, Richard, *The Memoirs of Richard Nixon*. Arrow Books, London 1979.

O'Brien, David, 'The Reagan Judges: His Most Enduring Legacy' in Jones, *The Reagan Legacy*, op. cit., pp. 60–101.

O'Neill, Tip (with William Novak), *Man of the House: The Life and Political Memoirs of Speaker Tip O'Neill*. Random House, New York 1987.

Ornstein, Norman, 'What Sununu Should Do', *The Washington Post*, National Weekly Edition (9–15 Jan. 1989), p. 29.

Ornstein, Norman (ed.), *President and Congress: Assessing Reagan's First Year*. American Enterprise Institute, Washington DC 1982.

Ornstein, Norman, 'The Open Congress Meets the President' in King, *Both Ends of the Avenue*, op. cit., pp. 185–211.

Ornstein, Norman *et al.*, *Vital Statistics on Congress 1984–85 Edition*. American Enterprise Institute, Washington DC 1984.

Osborne, David, 'On a Clear Day He Can See Massachussetts', ibid. (25 Apr.–1 May 1989), p. 24.

Osgood, Robert E., 'The Revitalisation of Containment' in Hyland, op. cit., pp. 19–56.

Palmer, John, Perspectives on the Reagan Years. The Urban Institute Press, Washington DC 1986.

Palmer, John and Sawhill, Isabel (eds), The Reagan Record. The Urban Institute Press, Washington DC 1984.

Peterson, Paul and Rom, Mark, 'Lower Taxes, More Spending and Budget Deficits' in Jones, The Reagan Legacy, op. cit., pp. 213–40.

Pomper, Gerald (ed.), The Election of 1976. David McKay, New York 1977.

Ranney, Austin, Channels of Power: The Impact of Televison on American Politics. Basic Books, New York 1982.

Ranney, Austin, 'The Political Parties: Reform and Decline' in King, The New American Political System, op. cit., pp. 213–47.

Ranney, Austin (ed.), The American Elections of 1980. American Enterprise Institute, Washington DC 1981.

Reagan, Ronald (with Richard Hubler), My Early Life or Where's the Rest of Me? Sidgwick and Jackson, London 1981.

Reedy, George, The Twilight of the Presidency. New American Library, New York 1970.

Reeves, Richard, A Ford Not a Lincoln. Harcourt Brace and Jovanovich, New York 1975.

Regan, Donald T., For the Record: From Wall Street to Washington. Harcourt Brace and Jovanovich, New York 1988.

Rieselbach, Leroy, Congressional Reform. Congressional Quarterly Press, Washington 1986.

Robins, Lynton (ed.), The American Way: Government and Politics in the United States. Longman, London 1985.

Robinson, Michael, 'The Media In 1980: Was the Message the Message?' in Ranney, The American Elections of 1980, op. cit., pp. 177–212.

Roettger, Walter and Winebrenner, Hugh, 'Politics and Political Scientists', Public Opinion (Sept./Oct. 1986), pp. 41–4.

Rose, Richard, The Postmodern President: The White House Meets the World. Chatham House Publishers, Chatham, New Jersey 1988.

Rossiter, Clinton, The American Presidency. Harcourt Brace and World, New York 1956.

Rothenberg, Stuart, 'Election '88: the House and the Senate', Public Opinion 11, No 5 (Jan./Feb. 1989), pp. 8–11.

Safire, William, *Before the Fall*. Belmont Tower Books, New York 1975.

Saikowski, Charlotte, 'What US Scholars Think of the Reagan Presidency', *Christian Science Monitor*, World Edition (12–18 January 1989), pp. 1–2.

Salamon, Lester and Lund Michael (eds), *The Reagan Presidency and the Governing of America*. The Urban Institute Press, Washington DC 1984.

Salmore, Stephen and Salmore, Barbara, *Candidates Parties and Campaigning*. Congressional Quarterly Press, Washington DC 1985.

Sandoz, Ellis and Crabb, Cecil (eds), *Election 84: Landslide Without a Mandate?* New American Library, New York 1985.

Schick, Allen, 'How the Budget was Won and Lost' in Ornstein, *President and Congress*, op. cit., pp. 14–43.

Schlesinger, Arthur Jr, *The Imperial Presidency*. Popular Library, New York 1974.

Schlesinger, Arthur Jr, *The Cycles of American History*. Andre Deutsch, London 1986.

Schlesinger, Arthur Jr, 'Seeing Daylight', *Playboy* (Mar. 1988).

Schlesinger, Arthur Jr, 'Reagan: Failed Revolutionary', *The Times* (17 Jan. 1989).

Schneider, William, 'The November 4 Vote for President: What Did it Mean?' in Ranney, *The American Elections of 1980*, op. cit., pp. 212–63.

Schneider, William, 'The Political Legacy of the Reagan Years' in Blumenthal and Edsall, *The Reagan Legacy*, op. cit., pp. 51–98.

Shannon, Wayne, 'Ronald Reagan's Unique Pattern of Public Approval', Paper delivered at the Conference of the American Politics Group of the Political Studies Association (Jan. 1987), University of London.

Shaw, Malcolm (ed.), *Roosevelt to Reagan: The Development of the Modern Presidency*. C. Hurst, London 1987.

Smith, Hedrick, *The Power Game: How Washington Works*. Random House, New York 1988.

Smith, Hedrick *et al.*, *Reagan the Man, the President*. Macmillan, New York 1980.

Speakes, Larry, *Speaking Out*. Avon Books, New York 1989.

Stockman, David, *The Triumph of Politics*. Hodder and Stoughton, London 1986.

The Tower, *Commission Report*. Bantam Books, New York 1987.

Tucker, Robert, 'Reagan's Foreign Policy' in Hyland, op. cit., pp. 1–27.

Turner, Michael, 'The Reagan White House, the Cabinet and the Bureaucracy' in Lees and Turner, op. cit., pp. 39–67.

Wayne, Stephen, 'Congressional Liaison in the Reagan White House' in Ornstein, *President and Congress*, op. cit., pp. 44–65.

Weinraub, Bernard, 'How Regan Runs the White House', *New York Times*, Sunday Magazine (5 Jan. 1986).

White, William S., *Citadel: The Story of the US Senate*. Harper and Brothers, New York 1956.

Wildavsky, Aaron, 'President Reagan as Political Strategist', *Society* (May/June 1987), pp. 56–62.

Williams, Robert, 'The President and the Executive Branch' in Shaw, op. cit., pp. 119–58.

Wills, Garry, *Reagan's America: Innocents at Home*. Doubleday, New York 1987.

Wright, Oliver, ' "Understanding America": Impressions of a Departing Ambassador', *Government and Opposition* **22**, No. 2 (Spring 1987), pp. 163–74.

Index